ELECTING A
PRESIDENT

*Copublished with the Eagleton
Institute of Politics
Rutgers University*

ELECTING A PRESIDENT
Information and Control

Paul A. Smith

American Political Parties and Elections

general editor:
Gerald M. Pomper

PRAEGER SPECIAL STUDIES • PRAEGER SCIENTIFIC

Library of Congress Cataloging in Publication Data

Smith, Paul Alan Lawrence, 1928-
  Electing a president.

  (American political parties and elections)
  Includes index.
  1. Presidents—United States—Election—1980.
I. Title. II. Series.
JK526 1980.S63   324.973'0926   82-5224
ISBN 0-03-059664-5   AACR2

324.913
Smbe
124702
may 1983

Published in 1982 by Praeger Publishers
CBS Educational and Professional Publishing
a Division of CBS Inc.
521 Fifth Avenue, New York, New York 10175 U.S.A.

© 1982 Praeger Publishers

23456789 052 987654321
Printed in the United States of America

For Schyler, Stacy, Todd, and Conant

And many future campaigns

Preface

In the course of a presidential election more events take place than can possibly be captured in a single book, or even in many books. Each candidate's campaign is a story in itself — a story that is like a constantly moving picture that never looks quite the same to different observers. Certainly this was true for the campaigns of 1980. My observations, readings, and interviews with participants and journalists turned up a host of diverse descriptions and interpretations.

Indeed, these were sufficient to make me thankful that this book is not the "full inside story" of 1980, but rather an examination of the campaigns from a particular theoretical perspective. My factual burdens were thus simplified, though far from relieved. Even if many small details might not be mentioned, the major event or point distilled from them could remain a composite of uncertain judgments. An incontrovertible version of what took place is, I suppose, a natural aspiration, but it is one that surely will not be fulfilled here. Different perspectives produce too many different "facts." Thus while I must confess to the eager search for new information, I am hardly grateful that it has not made the truth bright and clear and beyond contradiction. In short, for those who are fortunate enough to *know* the truth, there is no one to blame but me for either the interpretations or the facts that are wrong in this volume.

But if my gratitude for conflicting information is sparing, it is heartfelt and abundant for those who helped this project through to completion. Janet Sabel was an indefatigable research assistant. Her energy and spirit belied the frustrations of finding news in news magazines. To Joyce K. L. Smith, who proofread the manuscript as it came from the typewriter, caught endless typos, and made countless helpful suggestions, it is impossible to find words of appreciation that are adequate. Her aid and encouragement were immeasurable. I am also indebted to Frances S. Seto for her unusually conscientious work on the index. Needless to say, none of the people who have striven to correct my errors should share my responsibility for those that remain.

Finally, my deep appreciation to all those persons — family, friends, students, colleagues — for and with whom I failed to do as much as I should have because of this book. I can only hope the result is worthy of their forbearance.

Paul A. Smith

Contents

PREFACE   vii

INTRODUCTION   xi

1 THE RULES OF THE GAME IN AMERICAN CAMPAIGN
   POLITICS   1
   Demographic Changes   2
   Technical Changes   9
   Changes in Electoral Rules and Institutions   20
   The Changing Conditions of Political Parties   34
   Summary   40
   Notes   42

2 THEORY   48
   Alternative Approaches to Campaign Theory   50
   A Cybernetic Model   66
   Notes   81

3 THE PRENOMINATION CAMPAIGNS:
   THE DEMOCRATS   85
   Carter   86
   Kennedy   97
   A Note about the Media as a System   109
   Brown   113
   Notes   115

4 THE PRENOMINATION CAMPAIGNS:
   THE REPUBLICANS   119
   Reagan   120
   Bush   127
   Connally   131
   Baker, Crane, and Dole   135
   Anderson   139
   Notes   144

5 THE NATIONAL CONVENTIONS 146
The Republicans in Detroit 146
The Democrats in New York 155
Notes 165

6 THE GENERAL ELECTION 167
Carter 167
Anderson 181
Reagan 192
Notes 206

7 CONCLUSIONS 211
Notes 219

APPENDIXES 221

INDEX 232

ABOUT THE AUTHOR 241

Introduction

The saddest life is that of a political aspirant under democracy. His failure is ignominious and his success is disgraceful.

H. L. Mencken

Campaigning for public office is a critically important activity in democratic politics. Yet during the hoopla, exaggerations, attacks, and repetitions of a major competitive election, it often seems more appropriate to view the proceedings through the jaundiced eye of H. L. Mencken than to consider the basic political functions that are being served. It certainly is more fun, and the fact that we can join Mencken in seeing the ridiculous in campaigns — and do it publicly — constitutes a healthy skepticism about political authority. However, it also blurs the significance of what campaigns and elections are all about.

One reason for this is that in most of our social life, candidates (if there happen to be more than one) do no more than "stand" for office — making themselves modestly "available" as a community service. In small groups or organizations such noncampaign elections appear to meet the norms of popular choice because voters and candidates have considerable knowledge about each other and share common purposes. In short, there are few burning issues of collective policy or style of leadership, and, for their part, the offices to be filled may be an uncertain mixture of small honors and modest burdens. By avoiding active electioneering the group escapes the pain of interpersonal conflict, and those candidates not chosen are spared the embarrassment of defeat (because the whole matter is of so little consequence, or, "I didn't want the office anyway").[1]

As communities grow in size, however, policy interests and needs diversify, and the role of government becomes more formal. Personal acquaintance and communication no longer can be counted on to inform candidates about the desires of the electorate or voters about the pertinent qualities of the candidates. Moreover, since issues are now endemic, there is doubt about just what the "popular will" is. In such larger and more diverse constituencies competitive campaigns can identify and clarify issues and pose alternatives. Candidates have the opportunity to try out, shape, and adapt their policy positions, and voters can appraise the knowledge, positions, and skills of the potential office-holders, and they can make choices. For most citizens, caught up in the pressures of daily life, campaigns provide the most practical access to political participation.[2] They perform a mutual education function through which government has a better chance of working to the satisfaction of its constituents.

This picture of smooth and benign political education and involvement leading to governmental effectiveness and legitimacy may seem a bit remote from the campaign events and controversies one has witnessed. In fact, to the extent that these campaigns have been hard-fought, one might very well conclude that candidates are more interested in winning office than in educating the electorate, and voters are more concerned about finding good or evil in the candidates than in accurately assessing their policy positions and leadership abilities.[3] Election campaigns thus might appear to be serving rather different functions — notably those of personal ambition and public recreation — than the ones presented in my idealized portrait.

Nonetheless, the simple, idealized picture I have sketched not only depicts a certain amount of reality but also provides a set of norms or standards with which to judge campaigns in general. It emphasizes, first, the importance of true competition, for to the extent this is missing the political community is reduced to assuming the existence of leader-follower agreement when there are no reliable means for knowing whether underlying dissatisfactions simply have not been activated.

Second, it shows that insofar as campaigns do not reveal much about the candidate, or do not "reach" substantial portions of the electorate, their essential functions are not being performed. After all, in democracies, political campaigns are the road to public leadership. One of the key features of this road should be to expose candidates to public scrutiny in minimally controlled circumstances. So surprise and uncertainty are a benign part of those campaigns that reveal the various "sides" of their candidates.

As simple as these points are, they get to the heart of what political campaigns can do in democratic systems — whether the systems are large or small. They are a way of exposing and a way of choosing. Most of this book will deal with very large campaigns for the top office of a very large political system: the presidency of the United States. Yet the measure of their performance remains the flow of information between the candidates and their constituents — between the followers and the potential leaders. Because the scale is so large, however, just what is happening in campaigns, and how well they are performing their functions of mutual education, is far from obvious. So we shall search for ways of looking at and thinking about these electioneering activities in order that they will be more understandable, and perhaps more significant.

NOTES

1. Often these noncampaign situations are not as happy and effective as I have depicted them. The avoidance of controversy can be a short step from the loss of useful ideas and creative leadership, and also from the famous "village tyranny."

2. The relatively low political involvement of the American people has been demonstrated in numerous studies. More recent dynamics are shown in Norman H. Nie, Sidney Verba, and John R. Petrocik, *The Changing American Voter* (Cambridge, Mass.: Harvard University Press, 1976), pp. 15-17 and 271-77.

3. Marjorie Randon Hershey provides an unusually perceptive treatment of the functions of campaigns in *The Making of Campaign Strategy* (Lexington, Mass.: D. C. Heath, 1974), pp. 1-9.

1

The Rules of the Game in American Campaign Politics

Election campaigns do not take place in a vacuum, either political or otherwise. Every campaign is conducted for an electorate having certain characteristics, and within a context of events, technologies, and legal constraints. That these "contextual factors" exist is obvious, but their precise form and content are not. Indeed, if we start trying to list and describe all of them, they threaten to become so numerous and varied that every campaign becomes unique in itself (which, of course, it is) and the contextual factors become impossible to keep track of. So this approach leads not to science but to folklore as we search for generalizations about things that matter.

There certainly is plenty of folklore associated with election campaigns — this quality of the candidate, that method of attacking an opponent, this issue to be avoided — all formulas for success (or failure) based on usually unstated assumptions about what factors count. Our task is to identify those common factors that can be specified without getting lost in mindless details or unsubstantiated generalizations.

It is useful to think of an election campaign as a game — a game with players, rules, and payoffs or rewards. The rules are the most important part of any game because they establish how it is to be played, by whom, and with what probabilities of success.[1] We may take rules to mean *any* explicit constraint upon the players, so that for political games we think beyond deliberately formulated rules

1

such as laws and regulations. Using this definition, an obvious — though hardly trivial — example of rules governing campaign games is the physiological characteristics of human beings that limit the amount of continuous time that can be put into campaign activity (before falling asleep). Fairly evident consequences of this rule can be observed in the frequent references to candidate exhaustion in descriptions of campaigns. A specific and notable example occurred in the presidential campaign of 1960, when Richard Nixon, driving himself unmercifully, ended up losing valuable campaign days in the hospital and appeared haggard in his first and critical debate with John Kennedy.[2]

This illustration, however, is of a type of rule that has not changed for a very long time. Though obviously important, such rules are so numerous and "natural" that their relative effects on campaigns cannot yet be systematically measured (although interesting examples can always be found). Instead, we are interested in those contextual factors or rules that are distinctly related to campaigns *and* that have changed in more or less recent years. The time period is important because we are looking for clues to why campaigns are developing as they are, how they might develop in the future, and whether certain rules are particularly related to campaign success or failure. In the sections that follow I shall present elements of the campaign environment that have changed in the last decade or two and appear to me as rules of the game.

DEMOGRAPHIC CHANGES

The American people have always been noted for their mobility, part of which is a matter of geographic movement, and part of which involves patterns of birth rate, intermarriage, education, employment, and so on. The last decade has been no exception. Campaign strategists have long prided themselves on being sensitive to the distribution of political attitudes and opinions within the electorate. Increasingly since the 1930s these have come to be measured directly through large-scale public surveys, and, as we shall see, campaigns are often transfixed by them. But public attitudes (predispositions to respond in certain ways to given issues or events), while relatively stable, are generally not stable enough to be treated as political rules (although often they are). In some respects, however, there appear to be long-term relationships between certain attitudes and certain groupings of the population. This, in turn, has led to the association of distinct patterns of political behavior with basic social characteristics. To the extent that this is true, these social characteristics may take on the quality of rules, with their changes being relevant to campaigns.

Age

The American people are growing older. While the electorate of 1980 was on the whole a bit younger than that of 1970 (and before), those in the population that were 65 or older rose from 20 million in 1970 to about 26 million in 1980.[3] Between 1950 and 1980 the number over 65 doubled. Essentially, the effects of the post-World War II "baby boom" reached their peak in the early 1970s and began to recede. The largest age deciles of 1970, 5-14 and 15-24, were ten years older by 1980, and the falling birth rate in the 1960s and after produced smaller age groups under five in 1980 than in 1970. Meanwhile, advances in health care have continued to reduce the death rate among the elderly. The result: a national population that was in 1980 less skewed toward the young than in 1970, and that is definitely growing older.[4]

The political significance of this is *not* in the (false) old saw that Republicanism increases with age. It *is* true that in recent decades voters 65 or older have tended to be more Republican than other age groups, but this is because they adopted their party identifications in the predepression period when the Republican party was dominant. Even in this respect, the 1972 and 1976 presidential elections did not show the 65 and over age group to be much different from those immediately below them.[5] As for partisanship in general, while it remains uncertain whether party affiliation increases with age under all circumstances, it is clear that older age groups today are more partisan than younger.[6] Older voters are also more stable in their affiliations — less inclined, that is, to abandon their parties for independent or other party candidates. Virtually all age groups have grown independent during the last 20 years, and the youngest groups enormously so. For 1980, the age groups of 50 years and over provided a substantial block of committed partisans, but as these groups disappear and are replaced by those who came of age in the 1960s and 1970s, overall partisanship can be expected to decline further.

Of course the electoral impact of any population group depends on both the group's size and exercise. In this respect, voting turnout increases sharply by age until about 35, and declines gradually after 65.[7] On the average, a citizen of 50 is twice as likely to vote as a citizen of 18. Those in the 65 and over category hardly retire from the polling booth, their turnout percentage in 1976 ranking above all the groups under 35.[8] Thus the growing number of older Americans cannot be discounted because of low interest or turnout — something that might be justified for the very young groups. The extent to which age will be a factor in an election depends, of course, on the particular candidates and issues involved. For 1980 the age distribution appeared to be a relevant rule.[9]

Education

The rise in the average level of education of the American people in the last generation has been substantial, but it is less striking than the jump in numbers of college students and graduates. Figure 1.1 exhibits the changing "higher education shape" of the population as a whole. Of course, since education is positively related to political participation, the actual electorate would have an even higher line on the graph.[10] The meaning of this rise in education for campaigns is less clear. For example, it is reasonable to suppose that a better-educated population will vote more, be more Republican, and show more concern for policy issues. Yet in the postwar period of rising education, voting turnout and Republican identification have fallen; issue salience reached a high in the 1972 election and then dropped back.[11] We are left without consistent and simple match-ups between educational averages and political behavior. The reason is that many other factors are mixed with education in influencing the voter. It seems clear, however, that higher education *does* lead individuals to be more attentive to campaign events and more "independent" in their voting — therefore creating a potential in the electorate that was not there before.

Yet there is another element of this educational growth that is less frequently examined for its political effects. Since 1960 the number of universities and colleges offering four-year and higher

FIGURE 1.1
Education in the United States

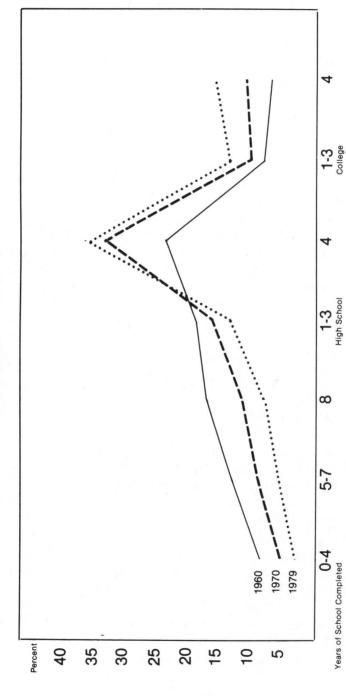

Source: U.S. Bureau of the Census, *Statistical Abstract of the United States* (Washington, D.C.: U.S. Government Printing Office, 1980), p. 149.

5

degrees increased from 1,400 to 1,800 in 1980 (two-year colleges doubled in number from 500 to 1,000). At the same time their enrollments rose even more — from 3.1 million in 1960 to 7.3 million in 1980 (two-year enrollment increased from .45 million to 4.2 million) — and their faculties almost tripled in size. Much of this growth occurred at a time of intense political concern among faculty and students, with the result that in communities throughout the nation colleges and universities may be found with traditions of political activism. Of course, these institutions exhibit great diversity in size, sophistication, educational purposes, and political "tone." Nevertheless, many of these institutions comprise substantial aggregations of young men and women who are interested in public affairs and relatively free to act. They are a potential source of participants for those campaigns whose candidates appeal to student values. Their faculties can be a source of technical expertise. Furthermore, larger institutions, especially, can provide appropriate settings for candidates seeking to gain attention for important policy statements.

Obviously, the ability of a campaign to exploit these collegiate resources is highly dependent upon the attractiveness of its candidate and the timing of the effort. Nonetheless, the last 20 years have demonstrated that the resource is real, and it is part of the educational factor, or rule, that campaigns should take into account.

Demographic Mobility

The U.S. population has always been mobile, yet this truism has taken on new freshness in the last decade. First of all, mobility can mean different things. The college students we have just been discussing are "moving upward" in terms of their educational levels. Similarly, persons who change to more desirable occupations, and in so doing receive higher incomes, are moving up the occupational and income ladders. Such changes in occupation and wealth have been going on in the United States for a long time, and they are politically significant, as can be seen in the gradual decline of industrial labor unions compared to the increase in numbers and organizations of white-collar and professional workers. Yet they are also familiar in American politics. Other movements of this type are less familiar, however. In 1980 women comprised almost 50 percent of the labor force, and in the 1970-80 decade the proportion of households in which both men and women were employed rose sharply.[12] Furthermore, during the same period the decline in household size continued unabated (the average number of persons per household was 4.1 in 1930, 3.1 in 1970, and 2.8 in 1980). Although the political effects of these latter social and occupational changes are likely to be subtle, they point to greater attitudinal independence of women and continuing increases in their political participation, and to the declining influence of the family as a political unit.[13]

A second type of demographic mobility involves geographic movement. This has been quite distinctive during the last ten years, and the political relevance is in some instances obvious. First there are what we might think of as local migrations — people moving out of their communities but not into another region of the country. One result of this has been a steep decline in numbers of whites, coupled with growing proportions of blacks, in the large cities of the nation. Indeed, between 1970 and 1980 black citizens became majorities in Baltimore, New Orleans, and Detroit (they already were in the majority in Atlanta and the District of Columbia), and moved close to being the majority in Chicago, Memphis, and St. Louis. Furthermore, if hispanics are added, such other large cities as Los Angeles have nonwhite majorities.[14] What happened during the 1970s was that both whites *and* blacks migrated out of the large cities, but whites did so in far greater numbers, leaving largely poor black people concentrated in central cities. As a result, at the very time central cities were declining in overall population (by about 10 percent), they were becoming occupied by growing concentrations of the poor.

But these changes did not occur equally around the country, although they were quite widespread. This brings us to long-distance movements of the population during the 1970s. The dominant pattern was the now well-known migration from the Northeast and Midwest to the "sun belt." What is more, those who moved were not the "Okies" of the 1930s, but members of the middle class, with considerable education, income, and skill (and, in the case of the migration to Florida, age). The economic result was a decided shift in productive wealth from and to the same regions. The compound difficulties of such cities as Boston, Chicago, and New York, while such others as Dallas and Houston were burgeoning, exemplify the changing situation.[15] Needless to say, a host of other factors were involved in these population movements — the price of oil, the development of "space-age" industries, and the refinement of air quality, for example — but for us the redistribution of the American people is of decisive importance.

Some of the political consequences of this geographic movement are direct and can easily be seen in Table 1.1. Fourteen congressional seats will be lost by states of the Midwest and Northeast and gained by states of the sun belt — the biggest loser being New York (5) and the biggest gainers being Florida (3) and Texas (3). Of course these seats are also electoral votes, so both congressional and presidential

TABLE 1.1
Congressional Seats Gained and Lost, 1970-80

States Gaining Seats	*1970*	*1980*	*Gain*
Arizona	4	5	1
California	43	45	2
Colorado	5	6	1
Florida	15	18	3
Nevada	1	2	1
New Mexico	2	3	1
Oregon	4	5	1
Tennessee	8	9	1
Texas	24	27	3
Utah	2	3	1
Washington	7	8	1
States Losing Seats	*1970*	*1980*	*Loss*
Illinois	24	22	2
Massachusetts	12	11	1
Michigan	19	18	1
Missouri	10	9	1
New Jersey	15	14	1
New York	39	34	5
Ohio	23	21	2
Pennsylvania	25	23	2
South Dakota	2	1	1

Source: Bureau of the Census, New York *Times*, July 21, 1981, p. B8.

campaigns are affected. Other implications for political campaigns are more indirect and subtle. For example, the wealth of the Southwest can be expected to aid conservative rather than liberal candidates. It can further be expected, in conjunction with the additional electoral votes, to draw the attention of all major presidential candidates to the region — including candidates who are incumbents. This is not to mention the political reach of the independent political action committees that have been, and will be, springing up in the region.

The local migrations I have mentioned mean the growth of suburbs and "outstate" areas at the expense of central cities as far as campaign attention is concerned — a development reinforced by the substantially lower political participation (for example, voting turnout) by the "disadvantaged" inner city populations. Clearly, the traditional centers of urban "machine" power will have fewer votes to bargain with. And all of this geographic mobility is likely to undermine further local political communities, thus adding to the disruption of long-term party loyalties and networks of communication and interest that produced geographic voting blocs and simplified campaigning.

Any student of American voting behavior will recognize that many of these political consequences are not new in American politics, just as population movements certainly are not. The point here is that within the last decade or two, certain demographic changes have been sufficiently distinct to constitute rules for campaign politics. Furthermore, they frequently occur in combinations. A good example is the selection of Florida as the place to live in retirement by many men and women from the North, especially the New York City area. Occasioned by the lapse of extended families, made possible by strong postwar incomes (and the social security program), and with numbers swelled by the growing post-65 cohort, this migration has not only contributed heavily to Florida's population growth but also produced an unusual concentration of Jewish voters in such areas as Miami. This has affected both the congressional candidates and campaigns in Florida and the state's presidential primaries as well.

TECHNICAL CHANGES

If some of the demographic changes that have emerged in the last 10 or 20 years are essentially continuations of long-term patterns, the technologies we shall review below might seem more clear-cut examples of new contextual factors. There were innumerable technological developments in the post-World War II United States, any number of which have made appearances in election campaigns (for example, the efficient walkie-talkie, commonly used at national conventions and in campaign field appearances). In what follows, however, I shall discuss only those that in my view constitute major changes that campaigns need to take into account — without implying that further analysis will not find others.

Television

Often called "the mass media" (thus leaving the other media in limbo), this is doubtless the most obvious public technology of the last 30 years. Although invented before the war, it was not until the mid-1950s that television was used to cover campaign events. Previously, in the 1930s and 1940s, campaign coverage was dominated by radio and of course the printed press.[16] However, with the completion of a coast-to-coast coaxial cable in 1951, television was able to achieve national coverage of the 1952 national conventions, and to some extent get into the field.[17] (Walter Cronkite began his career as "anchorman" at the Republican convention of that year.) Yet television news broadcasts were still based primarily on information supplied by the press and wire services.[18]

The advance, however, was rapid. By 1956 television was not only at the national conventions but also covering events in the field directly (as its physical equipment became less cumbersome and more efficient). Moreover, a great deal of commercial time was purchased by parties and candidates. Radio and newspapers were quickly outdistanced in popularity by this new medium, and television eventually responded by taking its news functions more seriously. In 1963 the major networks lengthened their 15-minute evening news broadcasts — the traditional length inherited from radio — to 30 minutes and became the dominant source of public information about political affairs. A more precise picture of the growth of television in American homes can be seen in the percentages of households that had at least one set in 1950: 9; 1960: 65; 1970: 95; and 1980: 98. During the same 30-year period the average number of sets per houshold increased from 1.01 to 1.71.[19] By

1980 more American homes had television than had telephones or indoor plumbing. The "depth" of the information being received by the public is suggested by what happened to daily newspapers during this period. From 1950 to 1979 the number of daily newspapers fell steadily from 1,894 to 1,744. Although daily circulation increased slightly, per capita "consumption" also fell from .476 to .360.[20]

The reactions of national candidates to this new technology were not long in coming, and have been widely studied.[21] An initial landmark was Richard Nixon's campaign of 1968, which was essentially organized around carefully constructed television appearances that were effective not only in projecting a favorable image of Nixon but also in keeping him separated from the press. Going far beyond what might be seen on network news programs, or what was the usual 30- and 60-second spot commercial, Nixon made highly sophisticated ads of various lengths, including the famous 30-minute "open meetings," in which he responded to questions from well-coached and selected audiences of "average" citizens.[22]

Although the manipulative aspects of Nixon's effort subsequently were widely criticized, it established the basic uses of television for the campaigns that followed. Campaign itineraries were drawn up so that the candidate's appearances would "catch" the network evening news broadcasts, campaign budgets were devoted overwhelmingly to television advertisements, and the entire formats of the national conventions were restructured with an eye to prime-time television audiences.[23] The notable exception to this scheduling occurred at the Democratic convention of 1972, when George McGovern ended up giving his acceptance speech to a few loyal (and weary) viewers in the early hours of the morning – an exception that has been taken to prove the rule.

Television has always been expensive, first because the technology itself was costly, and later because its effectiveness as a marketing vehicle in general drove up its price. Moreover, the basis of its great potential – bringing "words and pictures" of the candidate directly into homes – could also be a hazard if the overall image was not shaped with some skill. The result was that television did not immediately become a universal campaign medium. State and local campaigns were often intimidated by its cost and adopted it according to the size and shape of the candidate's district and budget. The most difficult decisions usually involved districts that were marginal in terms of the broadcast coverage of the available stations. (An illustrative example from national campaigns is: Should Boston television be used in the New Hampshire primary?) Then there were the countless local candidates who, whether in debates or interviews sponsored by others or in their own paid commercials, presented images that bordered on the ludicrous.

Nevertheless, during the decade of the 1970s the "reach" of television into campaigns at every level was spectacular — prompted by the "evidence" of national campaigns and by the growing availability of media consultants and other expertise that was part of the overall industry. All of this constituted a new contextual factor that few campaigns could ignore.

High-Speed Aircraft

Although television is the most obvious technology that has become a "rule" in the last 20 years, for national campaigns especially it has been joined by the jet airplane. As early as the 1950s the classic "whistle stop," developed in the 1920s and 1930s (remember that presidential campaigning of any kind tended to be very modest before the late 1920s),[24] and which Harry Truman used to such brilliant effect in 1948, was replaced by the airplane.[25] The large jet aircraft, by which not only candidates but also staff and news media can travel swiftly, have marked another change. Now candidates move from one section of the country to another in a few hours, while having clerical and communication facilities superior to those of the now outdated train. They are able to reach increasing numbers of smaller communities as airports have been enlarged and planes redesigned for shorter runways.

One effect of this technology is an expansion of the candidate's time. Appearances in different parts of the country that 40 years ago would have taken days, if not weeks, can now be made in a single day. Moreover, each appearance can now be given a visual reality for a national audience through the accompanying television. Thus a large jet airplane (chartered) adds greatly to a presidential candidate's ability to campaign in the field.

Of course, such transportation exacts a price. First there is the direct financial cost; but this is accompanied by the cost of the additional support services that are needed if such rapid transport is to be used efficiently. More staff, more communication, more speech writing, more decisions — the acceleration of the campaign's schedule must be matched by an expansion of virtually all its resources of decision and administration. In its way, the same thing may be said for television. And both technologies, in adding to and speeding up what must be done to employ them, increase the chances of error. The costs thus rise both directly and indirectly.

In congressional and state campaigns the advantages of chartered jet transportation vary widely, obviously depending on the size of the state or district. In the case of congressional candidates, high-speed transportation makes it easier for incumbents to reach their districts, adding to the ability of the House and Senate to stay in session during election years. Yet again, although the aircraft may be smaller at the state level, they are comparatively costly. This has led some candidates to adopt dramatically different modes of transportation — walking, for example, or a return to trains and the whistle stop.[26] (While walking is indeed an inexpensive method of travel, it is patently inefficient for any not-very-local district. Similarly, since trains, stations, and tracks are not as available as they were a generation ago, they are not a cost-cutting device.) Both alternatives, by being primarily means for getting free media attention for the campaign, actually demonstrate that the plane and the automobile are the common means of campaign transportation. For statewide and national campaigns, the technology of air travel is a new rule.

Mass Mailing

With the rising costs associated with the preceding (and other) technologies, and the limitations imposed on campaign contributions that we shall review later, campaigns have needed to enlarge their financial base.[27] There are various ways of doing this, including the use of the traditional grass-roots party organization, telephones, and television appeals. Except for local campaigns, however, the classic process of printing, folding, stuffing, addressing, and mailing letters by hand is not one of them. Yet the last decade has seen the growth of a computerized mailing list and machine processing technology that makes it possible to reach massive numbers of citizens by mail at a modest unit cost and with great accuracy. Moreover, mass mailing systems are able to "process" the information contained in the responses to the mailing in order to make improvements.[28]

Once again, the development of this technology was neither easy nor cheap, although much of the early costs were borne by nonpolitical enterprises, such as magazine and mail-order companies. It is not inexpensive today, but after the initial investment is made in the physical equipment and the mailing lists, implementation can be fast. Moreover, the effectiveness of a particular list, or letter of appeal, or cause is subject to systematic assessment because response rates can be determined precisely and compared.

As direct-mail campaigns proliferated during the 1970s, so did mailing lists. Particularly valuable to a candidate are lists of citizens who have already shown a willingness to contribute to similar candidates or causes. Thus there is some tendency for direct-mail specialists to concentrate on particular types of causes and populations — Republicans, liberals, conservatives, environmentalists, and so forth. This leads to considerable buying and selling and exchanging of lists between groups and candidates who appeal to similar attitudes and interests within the population.

Since direct-mail fund raising aims at the small contributor (that is, between $5 and $50), response rates are critically important. They are also highly variable, ranging from less than 1 percent to perhaps 20 percent, with returns of 5 percent from a national mailing considered very respectable (depending, of course, on the average contribution). The "quality" of a candidate's mailing lists thus becomes very significant, and considerable expertise is required to produce good lists for "center" candidates who do not appeal to deeply committed segments of the population.

While direct mailing operations have been in use for a long time, in the 1960s and 1970s they were increasingly computerized, making the analysis and refinement of lists easier. It was the McGovern campaign of 1972 that demonstrated how effective direct-mail fund raising could be in a major presidential campaign, and for a candidate who was not widely known when he began.[29] By 1976 most of the various presidential candidates used direct mail in one form or another. Every candidate considered it.

The technology of computerized direct mail clearly is not the solution to every candidate's financial woes. It is expensive, it is complex, and it certainly offers no guarantee of success to the user. By 1980 it cost about 40 cents to send a first-class letter through a direct-mail system, and it was common for national candidates to raise several million dollars via direct mail, only to find that the costs of the operation approached or exceeded the income.[30] Nevertheless, by 1980 the technology was in place and refined. It could reach the small contributor. It could be integrated with mass media appeals. It was effective in supporting organizations, such as the Republican National Committee. And it could work for some candidates who were unable to raise enough money through more traditional means. It had become a factor that no national campaign could ignore.

Public Opinion Polling

Although the computer plays a central role in massive direct-mail operations, that role is relatively simple compared to the part it plays in modern public opinion polling and analysis. It is the core of this information-gathering technology. Originated as a practical business enterprise by George Gallup in 1935, "scientific" public opinion polling arrived just in time to salvage the damaged reputation of preelection surveys after the famous *Literary Digest* poll of the Landon-Roosevelt election in 1936. The *Digest* sent ballots to a massive "sample" based in part on addresses drawn from telephone directories. Since only one out of three American households had phones in 1936, this nonsystematic procedure badly underrepresented lower income groups in the population. The *Digest* prediction of a Republican landslide confirmed the weakness of telephone polls for years. (Gallup, meanwhile, with a very much smaller yet systematic sample, accurately predicted Roosevelt's victory.)[31]

By 1970, however, 92 percent of U.S. households had phones, and 97 percent had them by 1980. This meant that with the technology of computerized random digit dialing, the advantages of telephone (as opposed to personal interview) polling far outweighed the marginal underrepresentation of very low income groups — underrepresentation made even more marginal by the low voting turnout of these groups.* The technology itself combined the

---

*By the late 1970s only the Gallup organization, of the major national polling organizations, was still using in-person interviews.

effective interconnection of numerous state and local phone companies and computerization. Thus a correctly programmed computer
is able to generate its own random sample of telephone numbers
(including those unlisted) from the entire nation and dial them on
demand. Once such an operation is developed, the mechanical
elements of public opinion surveys can be accomplished rapidly,
precisely, and at relatively low cost per interview. Instead of spending a week or more in the field going from door to door, current
technology makes it possible to complete a modest national survey
in a day or less. Furthermore, the responses can quickly be integrated with other types of data (such as voting records and census
results) in order to perform sophisticated analyses in a fraction of
the time that would have been required a generation earlier.[32]

The advantages of modern polling technology are therefore
much more than time-saving. Segments of the population, including
geographic segments such as states, can be singled out in terms of
census characteristics, past voting behavior, or public attitudes and
compared with other segments to determine whether they should
be targeted for special campaign efforts.[33] Series of polls, stretching
back for years if practicable, can be used to construct hypothetical
electorates. With these it is possible to *simulate* campaigns and
elections, thus "testing" the effectiveness of issues or events before
they occur.[34] In effect, modern polling not only enables a campaign
to respond quickly to opinion changes in the electorate, but also
the systematic information about *individual* members of the electorate that it provides is the raw material for complex analyses
that makes it possible to avoid or create events with greater
confidence than in the past. Polling and its associated technologies
have therefore altered the environment of information within which
campaigns are conducted. The competent use of this science and
technology gives any campaign an improved position.

So much for the positive side. Just as with the technologies
that we reviewed earlier, the benefits of polling are neither cheap
nor sure, and "competent use" is the exception rather than the
rule. More or less professional polling has been part of presidential
campaigns for 40 years, and it captured the public imagination
before that. From the beginning, the gaps between the scientific
bases of opinion sampling and innumerable polls actually being
conducted have been considerable. Each step of a poll — sampling,
questionnaire construction, interviewing, and the methods of analysis

and interpretation — is vulnerable to numerous pitfalls, any one of which can undermine the validity or reliability of the results. Because of this, good polling is a complex and relatively costly operation.

At the same time, the great publicity given to preelection polls — not surprising since the outcome of the "game" is intrinsically interesting and the professional pollsters want to sell their products — has led to the idea that polling is a natural, if not easy, part of any campaign. Consequently, in state and local communities throughout the nation, news media are on the lookout for polls covering their areas, whether these are done by a local college, political club, or themselves. However, because the basic requirements of good polling are essentially the same regardless of constituency size, the cost of a state or local poll should not be commensurately lower than that of a national poll. Yet it strains the credulity of the aspiring local pollster to learn that the sample needed to measure the town's presidential voting intentions is as large as that needed to poll the nation; that interviewers must be as carefully trained; and so forth. It also strains his budget. The result is a sort of Gresham's Law* of public opinion polls.

The same forces are at play at the national level, but there they are counteracted by competition and intense professional (and public) scrutiny, leading to much higher standards of design and operation. For example, to stop polling a week or more before a presidential election, which contributed to the acute embarrassment of the public polling organizations in 1948, is no longer considered acceptable.[35] In general, polling standards are established at the national level and then filter down to congressional, state, and local campaigns. Although this filtering is far from perfect, during the 1970s it was accelerated by the rapid growth of polling operations associated with the congressional campaign committees and, in some states, similar state party legislative committees. Professional political consultants specializing in state and local campaigns also became a growth industry that has had considerable impact on campaigns at these levels.

We can see in all of this an enormously irregular and mixed process through which the knowledge and technology of polling has been presented to and adopted by election campaigns. Plainly,

---

*Named after an English financier, Sir Thomas Gresham (1519-79), it is commonly stated as: "Bad money drives out good money."

the existence of the knowledge and technology as a "rule" has not meant that campaigns have made the appropriate adaptations in response. I have suggested that probably the worst response – which has been quite common despite numerous verbal expressions to the contrary – has been: "If it's a poll it must be right." Poor or inadequate polls can be a double hazard to campaigns, first in wasting valuable resources, and second in leading to the assumption that something is true about the electorate when it is not. Waste frequently occurs in polls that concentrate on discovering who is ahead. Even if accurate, such findings are of only minimal use, since what the campaign really needs to find out is how to improve such things as the candidate's style, issues, scheduling, or field organization. Obviously, a campaign that puts its trust in a poll that is wrong can be in serious trouble.

Finally, instead of the faults of poor design and execution that we have been discussing, there are the limitations to polling that remain after the best available knowledge and technology have been applied. Without prohibitive costs, polling cannot produce more than a close *approximation* of public opinion and action, such as voting behavior.[36] The reasons for this lie in the basic laws of probability and other inherent uncertainties. For example, there is no current agreement on the best way to correct for nonrespondents (persons in the original sample who cannot be reached or refuse to answer), to identify those among the respondents who actually will vote, and to assign "undecideds." How these things are done will measurably affect a poll's findings. The laws of probability dictate that a sample will be accurate within a given plus or minus percentage error (at a certain level of "confidence"), depending on its size.[37] Thus when in early September 1980 a New York *Times*/CBS poll found that from a sample of 1,417 registered voters 14 percent favored John Anderson for president, this meant that one could be 95 percent confident that in the national population of voters, no less than 11 percent and no more than 17 percent (that is, +/– 3 percent) would favor Anderson.[38] Taken as whole, this means that within the normal limitations of time, money, and knowledge, even the best of polls cannot be taken as absolutely precise or accurate.

We are left with a contextual factor that is both clear and obscure, depending on the perspective of the campaign. The existence of the polling theory and technology is clear. It is a campaign "rule." Even if a major campaign chooses not to poll, it will not be able to avoid the published polls of others, and these will affect its environment, if not its own personnel. The meaning of the rule will be one thing for a presidential campaign and another for a city council candidate, however. Hence for many campaigns in the United States, just what polling requires and how the results should be interpreted are matters of considerable variation and uncertainty.

The New Professional Consultants

I have already suggested that the preceding technologies cannot be used effectively without specialized expertise. In politics, such expertise is usually sold by those generally called "consultants." The advent of "professional" advisers or consultants for election campaigns has long since occurred.[39] However, the expertise required by the technologies of computerized direct mail, polling, and the various facets of television was by 1980 of a considerably higher order than a generation ago. The expense of the capital equipment was also more imposing than that in 1950 or 1960. Candidates, therefore, are likely to need not only professionals who know how to use the technology but also professionals who have the technology — in short, substantial business enterprises.[40] In this form, a young industry of political consultants has developed rapidly over the last two decades, providing brisk competition for the more generalized public relations firms.[41]

Professional consultants have affected campaigns in many different ways during the last 20 years because there was considerable diversity in the young industry during this time. Some were virtually one-man operations, often holdovers from an earlier period when their expertise was primarily political in nature and based on experience in party politics and past campaigns. In the main, however, the movement has been in the direction of technical expertise, larger size, and involvement in overall campaign strategy-making. Typically, the consulting firm will offer a package of services, including media advertising, polling, and direct mailing. Since major decisions about how to employ these services cannot be divorced from the rest of the campaign, such consultants will argue that their participation in overall strategy is necessary to make correct use of their expertise. Most political consulting firms thus include both technical specialists and the "names" — David Garth, Joe Napolitan, Richard Viguerie — who are ready and willing to "run the campaign."[42]

The result has been a steady rise in campaign budgets and recurring disputes over whether consultants are to be "on tap" or "on top." Neither the costs nor the disputes are surprising. Campaigns, after all, hire consultants in order to gain access to specialized knowledge and technology that is expensive (and hopefully effective). Consultants are in the business to make money; but since winning elections is the source of the consultant's reputation, every campaign becomes an investment. So it is natural for consultants to press campaigns to do well — to spend more money to raise more money to buy more advertising, and so forth. Conflicts over who is running the campaign are inherent in this situation, and they are not new. Since the advent of public relations firms being hired by campaigns to help the candidate's "image," such conflicts between the veteran political generalists — traditionally the "pols" — and the new advertising experts have been present.[43] Given the increasing importance of the complex technologies we have been discussing, it seems inevitable that specialists in these technologies will play expanding roles in campaign decision-making.

As we confront the 1980s, an interesting question is whether candidates will find themselves increasingly separated from the operations of their own campaigns by the technical complexity of the operations. Certainly there is no reason to expect that polling, or advertising, or fund raising will become simpler, or that the consulting industry will wither away. Quite the contrary. Thus the costs of campaigning will continue to rise (unless they are artificially limited), and "running" the operation will be less and less open to amateurs.

CHANGES IN ELECTORAL RULES AND INSTITUTIONS

In a little more than a decade, beginning roughly with the Democratic national convention of 1968, there have been major changes in the formal rules governing national election campaigns and their associated political party institutions. These rule changes have been more consciously shaped to achieve electoral purposes than the rules we have already considered. Nonetheless, some of their major effects on campaigns have been as unintended as those of their demographic and technologic counterparts. In both cases we are dealing with relatively new contextual factors that campaigns cannot ignore.

Rules of Candidate Recruitment

In the aftermath of its 1968 national convention in Chicago, the Democratic party embarked upon what was to become a decade of modifications of its presidential nominating procedures.[44] The initial purposes of these changes were clearly reformist in character. A party generally priding itself on being open to new ideas and for the "little man" in American politics was being disparaged by some of its own leaders as unrepresentative and closed. The Chicago convention — and a national television audience — had witnessed harsh recriminations on the floor and police brutality in the streets (under orders of Mayor Richard Daley, one of the party's own chieftains).[45] There were accusations on all sides that Democrats seeking to end the Vietnam War could not have a proper voice at the convention because of the party's regressive delegate selection procedures. It was a sorry image of a presidential nomination, and a bitter pill for the party — made worse by Hubert Humphrey's loss to Richard Nixon in November.

The fact was that the innumerable laws and regulations, party rules, and local usages under which convention delegates were selected in the 50 states reflected no overall design, but a hundred years of disjointed state and national history. It was a hodgepodge; and in many cases it also allowed a handful of party leaders to select and control state delegations. Whether or not different procedures would have produced a different platform or a different nominee, there was no denying that Humphrey had been nominated without entering a single primary — while a series of primaries had been contested by other candidates, in particular Eugene McCarthy and Robert Kennedy, who was assassinated on the night of his victory in the California primary.

The convention responded in a classic manner by establishing a Commission on Party Structure and Delegate Selection, which was authorized to review the party's nominating procedures and to recommend changes that would soothe the divisive factions. Initially chaired by Senator George McGovern, and then by Congressman Donald Fraser, the commission lost no time in getting down to work.

Holding numerous public hearings around the country, which were unusually well covered by the press, the commission quickly made it evident that it did not intend to paper over the problems. Its report (which became the rules for the 1972 campaign) set forth 17 guidelines designed to ensure "all Democratic voters . . . a full, meaningful and timely opportunity to participate" in the selection of convention delegates.[46] State Democratic parties were *mandated* to implement these guidelines in their delegate-selection procedures — an important point, since in many cases formal state action was required, and state parties were the natural vehicle with which to bring national policy into state reality.[47] Among other things, convention delegations were required to accurately represent the demographic characteristics (especially with respect to age, race, and sex) of state party members, were to be selected in the year of the convention, and were to be chosen through procedures that involved the participation of the party's rank and file.

The McGovern-Fraser Commission (1969-72) set in motion a series of party decisions that restructured the nomination process and the party's organization. Running parallel to it was the O'Hara Commission on Rules* (which worked more quietly, mainly on convention rules). These were followed by the Mikulsky Commission (1973-74); the Compliance Review Commission (1974-76); the Sanford Charter Commission (1973-74); and the Winograd Commission (1975-78). In addition, the national conventions, the new midterm conventions of 1974 and 1978, and the national chairmen (and committees) all played both authorizing and modifying parts in this highly political process of rule change. The changes that were made in this ten-year period were by no means all of a piece. Each new commission worked in part to correct problems that had not been solved, or had been created, by the previous commissions. It is fair to say that "the tide of reform" crested in 1972, and that the subsequent commissions worked either to fit the McGovern-Fraser changes into the party organization (the Charter Commission) or to rework the rules so that certain elements of the pre-1970 period were brought back.[48]

---

*Representative James O'Hara of Michigan. The other Chairmen were: Representative Barbara Mikulsky of Maryland; Governor Terry Sanford of North Carolina; and Morley Winograd of Michigan (former state party chairman).

Keeping in mind that most of the major controversies that marked this decade of rule changing linger on, and thus may affect the actual behavior of politicians, let us summarize the principal changes of concern to presidential candidates in 1980:[49]

The presidential nominating system must be open to participation by all Democrats. In practice, participation means the opportunity both to become a national convention delegate and to vote for delegates. This in turn means that the ability to secure delegates in a state by dealing with a few state leaders is, at best, very limited. Instead, candidates must recruit delegates and appeal to the party's rank and file, usually in caucuses or primaries, to get their delegates elected; and in a number of states there will be a combination of caucuses or primaries and conventions. In choosing slates of delegates, the candidate must take care that in each state his slate reflects the party's demographic characteristics, in particular age, race, and sex. However, 10 percent of the eventual delegation (assuming enough delegates are won in the initial caucuses or primary) must be composed of party leaders and elected Democratic officials.

Delegates will be identified with the presidential candidates they support and will vote for their candidates in the convention. This ends the practice in some states of presenting lists of delegate candidates in a primary with no indication of which delegate represents which candidate. Obviously, this rule makes it easier for the party rank and file to vote for the presidential candidate of their choice. But it also binds the delegates pledged to a candidate to vote for that candidate at least through the first convention ballot (unless released by the candidate). The potential conflict in this lies in the possibility that between the time delegates are selected and the time they vote at the convention, events have changed their (and the electorate's) minds. As we shall see, this became a major issue at the Democratic convention in 1980.

Delegates will be fairly apportioned to reflect the presidential preferences of the primary/caucus/convention voters. Thus proportional representation replaced the "unit rule," which had been with the Democratic party virtually since its birth.[50] The rule was applied to both delegate apportionment (for example, winner-take-all primaries) and convention voting by state delegations, so that all the votes of a state might be cast for one candidate despite delegates who, though in a minority, supported other candidates. (It is also practiced in the Electoral College.) Proportional allocation is not total, however. A candidate must first reach a certain minimum "applicable percentage" of the votes cast, whatever the level of election, in order to qualify for *any* delegates. (The applicable percentage may vary from state to state, but cannot exceed 25 percent, and commonly will be between 15 and 20 percent.) Thus in a multi-candidate field, it is quite possible for a candidate to receive no delegates at all — serving to discourage candidates without broad popular support from continuing.

For campaigns, the new rule also means that even strong candidates will be motivated to run in as many states as possible, since even a losing effort will produce some delegates (as long as the applicable percentage is reached), and winning a clear majority of convention delegates is unlikely to occur before the last major set of primaries in June — assuming, of course, that there is more than trivial opposition. The rule further suggests that candidates, rather than concentrate a disproportionate amount of their resources in the large competitive states (as was the case under the winner-take-all rule), make a special effort in those states where they can expect to do very well — picking up an extra dividend of delegates for their efforts.[51] It also has been argued that the new rule favors candidates that express more extreme ideological positions, but this is less certain given all the other forces at play in preconvention politics.[52] In any case, since proportional representation is relatively uncommon in American politics, yet generally recognized as a significant factor by political scientists, the impact of this rule upon preconvention campaigns is likely to be considerable.

Participation in the delegate selection process will be restricted to Democratic voters. It is difficult to anticipate how soon this "closed primary" provision will actually become universally effective. This is because among the states open primaries take a number of different forms, sometimes allowing only independent voters to "cross over," for example. Furthermore, some states do not have formal voter registration, thus making the mechanics of a closed primary more difficult. The effects of cross-over voting vary substantially with the particular candidates and issues involved in a primary. Nevertheless, the purpose of this rule was twofold: to prevent Republican partisans from entering Democratic primaries for Republican purposes (for example, to nominate the weakest Democratic candidate), and to generally strengthen the organization.

In one form or another, the open primary was still present in 18 states by 1980 (see Appendix C), although Democratic officials found only Montana and Wisconsin in violation of the party rule — but both states went to court to defend their primaries in 1980. Wisconsin, widely considered the mother of primaries since it adopted an open (though not a presidential) primary in 1903 during the administration of Governor Robert M. La Follette, had been given an exemption from the national rule in 1976; but for 1980, the party decided that the state would finally have to comply.[53] When all was said and done, however, the party usually backed off from a strict enforcement of its rule during the 1970s. Given the inherent complexities of defining "party voters" in different states, and a reluctance to offend local organizations, it normally accepted any public declaration by voters that they were Democrats when they went to the polls.[54]

Whatever the case, by 1980 Democratic candidates could anticipate few problems from cross-over Republicans, except in the two states just mentioned. Republican candidates, on the other hand, were faced with a significant number of potential independent and Democratic cross overs in about half the states. As we shall see, this became an important factor in the 1980 campaign in the person of John Anderson — adding to the uncertainty caused by the electorate's growing instability as party attachment declined.

State parties must adopt and publish explicit rules and procedures covering their delegate selection processes, and these must conform to national party rules. The Democratic party's moves to "nationalize" its nomination process were a very significant feature of its 1970s rule changes.[55] By 1980, national party policies that generations earlier would not have even been discernible in the practices of some states were easy to see across the nation. The formal authority of the national party was established by the Supreme Court in the case of *Cousins* v. *Wigoda*, 419 U.S. 477 (1975), involving a challenge by Mayor Richard Daley's Chicago machine to the McGovern-Fraser guidelines for 1972. The Court declared that the rules adopted by the party's national convention prevailed over those of the Illinois state law.[56] Given the federal structure of political parties in the United States, this decision was an important legal precedent in support of national party authority* It was basically reaffirmed in *Democratic Party of the United States*

---

*Of course, it is the national convention's ability to seat or refuse to seat state delegations, supported by *Cousins* v. *Wigoda*, that provides the immediate sanction against those who refuse to comply with the national rules.

of America v. *Bronson C. La Follette*, 449 U.S. 897 (1981), when Wisconsin's challenge to the party's 1980 closed primary rule finally reached the Supreme Court.[57]

For candidates, the fact that the states must publish their procedures for delegate selection, and do it early (no later than January 1 of the election year), is a convenience, for it eases the operations of their state grass-roots campaigns. Of course, "publication" leaves much to be desired in some cases yet even so, the existence of written rules simplifies matters for candidates who are not familiar with the state, or are not on good terms with local party officials. This is not to imply that the rule changes have simplified matters for preconvention campaigns overall. In the proliferation of primaries and the details of affirmative action and pledged delegates, they have done just the opposite. Nevertheless, this particular provision of the rules should make things easier, and certainly will help protect candidates against the manipulation of petitions, quorums, and slate-making that long-established local organizations have engaged in previously.

I have addressed the rule changes of the Democratic party during the 1970s not only because they received considerable public and professional attention but also because they have affected the electoral system as a whole in the United States. Naturally, the Republican party was perfectly aware of the Democratic rule changes, and in the earlier part of the reform period responded to similar pressures with changes of its own. But the Republicans were quieter and less peremptory about changing their rules, and also less interested. Two reform commissions were created. The Delegates and Organization (DO) Commission served from 1969 to 1972, and the Rule 29 Commission from 1973 to 1974. Both dealt with the same types of issues as their Democratic counterparts. However, as Cotter and Bibby point out, the organizational philosophy and political conditions of the Republican party were substantially different from those of the Democrats, with the result that the Republican delegate selection rules experienced only modest changes.[58] State parties were called upon to take "positive action" to increase the proportion of black, female, and young delegates, for example, but serious enforcement mechanisms were lacking. Consequently, between 1968 and 1976 the general increase in such delegates was considerably greater in Democratic than in Republican conventions.[59] The Democrats also experienced a greater increase in inexperienced (as opposed to veteran) delegates. Basically during the 1970s the Democratic party proceeded by *mandating* changes in state party delegate selection, while the Republicans achieved some of the same effects by having their national committee provide services and support for the state and local organizations.[60]

One result of this different approach was substantially stronger state and local Republican campaign organizations ready for the 1980 election. For the moment, however, let us return to the "spill-over" effects of the Democratic rule changes. As the national Democratic party called upon its state parties to bring their delegate selection procedures into compliance with the national rules, this required action on the part of the state governments (since state election laws were involved). In responding — and remember, this was a period of strong pressures for reform generally — many state governments found it simpler to adopt direct primaries than to make the necessary modifications in their caucus or convention systems. This meant that Republicans as well as Democrats were affected by the new procedures, thus greatly expanding the impact of the Democratic rules. (Rules governing independent candidates were an exception. The consequence was that independents were almost always left in a more ill-defined and difficult position, a fact that would affect the candidacy of John Anderson in 1980.)

In any case, for the Democrats the number of primaries increased from 17 in 1968, to 23 in 1972, 30 in 1976, and 35 in 1980 (see Appendix C). Equally significant, the percentage of delegates chosen in these primaries rose from 40 to 65, 76, and over 85 when the "grass-roots caucuses," such as Iowa's, are added.[61] For candidates this means that instead of being faced with a handful of important primaries (before 1972 some were not linked to delegate selection and others were not worth the effort because they were winner-take-all, so there might be four or five a candidate would find it useful to enter), they now confront an extended series of primaries, caucuses, and conventions, few of which can be missed without losing needed delegates. To garner these delegates the candidate of the 1980s cannot rely on the influence of a few key leaders in each state, but instead must prepare for intensive campaigning in state after state — and sometimes in several states at the same time — since there is no substitute for the steady accumulation of delegates at the grass-roots level. Clearly, the new rules place a premium on the ability to attract not just the chiefs, but also the Indians; so time, travel, careful scheduling, mass media advertising, local organization, and the resources to make all of this possible are required. To a significant extent, the components of a general election campaign are now needed to compete for delegates in the preconvention period.

Rules for the Collection and Expenditure of Money

The same forces of protest and reform that led to new delegate selection rules were also part of those that pressed for major changes in the rules of campaign finance during the 1970s. In this case, however, the resulting rules were not those of political parties and the states but of the federal government. The history of attempts to regulate the financing of federal election campaigns stretches back to the nineteenth century, and it is not a proud record of success.[62] Two general points can be made at once: the pressures to increase campaign expenditures are unrelenting; and the law separating needy politicians from greedy contributors (or vice versa) that is without loopholes has yet to be framed.

Partly as the result of the sharply increasing costs, and partly because of rising concern about the political influence of large contributors, which obviously were not being effectively constrained by existing laws, Congress passed the Federal Election Campaign Act (FECA) of 1971. This act, in turn, did not prevent the excesses of the 1972 campaign that were gradually exposed in the Watergate investigations. These revelations led to the 1974 amendments to the 1971 act that for the first time provided public financing for presidential campaigns. Just as the 1976 campaign was getting under way, portions of the amended act were declared unconstitutional in the case of *Buckley* v. *Valio*, 424 U.S. 1 (1976). Both Congress and the President reacted with comparative dispatch, and the 1976 amendments took effect in May — in time for the remaining primaries and general election of that year. Altogether, the 1971 act (and the Revenue Act of 1971 that provided the funds from an income tax check-off) and its 1974, 1976, and 1979 amendments constitute an unprecedented restructuring of federal campaign regulation and financing.

Contributions

Individuals, political parties, and political action committees (PACs) are all limited in what they may contribute to federal campaigns. Individuals may contribute no more than $1,000 to a candidate in an election, and $25,000 to all federal candidates in any one year. They may give up to $5,000 to a PAC, and up to $20,000 to a party's national committee. PACs may contribute no more than $5,000 to a candidate in an election and $15,000 annually to a national committee. Multicandidate committees may give up to $15,000 to a national committee, and up to $5,000 per election per candidate. Political party committees, such as congressional campaign committees, may contribute no more than $17,500 to a federal candidate in an election (with the exception of the national committees given below). However, certain state and local party expenditures for buttons, leaflets, posters, and so on, in behalf of federal candidates are not counted as contributions. Presidential candidates may contribute up to $50,000 to their own campaigns.

Expenditures and Public Financing

Presidential candidates who seek public financing, in order to qualify for public support in the primaries, must collect at least $5,000 in each of 20 states in contributions of $250 or less (and a total of at least $100,000). After qualifying, they are eligible for public matching funds covering all individual contributions again up through $250, although not beyond their expenditure limits. Candidates may spend no more than $14.7 million* before the nomination (which also includes national convention expenses), with specific limits in each state based on the size of the state's voting population. For example, the 1980 spending limit in New Hampshire was $294,400.[63] Candidates may also spend an additional 20 percent (about $2.9 million) on fund raising, but this is not covered by matching funds. The two major parties are each given $4.4 million to help finance their national conventions.

For the general election, the major party candidates each receive $29.4 million in public funding, and no private contributions are permitted. However, the two major parties may each spend up to $4.6 million on their presidential candidates, making a total of $34 million available for campaign expenses in 1980. (Both candidate and national committee expenditures on services required to comply

---

*All the figures in this section are for 1980. The level of federal support is indexed to match inflation.

with the FECA are exempted from the spending limits.) Minor-party and independent candidates are eligible to receive a proportion of full funding based on the number of votes they receive(d) either in the current or last election.

Presidential candidates who do not seek public financing are not limited in their expenditures, but the contribution limits are the same. Political action committees (or anyone else) are allowed to spend unlimited amounts opposing or supporting candidates as long as these expenditures are "independent" of candidate campaigns. As one might guess, this loophole in the FECA, which resulted from the *Buckley* decision and the resulting 1976 amendments, has encouraged large independent expenditures and was a major factor in the 1980 elections.

Reporting and Disclosure

Although by the decade's end some of the more burdensome reporting requirements had been lightened, federal campaigns faced record-keeping and reporting requirements that were unheard of a short generation earlier. Any person seeking federal office who raises or spends more than $5,000 must report to the Federal Election Commission (FEC). These reports must follow a regular quarterly schedule and cover contributions received and expenditures made (unless these are less than $5,000 in a quarter). Nine reports must be made during a two-year election cycle, with modest distinctions between election and nonelection years. Presidential campaign committees, with contributions or expenditures over $100,000, must report monthly. Contributions and expenditures over $200 must be itemized, and contributions over $1,000 made less than 20 days before an election must be reported within 48 hours.

Not only do the new rules require an imposing amount of record-keeping to marshal the preceding and other information, but also they do not leave this to chance. Each campaign committee *must* have a treasurer; it must establish internal procedures so that contributions of more than $50 are reported to the treasurer within ten days; it (the treasurer) must see to it that financial records are preserved for three years; and it must have the candidate's name in its title. In short, the new rules require an explicit set of procedures and personnel for collecting and disclosing financial information.

A sizable apparatus is involved, and its demands are not to be taken lightly.[64] PACs are subject to the same type of organizational requirements, as are national party committees. Significantly, in its 1979 FECA amendments, Congress recognized the excessive burden of these rules on local party organizations and exempted them from filing reports if expenditures for activities associated with federal campaigns are less than $5,000 a year.

Administration: The Federal Election Commission

An independent agency composed of six bipartisan members, the FEC is the first specialized agency the nation has had to implement its campaign finance regulations.[65] Its members are appointed to six-year terms by the President and confirmed by the Senate. It has authority to conduct audits, issue subpoenas and advisory opinions, frame regulations, and sue for civil injunctions.[66]

Not surprisingly, considering its central role in the elaboration and administration of the FECA, the FEC has been subject to continuing controversy during its short life. As originally created by the 1974 amendments, it was declared unconstitutional in *Buckley* v. *Valeo* scarcely a year after it was organized in April 1975 (because some of its members were appointed by Congress, it violated the separation of powers). Among the recurring issues surrounding the agency are the extent of its independence, the character of its advisory opinions, its use of its auditing authority, and the level of its budgetary support.[67] The issue of independence has arisen whenever there are appointments to the FEC, as both conservative and liberal wings of the parties, and public interest groups, are on the lookout for proposed new members who might be in the thrall of some opposing point of view. It has arisen, too, out of the authority Congress has retained to disallow (within 30 legislative days) FEC regulations before they take effect. And Congress has exercised this authority in cases affecting its campaigns. As Jacobson puts it, "Members of Congress appreciate regulation no more than anyone else, and they are in a position to do something about it."[68]

By 1980, issues involving the FEC's audits and advisory opinions (AOs) had led to a narrowing of both its authority and its practices in these functional activities. In the case of audits, first priority was given to candidates and committees that asked for assistance (Are we doing it right? Is your judgment of our condition the same as ours?), and Congress had removed the authority to do random audits. The problems with early advisory opinions (which are very handy for campaigns uncertain about whether some procedure is within the law) grew out of similar uncertainties about their authority and breadth. Thus by the end of the decade the FEC was issuing formal AOs in response only to very specific questions, and informal "advisory opinion responses" (AORs), which were estimations of the applicability of *proposed* regulations, and which did not carry the authority of AOs.[69] In short, the FEC was taking care that its advisory opinions did not take the place of regulations.

Given the close relationship between the FEC's budget and its level of activity, and the forces, both in and out of Congress, that are strongly for or against the regulation of campaign finance, the level of budgetary support for the FEC has been, and doubtless will be, a point of controversy. Even a casual review of FEC activities shows that they are intertwined with manifold political interests that have something to win or lose from elections. Thus the extent of campaign audits and financial disclosures can be of great importance to campaigns in terms not only of the resources they must devote to keeping records and making reports but also of the public exposure contributors are willing to risk. Congress has bestowed an impressive amount of formal authority on the FEC, but in the practical world of campaign politics there is a vast difference between a commission that is abundantly funded and one that is starved — and the agency can be counted on to be a continuing object of budgetary conflict.[70] Nevertheless, both before and after the 1980 election, it is safe to say that while underfunded in the eyes of those favoring more financial regulation, the FEC has achieved an unprecedented administrative effectiveness that will be politically difficult to reverse.

It is evident that the federal regulations of campaign contributions and expenditures, and the provisions for public financing of presidential campaigns, adopted during the 1970s constitute important changes in what campaigns must do. Presidential candidates, for example, must not only act early to acquire campaign personnel who will enable them to meet the various record-keeping and reporting requirements but also put into play strategies for taking advantage of the matching funds provided by public financing. This is no mean feat given the combinations of caucuses and primaries, and the uncertainties about opponents' strategies – *especially* for candidates who begin with limited resources. Therefore, if the inherent logic of campaign finance possibilities seems to attract candidates of modest wealth, they also impose unequal burdens upon certain types of candidates – such as those who begin with weak grass-roots organizations or little financial expertise. The new rules of the 1970s thus cut both ways by first encouraging candidates to enter the fray, and then confronting them with rules that require more resources of organization and support than they are able to marshal. We shall see this occur in the 1980 campaigns.

Although it cannot be reviewed in detail, a substantial body of new state campaign finance legislation was also in place by the 1980 elections. Just as the states reacted to changes in national party rules, many also modified their campaign finance laws both to follow federal practices and to comply with the *Buckley* v. *Valeo* decision.[71] As always, there is enormous diversity among the states with respect to campaign financing – diversity that is not reflected in the summary figures that follow. Of the states, 25 have contribution limits and 24 forbid or sharply restrict corporate giving. At the same time, almost all the states allow the operation of PACs. There are disclosure requirements in 49 states; 29 have bipartisan independent election commissions; 17 have public financing of campaigns; and 11 channel public funds through political parties. While this last provision shows that some states have adopted policies distinct from those of the federal government, the overall patterns suggest definite federal policy leadership. And to a large extent the same type of political controversies that have surrounded the operations of the FEC also have been common at the state level, with underfunding and understaffing of the election commissions being the normal state of affairs.

Finally, it is prudent to keep in mind that, along with the continuing readjustment of party rules, campaign finance laws and regulations also remain in a condition of fluidity. For this reason, particular provisions of the rules, such as individual contribution limits or expenditure ceilings for specific primaries, are almost certain to change before the next presidential election.[72] And even more changes can be expected among the states, as each in its way responds to the pressures for more or less control over money in its campaigns. As a whole, however, the basic thrust of the campaign financing rules of the 1970s appears to be difficult to reverse; and in any case the rules were in effect for the 1980 campaigns.

THE CHANGING CONDITIONS OF POLITICAL PARTIES

One of the recurring points that has emerged as we have considered different rules changes affecting campaigns is that they also have affected political parties, usually in a negative way. Of course some of the rules, such as procedures of delegate selection, have been those of the parties themselves, but in other cases the forces of change have come from outside the parties. Public financing of presidential campaigns, for example, channels money directly to candidates, not via parties. It is true that the two major parties receive public funds to help conduct their national conventions; that there are special provisions in the FECA that allow parties to give more to their candidates than individual or group contributors may; and that they (the major parties) also enjoy reduced postal rates not shared by minor parties. Yet during the critical preconvention period, when nominations are now won or lost, federal matching funds flow to candidates on the basis of what *they* − not their parties − do.

Does the particular form of public financing of presidential campaigns thus have the effect of downgrading the role of party organizations in the electoral process? It would seem so; but to say it is a "cause" of general party decline is more difficult, for we are dealing here with complex political institutions of great subtlety and variety. Hence simple cause-and-effect relationships, say between specific delegate selection rules and the flabbiness of party muscle generally, are hard to establish with much confidence. Evaluations of such connections are more complicated still because of conflicting judgments about the proper character of party organizations.[73] Suffice it to say that particular linkages between various "reforms" of the 1970s and the condition of U.S. political parties are matters of considerable dispute.[74]

Relatively consistent patterns, however, are quite clear, and what is not in dispute is the overall decline of political parties during the 1960s and 1970s. This can be seen in both the fall off in citizen "loyalty" to the two major parties and the inability of party organizations to exert influence over political events, such as the recruitment of party candidates. Obviously, these two functions − of "structuring the electorate" and controlling public leadership recruitment − are interrelated, since the capacity to mobilize voters helps to win elections. Nonetheless, let us examine these two aspects of political parties separately.

Earlier we observed that as the American electorate became younger during the 1970s it also became more politically independent. Other age groups became more independent as well, and the overall extent of this decline in partisanship can be seen in Table 1.2, where patterns of party identification since 1940 are presented. Preceded by a drop-off in Republican partisanship in the 1940s, and again in 1964, independence rose sharply in the period between 1965 and 1972, at the cost of strong party identification.

Acknowledging that what is being measured in Table 1.2 is quite complex,[75] its significance to candidates is relatively plain. Not surprisingly, individuals who identify more strongly with their parties are not only more likely to vote, but also more likely to vote for their party's candidates. In 1976, for example, 95 percent of strong Democrats and 98 percent of strong Republicans reported having voted for their party's presidential candidate, while about 77 percent of weak partisans voted "loyally" — a difference between strong and weak partisans that was smaller than usual. Also important, however, has been the increasing willingness of even strong partisans to defect from their party in one election or another. (Generally, Republicans are more loyal than Democrats.) Thus in 1952 fewer than 12 out of every 100 strong partisans admitted to *ever* having voted for any candidate from another party, while in 1976 that number had climbed to 31 percent.[76] Among weak partisans, less than half always stayed with the party. In short, no longer can the presidential (or other) candidate be assured of support (or opposition) from a very large proportion of the electorate because of party. Campaigns must be fashioned in the face of greater uncertainty, and to make more direct appeals to voters based on their interests in public policies and the candidate. Nimmo and Savage describe what happens in this weaker party situation as follows: ". . . the voter formulates images of the candidates and parties and votes for the candidate with the most favorable image; if there is none, his partisan self-image takes over. Voters with neither candidate nor partisan self-images reach null decisions; that is, there is no basis to say how they will vote."[77]

The strength of party organizations in the electoral process cannot be measured with the same precision as party identification

TABLE 1.2
Party Identification of the American Electorate

	1940	1944	1947	1952	1956	1960	1964	1968	1972	1976	1980
Strong Democrats				22	21	20	27	20	15	15	17
Weak Democrats	41	41	46	25	23	24	25	25	26	25	23
Independents	20	20	21	22	23	22	22	29	35	36	34
Weak Republicans	38	38	27	14	14	14	13	14	13	14	14
Strong Republicans				13	15	15	11	10	10	9	9
Other	1	*	7	4	4	5	2	2	2	2	3

*Unavailable.

Sources: William H. Flanigan and Nancy H. Zingale, *Political Behavior of the American Electorate*, 4th ed. (Boston: Allyn and Bacon, 1979), pp. 54-55; and Warren E. Miller, "Policy Directions and Presidential Leadership: Alternative Interpretations of the 1980 Presidential Election," paper presented at the 1981 Annual Meeting of the American Political Science Association, New York, September 3-6, 1981, Table 2.

among voters. Nevertheless, the ability of these organizations to perform electoral functions can be at least roughly assessed in terms of the resources and rules we have already discussed. Once again, consider presidential candidates. Confronted very early in the prenomination period with the need for a substantial and expert campaign organization in order to optimize public matching funds, while competing in a lengthy and costly series of caucuses and primaries, they obviously cannot rely on party organizations that have limited control over either money or votes (and are also deterred by other rules of the game restricting prenomination intervention) to pull them through. They must build their own organizations.

(They may, of course, opt not to seek public financing, thus avoiding FECA expenditure limits; but this does not free them from the contribution, record-keeping, and disclosure requirements, or make them more able to draw support from their parties. Instead, candidates eschewing federal matching funds must put together even more formidable organizations able to collect individual and PAC contributions large enough to somehow overcome the stigma of representing the very rich.)

True, once nominated, a presidential candidate may designate his party's national committee as his "principal campaign committee" and adopt its staff as his own; but by then it is late in the game — too late to displace the candidate's prenomination organization, built from primary to primary, and based on intense mutual experiences and trust, with an unfamiliar staff of uncertain loyalties. Naturally, if the candidate is an incumbent president it will be easier to make the national committee an arm of the campaign; yet even so, organizational dynamics and intraparty sensitivities impose practical limits upon the capacity of a party's national committee to serve as the core of any candidate's campaign before and after the nomination.

Interestingly enough, another result of the campaign finance rule changes of the 1970s has affected the ability of party organizations to influence (and protect) their candidates. This has been the explosive growth of political action committees, the early development of which was noted earlier. Following the *Buckley* v. *Valeo* decision, and the ensuing 1976 FECA amendments, the growth of these committees, and especially of those representing corporations, accelerated. Between 1974 and 1980, the total number of PACs increased from 608 to 2,387, and corporate PACs from 89 to 1,127.* In comparison, the number of labor PACs grew from 201 to 276 during this same period. Understandably, in view of FECA contribution limitations ($5,000 to a campaign), PAC contributions were aimed primarily at congressional campaigns. Compared to $22.5 million in 1976, PACs gave almost three times that amount — approximately $56 million — to House and Senate candidates in 1980. The availability of funds on this scale causes congressional and state candidates to expand their search for money outside their constituencies, just as the individual campaign contribution limit leads rich PACs to search across the nation for candidates sharing their interests and values.[78]

Equally significant are the burgeoning "independent" expenditures by individuals and PACs that I mentioned earlier. Unrestricted by FECA regulations as long as they are not coordinated with candidate campaigns, so-called independent PACs spent $16.1 million in the 1980 elections — expenditures that were overwhelmingly in support of conservative candidates.[79] Moreover, a number of the largest and most sophisticated committees began their independent expenditures in opposition to and support of candidates before 1980. The National Conservative Political Action Committee, for example, spent $7,463,833 in the two years between 1979 and 1980, followed closely by the Congressional Club (formed by supporters of Jesse Helms, a conservative senator from North Carolina), which spent $7,212,754.[80] In contrast to direct campaign contributions, independent expenditures are not only unlimited but also may target individual candidates, thus easily displacing political parties as the principal source of resources affecting a candidate's chances of election. For example, independent committees spent approximately $10 million on the election of Ronald Reagan, while the Republican National Committee was able to spend only $4.6 million, its legal limit.

Thus by 1980 the declining role of political parties in marshaling support for campaigns was counterbalanced by the rise of incipient alternative institutions of campaign financing.[81] As their parties have lost the ability to deliver money, workers, and votes, candidates have found themselves increasingly on their own and vulnerable to the threats and promises of large PACs — groups that in contrast to parties tend to represent narrow interests in the society. Consequently,

---

*The source of these data is the FEC, and I have noticed that the numbers vary slightly depending on who retrieves them from the FEC's computer.

the weakened ability of parties to mobilize the electorate and to provide other campaign resources in the 1970s has presented an opening that other political organizations have exploited.

The import of this situation has not been lost upon the major parties. Democratic and Republican national chairmen alike have expressed their opposition to the unrestrained intervention of independent PACs in campaign financing — which is significant in view of the preponderance of independent expenditures going to Republican candidates in 1980.[82] The public-interest reform groups that initiated and gave heavy support to the campaign finance rules of the 1970s — rules intended to restrain the political influence of large concentrations of wealth — ended the decade in a state of outrage at the unintended consequences that the ensuing independent expenditures have brought about.[83]

There is little doubt that by the 1980 elections changes in the major political parties that took place during the preceding 10 or 15 years confronted many federal candidates with substantially different rules of the game than existed a short generation earlier. Generally, these new rules have led candidates away from a reliance on their parties and toward a reliance on their own resources and endeavors. We must take care not to conclude more than the evidence can justify, however. The decline of parties has not been the same in every constituency throughout the land, since in many states and districts parties have never been vigorous, and in others party organizations remain formidable. What is more, it is too soon to leap to the conclusion that the national parties are disintegrating. To paraphrase Mark Twain, rumors of their death are premature — grossly premature in the case of the Republican party, which a number of times during the last decade appeared on the verge of losing so many of its identifiers as to be a stretcher case. During the last half of the 1970s the Republican national committee mounted a determined effort to rebuild the party's organization from top to bottom. It used the technology of direct mail to construct an impressive financial base, and from the resulting resources major contributions were made to its congressional and state candidates.[84] By 1980 it was able to conduct an extensive media campaign, *as a party*, to undermine Democratic candidates *before* the traditional campaign period began.

As we shall see in greater detail later, the result was that in the 1979-80 two-year period the national Republican party raised more than $110 million (compared to less than $20 million by the Democrats) and was able to organize a revitalized local get-out-the-vote operation for the November elections. In the aftermath of the elections, the national staff utilized the party's computer facilities to develop elaborate redistricting maps, covering both Congress and the states, to take advantage of the redistricting required by the 1980 census. And also in the postelection period it even appeared that the party was at last increasing its proportion of identifiers in the electorate, and specifically among young potential voters.[85]

For the Democratic party the organizational picture was far less bright as the 1980s began. The party's national committee lagged badly behind its Republican counterpart in raising money, supporting congressional candidates, and building state and local organizations before and during 1980. Following the election it (and various adjunct organizations) began vigorous efforts to improve its direct-mail fund-raising capability, but the returns continued to lag considerably behind those of the Republicans. Nevertheless, with a new national chairman, the party gave numerous indications that it was sensitive to its decline as an organization. Authorized by the national convention in 1980, still another special commission was established in 1981 to "reform the reforms" of presidential nominating and other procedures; its chairman is Governor James B. Hunt, Jr., of North Carolina. At this point the indications are that the Hunt Commission will attempt to strengthen the role of the party in future campaigns.[86] In the 1980 campaigns, however, the Democratic party represented the sagging political institution that we pictured earlier.

SUMMARY

In this chapter we have considered some of what I have called "rules of the game" that affect electoral campaigns. In one way or another these are elements of the political environment that campaigners cannot control and cannot ignore. They must play by these rules in order to optimize their chances of election.[87] Bear in mind, of course, that I have by no means presented *all* the rules of the campaign "game," for this would be exhausting.[88] Instead, I have concentrated on those rules that appear to have changed in recent years (or at least since 1960) and to be of significance. Some of the rules are characteristics of the population; others are technological in nature; and still others are directly man-made, and more liable to manipulation, especially by incumbent officeholders. In such cases we are obviously in some conceptual difficulty, since a game disintegrates if the rules can be changed by the players — as Lewis Carroll pointed out in *Alice in Wonderland*.

We have seen that the electorate has become older, better educated, redistributed, and more sensitive to candidates and issues rather than political parties. Technologies of mass communication, poll taking, computer analysis, machine processing, and high-speed travel have become key instruments available to campaigns. Political parties have lost much of their organizational muscle and have become lighter political anchors for individual voters. Formal procedures for presidential nominations have been modified so that they are "open" to more segments of the population, with the result that campaigns are pressed to be longer, larger, and more expensive — characteristics that are also consistent with new requirements of campaign financing. Yet while the new rules call for campaigns to reach out to "small" contributors, they also have led to enormous concentrations of financial resources in the hands of PACs, whose legal ability to spend is virtually without formal restraints.

In examining these rules I have tried to indicate the impact they can be expected to have on campaign operations; and such effects often can already be seen. In other cases, however, they are just elements of the campaign environment that rational candidates can be expected to adapt to in given ways in order to make the best of their electoral situation. This does not mean that the rules are "fair." A Republican candidate in the borough of Manhattan (New York City), for example, is very unlikely to get as many votes as a Democrat because the overwhelming number of registered Democrats comprise a rule that places the Republican at a distinct disadvantage. Yet playing by the rules allows the Republican the best chance of minimizing his or her losses. In short, if we think of the various environmental factors that affect electoral politics as rules, we are able to assess the *quality* of political campaigns apart from the eventual electoral outcome. It will be useful to keep this in mind as we review the various approaches to campaign analysis in the next chapter.

NOTES

1. John Von Neumann and Oskar Morgenstern, *Theory of Games and Economic Behavior* (New York: John Wiley, 1964), pp. 48-49.

2. Theodore H. White, *The Making of the President 1960* (New York: Pocket Books, 1961), pp. 326-30; 342-43.

3. U.S. Bureau of the Census release, as reported in the New York *Times*, May 24, 1981, p. A44.

4. Gerald M. Pomper with Susan S. Lederman, *Elections in America*, 2d ed. (New York: Longman, 1980), p. 57.

5. Bruce A. Campbell, *The American Electorate* (New York: Holt, Rinehart, & Winston, 1979), pp. 228-29; William H. Flanigan and Nancy H. Zingale, *Political Behavior of the American Electorate*, 4th ed. (Boston: Allyn and Bacon, 1979), pp. 26 and 70; and Pomper and Lederman, *Elections in America*, p. 57.

6. Flanigan and Zingale, *Political Behavior*, pp. 68-72. More intensive analyses are presented to Paul R. Abramson, "Generational Change in American Electoral Behavior," *American Political Science Review* 68 (March 1974): 93-105; and Philip E. Converse, *The Dynamics of Party Support: Cohort-Analyzing Party Identification* (Beverly Hills, Calif.: Sage, 1976).

7. Flanigan and Zingale, *Political Behavior*, pp. 26-27.

8. Ibid., p. 26.

9. Considering only the elderly group, and apart from the obvious issue of Reagan's age, samples that come immediately to mind are policy issues of retirement age, medical care, social security, tax structure, and many more. In 1981, as reports of the 1980 census became available, there were numerous discussions of these age-related issues — all of which were relevant to 1980 campaign decisions. See, for example, Warren Weaver, Jr., "Retiring at Age 65 is a Receding Good," New York *Times*, March 9, 1981, p. 1.

10. Campbell, *The American Electorate*, pp. 225-27.

11. Norman H. Nie, Sidney Verba, and John R. Petrocik, *The Changing American Voter* (Cambridge, Mass.: Harvard University Press, 1976), esp. p. 304; and Pomper and Lederman, *Elections in America*, pp. 59-68.

12. While less than one-third of American housewives planned to become employed in 1970, in 1980 the proportion was over one-half. Also, almost two-thirds of all adult American women worked outside their homes. Marlene Ellen and Thelma Anderson reported these findings in a study done for the Newspaper Advertising Bureau, Inc., Binghamton (N.Y.) *Sun-Bulletin*, July 31, 1979, p. B1.

13. The relationships here are discussed in Flanigan and Zingale, *Political Behavior*, p. 72.

14. New York *Times*, April 5, 1981, p. A1; and U.S. Department of Commerce *News*, Bureau of the Census (Washington, D.C.: Public Information Office, August 20, 1981).

15. New York *Times*, May 3, 1981, p. A30. By 1980 a majority of the eligible voters lived in the South and West.

16. This is shown at length in the landmark study by Paul F. Lazarsfeld, Bernard Berelson, and Hazel Gaudet, *The People's Choice* (New York: Duell, Sloan and Pearce, 1944).

17. Stanley Kelley, Jr., "Campaign Debates: Some Facts and Issues," *Public Opinion Quarterly* 26 (Fall 1962):352-59. Various selections covering the topic are presented in Robert Agranoff, *The New Style in Election Campaigns* (Boston: Holbrook Press, 1972), Section 4.

18. Thomas E. Patterson, *The Mass Media Election* (New York: Praeger, 1980), p. 4.

19. U.S. Bureau of the Census, *Statistical Abstract of the United States* (Washington, D.C.: U.S. Government Printing Office, 1980), p. 589.

20. Ibid., p. 592.

21. F. Christopher Arterton, "Campaign Organizations Confront the Media-Political Environment," in *Race for the Presidency*, ed. James David Barber (Englewood Cliffs, N.J.: Prentice-Hall, 1978). Much of this literature is summarized in Doris A. Graber, *Mass Media and American Politics* (Washington, D.C.: Congressional Quarterly Inc., 1980), esp. Chapter 6. A particularly insightful treatment is by Stephen Hess, *The Presidential Campaign* (Washington, D.C.: Brookings Institution, 1978), pp. 67-80.

22. Still the best description of this is Joe McGinniss, *The Selling of the President 1968* (New York: Pocket Books, 1970).

23. Patterson, *The Mass Media Election*, pp. 3-6; and Stephen J. Wayne, *The Road to the White House* (New York: St. Martin's Press, 1980), p. 31.

24. Wayne, *Road to the White House*, pp. 155-56.

25. A touching portrayal of that Truman campaign is given by TRB, "When It Was Good," *The New Republic*, November 1, 1980, p. 3.

26. In his 1978 reelection campaign, Governor Hugh Carey of New York chartered a train and whistle-stopped through large areas upstate, once again confirming the utility (and novelty) of this mode of transportation for modest distances between populated areas.

27. Robert Agranoff, *The Management of Election Campaigns* (Boston: Holbrook Press, 1976), pp. 246-49; Herbert E. Alexander, *Financing Politics: Money, Elections and Political Reform*, 2d ed. (Washington, D.C.: Congressional Quarterly Press, 1980), Chapters 1 and 3; and Wayne, *Road to the White House*, pp. 27-32.

28. Alexander, *Financing Politics*, pp. 59-62.

29. Ibid., pp. 59-60.

30. Agranoff, *Management of Election Campaigns*, p. 248.

31. Wayne, *Road to the White House*, pp. 226-27.

32. Jonathan Robbin, "Geodemographics: The New Magic," *Campaigns and Elections* 1 (Spring 1980):25-45.

33. Ibid.

34. Ithiel de Sola Pool, Robert P. Abelson, and Samuel Popkin, *Candidates, Issues and Strategies* (Cambridge, Mass.: M.I.T. Press, 1964 and 1965).

35. Wayne, *Road to the White House*, pp. 228-30.

36. Everett C. Ladd and G. Donald Ferree, "Were the Pollsters Really Wrong?" *Public Opinion*, December/January 1981, pp. 13ff. Scholars have long known and written about the requirements, pitfalls, and limitations of systematic public opinion polling. See, for example, Bernard C. Hennessy, *Public Opinion*, 4th ed. (Monterey, Calif.: Brooks/Cole, 1981), Chapters 4, 5, and 6.

37. Seymour Martin Lipset, "Different Polls, Different Results in 1980 Politics," *Public Opinion*, August/September 1980, p. 60. This article refers specifically to 1980 cases. A much fuller explanation can be found in any standard textbook on public opinion or basic statistics. For example, see Hennessy, *Public Opinion*, p. 53.

38. New York *Times*, September 17, 1980, p. B10.

39. Stanley Kelley, Jr., *Professional Public Relations and Political Power* (Baltimore: Johns Hopkins University Press, 1956).

40. Agranoff, *New Style in Election Campaigns*, pp. 52-69.

41. Sidney Blumenthal, *The Permanent Campaign* (Boston: Beacon Press, 1980). More analytic and comprehensive is Melvyn H. Bloom, *Public Relations and Presidential Campaigns: A Crisis in Democracy* (New York: Crowell, 1973).

42. Blumenthal, *The Permanent Campaign*, Chapters 4, 7, and 12. Some, such as Garth, insist on it.

43. Karl A. Lamb and Paul A. Smith present an early example of this conflict in *Campaign Decision-Making: The Presidential Election of 1964* (Belmont, Calif.: Wadsworth, 1968), pp. 159-62. There are many others.

44. Actually the changes were begun before the 1968 convention. See William Crotty, *Decisions for Democrats: Reforming the Party Structure* (Baltimore: Johns Hopkins University Press, 1978), pp. 14-19; and James W. Ceaser, *Presidential Selection: Theory and Development* (Princeton, N.J.: Princeton University Press, 1979), especially Chapter 6.

45. Theodore H. White, *The Making of the President 1968* (New York: Atheneum, 1969), pp. 297-98.

46. Crotty, *Decisions for Democrats*, Chapter 3.

47. This does not mean that all states responded to the "mandate." In fact, the response was gradual and often grudging. See ibid., pp. 105 and 109.

48. Virtually all those who have studied these rule changes agree with this point. For example, see Herbert Asher, *Presidential Elections and American Politics*, rev. ed. (Homewood, Ill.: Dorsey Press, 1980), pp. 306-12; and Wayne, *Road to the White House*, pp. 97-100.

49. Most of the information about the rules in what follows is drawn from *Delegate Selection Rules for the 1980 Democratic National Convention* (Washington, D.C.: Democratic National Committee, 1978).

50. Crotty, *Decisions for Democrats*, pp. 288-90.

51. Nelson W. Polsby and Aaron Wildavsky, *Presidential Elections*, 5th ed. (New York: Charles Scribner's Sons, 1980), pp. 88-92.

52. William Cavala, "Changing the Rules Changes the Game: Party Reform and the 1972 California Delegates to the Democratic National Convention," *American Political Science Review* 68 (March 1974):27-42; and James Lengle and Byron Shafer, "Primary Rules, Political Power, and Social Change," *American Political Science Review* 70 (March 1976):25-40.

53. E. J. Dionne, Jr., "Crossover Vote Looms in 8 More Races," New York *Times*, April 10, 1980. Wisconsin proceeded to challenge the party but eventually lost before the Supreme Court in *Democratic Party of the United States of America* v. *Bronson C. La Follette*, 449 U.S. 897 (1981).

54 Ibid. Also see Frank J. Sorauf, *Party Politics in America*, 4th ed. (Boston: Little, Brown, 1980), pp. 205-08.

55. The nationalization concept is discussed by Xandra Kayden, "The Nationalizing of the Party System," in *Parties, Interest Groups, and Campaign Finance Laws*, ed. Michael J. Malbin (Washington, D.C.: American Enterprise Institute, 1980), pp. 257-82; and Charles H. Longley, "Party Nationalization in America," in *Paths to Political Reform*, ed. William J. Crotty (Boston: D. C. Heath, 1979).

56. The Court's emphasis was on the vital role the national convention played in the process of choosing presidential and vice-presidential candidates. "The Convention serves the pervasive national interest in the selection of candidates for national office, and this national interest is greater than any interest of an individual state." 419 U.S. 477, 490.

57. See Antonin Scalia, "The Legal Framework For Reform," *Commonsense* 4, no. 2 (1981):40-49.

58. Cornelius P. Cotter and John F. Bibby, "Institutional Development of Parties and the Thesis of Party Decline," *Political Science Quarterly* 95 (Spring 1980):1-27.

59. Asher, *Presidential Elections and American Politics*, pp. 300-03.

60. Cotter and Bibby, "Institutional Development of Parties."

61. For the Republicans the numbers were comparable, although the proportions of primary delegates were a bit lower. The source for the pre-1980 data is F. Christopher Arterton, "Campaign Organizations Face the Mass Media in the 1976 Presidential Nomination Process," paper delivered at the Annual Meeting of the American Political Science Association, Washington, D.C., September 1-4, 1977. Also see "The Making of the Delegates, 1968-1980," by Warren J. Mitofsky and Martin Plissner, in *Public Opinion*, October/November 1980), pp. 37-43.

62. Alexander Heard, *The Costs of Democracy* (Chapel Hill: University of North Carolina Press, 1960); and Alexander, *Financing Politics*, pp. 25-28. I also benefited in this section from research of Paul S. Herrnson, "Campaign Finance Reform and Political Contributions: An Analysis of the Federal Election Campaign Acts and the 1971 Revenue Act," honors thesis, Department of Political Science, SUNY, Binghamton, N.Y., May 1981.

63. State limits are all given in *Congressional Quarterly Weekly Report*, February 23, 1980, p. 570.

64. "Reform-Spawned Agency Stirs Discontent," *Congressional Quarterly Weekly Report*, April 19, 1980, pp. 1019-26.

65. Alexander, *Financing Politics*, pp. 163-76 (Appendix). The information about the content of these laws that follows is drawn mainly from this source.

66. Gary C. Jacobson, *Money in Congressional Elections* (New Haven, Conn.: Yale University Press, 1980), pp. 182-3.

67. Alexander, *Financing Politics*, pp. 31-32 and 38-43.

68. Jacobson, *Money in Congressional Elections*, p. 182.

69. Alexander, *Financing Politics*, pp. 38-42. Also see two studies of FEC auditing: Arthur Anderson and Co., *Federal Election Commission: Review of*

the *Political Campaign Auditing Process*, (Washington, D.C., September 1979); and Accountants for the Public Interest, *Study of the Federal Election Commission's Audit Process* (New York, September 10, 1979).

70. "Reform-Spawned Agency Stirs Discontent," pp. 1019-26.

71. What follows is drawn from Alexander, *Financing Politics*, Chapter 7; and Rita Reimer and Jay Sharpansky, *Analysis of Federal and State Campaign Finance Law – Summaries and Quick Reference Charts*, prepared for the Federal Election Commission by the American Law Division of the Congressional Research Service (Washington, D.C.: Library of Congress, 1978), Chart 8, pp. 275-85.

72. For example, Gary R. Orren, "Presidential Campaign Finance: Its Impact and Future," *Commonsense* 4, no. 2 (1981):50-66.

73. The various aspects of this long-standing controversy can be seen in "Toward a More Responsible Two-Party System: A Report of the Committee on Political Parties, American Political Science Association," *American Political Science Review* (Supplement) 44, no. 3, Part 2, (September 1950); and Evron M. Kirkpatrick, "Toward a More Responsible Party System: Political Science, Policy Science, or Pseudo-Science?" *American Political Science Review* 65 (December 1971):965-90.

74. For example, William J. Crotty, *Political Reform and the American Experiment* (New York: Crowell, 1977); in contrast to Austin Ranney, "The Political Parties: Reform and Decline," in *The New American Political System*, ed. Anthony King, (Washington, D.C.: American Enterprise Institute, 1978), pp. 213-47.

75. Jack Dennis has done several studies of how partisanship can best be measured, finding that alternative measures are more sensitive than that used here. See "Some Properties of Measures of Partisanship," paper presented at the Annual Meeting of the American Political Science Association, New York, September 3-6, 1981.

76. Flanigan and Zingale, *Political Behavior*, p. 56.

77. Dan Nimmo and Robert L. Savage, *Candidates and Their Images* (Santa Monica, Calif.: Goodyear, 1976), p. 207.

78. Corporate PACs often make a practice of supporting incumbents, regardless of party, and both candidates in close elections. Details about how a particular large PAC operates are given by James Barron, "How Grumman Spends its Campaign Fund," New York *Times*, October 26, 1980. Jacobson, *Money in Congressional Elections*, Chapter 3, makes the same point about PAC strategies of support.

79. Jane Stone, "New Right Exploits Campaign Loophole," *Congress Watcher*, March/April 1981, pp. 8-9.

80. New York *Times*, May 31, 1981, p. A26.

81. In 1981 both national parties established task forces to examine how independent expenditures – which Republican Chairman Richard Richards said "create all kind of mischief" – could be controlled. See Fred Wertheimer, "Fixing Election Law," New York *Times*, September 3, 1981, p. A19.

82. New York *Times*, November 23, 1980, section 4; and Adam Clymer, "Conservative Political Committee Evokes Both Fear and Adoration," New York *Times*, May 28, 1981, p. A1.

83. Perhaps the most outraged is the public interest group, Common Cause, which pushed hard for financial regulation and public financing throughout the 1970s. The group's views are expressed in its publication, *In Common*, and frequently elsewhere as well.

84. "Republican Groups Dominate in Party Campaign Spending," *Congressional Quarterly Weekly Report*, November 1, 1980, pp. 3234-39; also, Margaret Ann Latus, "Direct Mail Fund-Raising and the National Parties: Threat or Boon?" paper delivered at the Northeastern Political Science Association Annual Meeting, Newark, New Jersey, November 12, 1981.

85. New York *Times*, May 3, 1981, p. A1.

86. Drummond Yates, Jr., "Democrats Assess Nominating Rules," New York *Times*, August 22, 1981, p. A7. Furthermore, a number of other "reviews" of political parties and the presidential nomination process were held in 1981, involving both scholars and practitioners. For example, the American Bar Association's Conference on the Presidential Selection Process, Wingspread, Racine, Wisconsin, July 16-18, 1981; the Duke University Forum on Presidential Nominations, Fall 1981; and a conference on "The Parties and the Nomination Process" in Cambridge, Massachusetts, December 4-6, 1981, sponsored by the Republican and Democratic National Committees and Harvard University's Institute of Politics. An entire issue of the Republican Journal, *Commonsense* 4, no. 2 (1981) was devoted to preliminary papers by various scholars for this conference.

87. In games of strategy rational moves require an explicit understanding of the rules. Von Neumann and Morgenstern, *Theory of Games and Economic Behavior*, pp. 32-33.

88. This is made dramatically clear when formal game theory is applied. See Steven J. Brams, *The Presidential Election Game* (New Haven, Conn.: Yale University Press, 1978).

2
Theory

When Karl Lamb and I began our study of the presidential election campaigns of 1964, we found a striking contrast between the commonly accepted ideal of tight, centralized, machine-like operations and what actually seemed to be happening — both in the campaigns we saw and those we reviewed in the literature.[1] This discrepancy between ideals and practices appeared to be at least in part related to a lack of systematic theory dealing with how campaigns work and why. To be sure, there were numerous descriptions of campaign events and analyses of what they meant; and some of these covered entire campaigns. A few, such as Theodore H. White's *The Making of the President* series that started in 1960, reached heights of personal insight and eloquent writing.[2] Yet the very richness of this work pointed up the relative absence of rigorous theories to go along with the detailed descriptions.

For our part, Lamb and I applied two models of decision-making to the campaigns of Barry Goldwater and Lyndon Johnson. We concluded that a disjointed-incremental model of decisions and organization was much better suited to the vagaries of American politics than the alternative model of centralized, synoptic management often applied to business firms and military organizations — and which also was the base of the imagined ideal mentioned above.[3] This, we felt, was a useful step in the direction of theoretical development.

Since that time the study of election campaigns has moved ahead with considerable vigor, if in fits and starts.[4] The variety has also been considerable, both because of different types of campaigns at different levels of government, and because campaigns and voting are often mixed together. In the first instance, the variety, while now perhaps distracting, can be of definite value in helping us move toward theories that encompass campaigning at all levels. In the second, although it must be emphasized that campaigns and elections are obviously interrelated, the distinction between what voters do and candidates do must also be kept analytically clear. Generally, campaign theory starts with the latter. Thus in sorting through the various studies it will be useful to separate those that concentrate on the behavior of voters from those that focus on campaigning itself. In some cases this will be easier said than done, because empirical research on public opinion and voting behavior has made massive amounts of data readily available, leading scholars of "campaigns and elections" to spend more time on the elections and less on the campaigns.

As far as the nature of theory is concerned, it is wise not to be pretentious about it. We know that theoretical development can proceed in different ways and take different forms.[5] I take theory to be a set of interrelated propositions (generalizations) that provide comprehensive explanations and relatively accurate (thus testable) predictions of events. Even the most detailed descriptions of campaigns therefore are not theories, although they may enable us to induce generalizations and test hypotheses on the way to theory. Separate insights about the causes and effects of events also may be the raw material for theoretical generalizations, but again are not in themselves theories. Theory becomes more "rigorous" to the extent that its propositions can be derived from more general axioms and related to other propositions using strict rules of logic (the ultimate rigor being mathematical); and it becomes more "systematic" to the extent that its deductive hypotheses are tested and confirmed with empirical evidence (data) collected according to equally strict rules (for example, of sampling) that provide confidence that the evidence represents what it is supposed to.

Unfortunately, this definition of theory might seem a bit much, and it is. While it constitutes an effective measure of achievement, we shall find that it does not offer enough ways to distinguish among the campaign studies to be reviewed. Therefore, I shall categorize these studies in terms of the "conceptual approaches" they take to campaigning, at the same time asking how well each approach lends itself to theoretical development. More precisely, in the case of each of the approaches that follow, I shall comment on four qualities:

> Its theoretical development. How strong are the theories under-lying the approach, and to what extent have these been exploited?
>
> Its contextual linkages. Does the approach lend itself to linking campaigns to environmental factors, such as the rules covered earlier?
>
> Its ability to connect campaigns to their electoral and policy consequences. To what extent do campaigns affect voting behavior, or have an impact on the actions of government?
>
> Its capacity for integration with other approaches. Can it encom-pass or take the place of other approaches, so that it can be used to build a "larger" understanding of campaigns instead of producing isolated findings of limited relevance?

ALTERNATIVE APPROACHES TO CAMPAIGN THEORY

The Campaign Management and Organization Approach

In many ways the most traditional and well-traveled, this approach ranges from versions that are how-to-do-it manuals to those that involve relatively sophisticated organization and decision theory (the decision theory will be considered later). One reason why this approach covers so much territory is that conventional concepts of good organization and management are widely shared among journalists, retired politicians, and political consultants who are considered knowledgeable because of personal experience rather than disciplined research. Trading on "practical" expertise, these writers usually start with a set of unstated assumptions about the characteristics of "good" organization and management, including the following:

> Good organizations are hierarchic, with a small number of leaders making decisions, the implementation of which is a matter of effective management.

Good organizations have a minimum of internal conflict, especially after the leaders have decided what to do.

Good organizations run well because they are managed by persons who know exactly what is going on and what to do.

Good organizations are flexible – quick to adapt to changing conditions and circumstances.

Good organizations run like (well-oiled) machines. (The machine metaphor has a firm hold on this version of the approach.)

So powerful are these assumptions that internal contradictions and observed inconsistencies with field experience tend either to be overlooked or to be treated as failures in the campaigns under observation. The result is that this version of the approach is highly programmatic – prescribing how campaigns ought to be run rather than attempting to clarify the conceptual and empirical bases of the prescriptions.[6] As for the organization prescribed, it is usually in the form of functional activities – finance, publicity, research, developing strategy, and so on – with various topics broken down into impressive detail: for example, what the campaign colors or the candidate's wardrobe should be.[7] Analysis tends to be commonsensical in nature, and generalizations are rarely linked to systematic research findings or deductive propositions. Thus this version of the approach is essentially atheoretical.

On the other hand, this version shows a keen awareness of environmental factors. The reader is told how to use polling and television, to raise money, to deal with new and old population groups, and to cope with FEC regulations. Since electoral results are the given purpose of the enterprise, connections between the proposed campaign operations and resulting votes are frequently referred to, but seldom by reference to systematic studies demonstrating specific effects of certain campaign techniques. I must add that in recent years this version has reflected an influx of academically trained social scientists, and its prescriptions have shown the influence of modern research findings and analyses – particularly of those dealing with public opinion and voting behavior. This is especially true for the campaign manuals put together by party organizations, such as congressional campaign committees.

This brings us to the more "academic" versions of this approach. Among these the work of Robert Agranoff is probably the best example. His *Management of Election Campaigns*, however, goes far beyond material usually associated with straightforward organization and management, and it presents a comprehensive review of research about both campaigns and elections.[8] Throughout, he strives to demonstrate how this array of information can contribute to more "professional management" of campaigns. In a true sense, the book is a campaign manual done in great depth. It reflects a high level of scholarship and sensitivity to the contributions of theory.[9]

Xandra Kayden's *Campaign Organization* is a study of three statewide campaigns – two gubernatorial, one senatorial – of 1974 from an explicitly organizational perspective.[10] Her treatment is much like Agranoff's in covering the various functional units of campaign organization, although Agranoff is more conceptual about different types of organization, while Kayden provides more comparative detail from her case studies.

Even more comparative are Burdett A. Loomis, *Campaign Organization in Competitive 1972 House Races*,[11] and Robert J. Huckshorn and Robert C. Spencer, the *Politics of Defeat*,[12] which is also more analytic about the nature of organizational alternatives. The Huckshorn-Spencer study includes important elements of other approaches, serving to emphasize that my categories of approaches must not be taken as tight descriptions of all the material the various books contain. Both of these studies address congressional campaigns and cover variables that bear upon the elections as well as the campaigns. Huckshorn and Spencer in particular identify a host of factors associated with losing efforts, the most important of which is *non*incumbency.[13]

It is evident that the theoretical development of this general approach is quite a mixed bag. I have already indicated that the descriptive and how-to-do-it writings are generally atheoretical, sometimes aggressively so. The studies done by academic scholars are, for the most part, based on an explicit awareness of certain organizational forms, but these are not well explicated in terms of their theoretical underpinnings or significance. For example, the classic theories of organization, such as those of Max Weber, are only occasionally brought to bear, much less the work of more recent theorists such as James March and Herbert Simon. Thus theory is underdeveloped in this approach, although there is little doubt that the potential is there.[14]

Contextual linkages are by and large a strong feature of this approach. Agranoff, for example, goes to great lengths to show how

campaign management can and should take account of the demographic, partisan, technological, and other characteristics of the
political environment. In whatever version, the approach seems to
lend itself to these linkages.

Connecting campaigns to their electoral and policy consequences
is another matter. Those taking this approach leave little doubt about
the central importance of electoral outcomes. Huckshorn and
Spencer are very explicit about this. Yet the analytic focus is on
internal structures and dynamics and not on matching responses by
voters (and nonvoters). Ironically, the less rigorous versions of the
approach are more likely to make electoral and less often policy
connections, but in the form of offhand assertions rather than
systematic analysis.

As a whole, the strengths of this approach are, on the one hand,
the familiarity of its central concepts, and on the other, the availability of a strong body of formal organization theory. These
strengths, especially the first, are also its weakness, since what
"everybody knows" about the elements of good organization and
management makes the concepts analytically flabby and empirically
imprecise. The accumulated formal theory, if care is not taken in
selecting it, appears too rigid or inapplicable because campaign
organizations seem so distant from those of business firms, government bureaucracies, or patterns of military authority. How does
one take a line and staff model, with specialized functions and
hierarchic relationships, and apply it to a congressional campaign
where the candidate and a few aides are the only organization
that can be identified?[15] The answer, of course, is that appropriate
selections must be made from the rich pool of organization theory,
and also that theories of campaign organization need to be treated
not only as something to be applied, but also as something to be
developed. For the time being, however, the theoretical development
of this approach appears to have reached a plateau.

The Decision-Making (and Organization) Approach

Overlapping the preceding category's elements of formal organization, this approach focuses on how decisions are made, and how
campaigns are organized for the purpose of collective decisions. Far
less popular than campaign management and organization, this

approach has been taken in only one major study, *Campaign Decision-Making: The Presidential Election of 1964*, by Lamb and Smith. The authors draw on a pioneering formulation by Charles E. Lindblom,[16] itself grounded on earlier work in both decision-making and formal organization, to construct two contrasting models of decision that are then applied to the Goldwater-Johnson campaigns. As stated earlier, they find that "disjointed-incremental" decisions are superior to those approximating the "comprehensive" model under most conditions of U.S. campaign politics.[17]

Because their models apply to both individual and collective decisions, Lamb and Smith are able to deal with both the behavior of candidates and the character of campaign organizations — thus covering some of the same territory as the management and organization approach. While decision-making analysis has not been used formally since the Lamb and Smith effort, its theoretical development is relatively advanced because theory-based models were employed in the original study — models that have been widely applied to other business and government cases. Thus the development of this approach in comparative studies outside of political campaigns has been considerable, adding to its potential.[18]

The approach is also well-suited to making contextual linkages, since all the factors decision-makers consider, or might consider, are automatically part of the analysis. The same is not necessarily true for the electoral and policy effects of campaigns, for while Lamb and Smith do reach conclusions about electoral effects, they do not do this on the basis of systematic analysis, specifically of voter decision-making. Obviously, the approach invites this additional analysis that a focus on the internal mechanisms of the campaign alone does not accomplish. Similarly, the impact of campaigns on public policy can be analyzed through the decisions of policy makers — where the approach is well established.[19] The capacity of decision-making to be integrated with other approaches is also high, as indicated with respect to the management and organization approach. Indeed, the activity itself is commonly referred to in descriptions of campaigns in action.

This leads us to one of the problems with the approach, for if the activity of decision-making is so ubiquitous, how does the analyst choose those decisions that are to be studied? Lamb and Smith answer that they "must be significant" — which Hershey points out can in turn lead the analyst to concentrate only on major events, thus slighting perhaps more normal campaign operations during quieter times.[20] Lamb and Smith go on to say that decisions to be studied should be part of "a process of action,"[21] so that *patterns* of decision, not single, isolated events, become the basis of analysis.

A second problem has to do with the "ideal type" models applied in *Campaign Decision-Making*; for while the Goldwater-Johnson campaigns provided adequate contrasts between comprehensive and incremental decisions, studies of other campaigns suggest that in most cases differentiations of this type might be too subtle to be useful. Of course, this points to the construction of new or refined models. In sum, this approach appears to have considerable potential in terms of theoretical development and analytic reach, yet it has been little used, and its existing models of decision may not be widely applicable.

The Strategies of Election Approach

What strategic "moves" does a campaign make that lead it to success or failure? A number of analysts approach campaigns with this question foremost in mind, and in comparison with the preceding approaches, they tend to concentrate less on the inner workings of the campaign than on its electoral outcome. For example, in *The Party's Choice*, William Keech and Donald Matthews analyze a large number of presidential prenomination conditions and campaigns to identify those elements of each that are most closely associated with a candidate's success.[22] Their study thus provides a host of strategic clues to the prospective campaigner. Partly because the notion of candidates developing comprehensive plans of action, or strategies, seems so natural, it is relatively popular. Therefore, I shall break it down into two major versions.

Rational Choice Theories

This version of the approach could be classified under decision-making, but its focus is not on the internal processes or structures of decision. Instead, campaign strategies are analyzed through models of rational choice. This use of formal deductive models is fairly recent in studies of parties and elections, and it follows the pioneering work of Anthony Downs[23] and William H. Riker.[24] It is now found in an extensive set of election studies. Three recent examples are Steven J. Brams, *The Presidential Election Game*,[25] John Aldrich, *Before the Convention: Strategies and Choices in Presidential Nomination Campaigns*, and Benjamin I. Page, *Choices and Echoes in Presidential Elections: Rational Man and Electoral Democracy*.[26] In addition, there are analyses of national convention decisions alone.[27]

Each of these studies utilizes rigorous, and in varying degrees abstract, formal analysis. Brams, who applies formal game theory to the entire pre- and postnomination process, is the most abstract, and thus distant from the nitty-gritty details of campaign operations. What is more, he repeatedly cautions against using his models to predict specific campaign events, which, he points out, is not their function:

> In contrast to the hindsight approach, I have attempted to develop scientific models that can impart a deeper and more general understanding of the underlying factors at work in the presidential election process. . . . By deducing consequences from models, one can see more clearly what is happening than one can by trying to deal with reality in all its unmanageable detail.[28]

Aldrich also uses game theory, and a selection from other rational choice decision theories, but with less rigor than Brams. Ambition of candidates, campaign resources, the behavior of voters, and the inner dynamics of campaigns are analyzed, with games often used metaphorically. Aldrich finds that the "moves" of the candidates were indeed consistent with models of rational strategy — thus explaining the basic nature of candidate decision-making and the workings of the electoral system in the 1976 presidential nomination campaign. Similarly, Page uses an elaboration of Downs' model of rational economic decisions to analyze presidential elections since 1932, concluding that given the conditions of information, both candidates and voters made decisions that can be explained by the prescriptions of rational choice. Since Downs' model is also less rigorous than formal game theory, both Page and Aldrich deal with more specific elements of electoral politics than Brams.

More than any other approach, this version rests upon, and strives to develop, formal theory — theory that characteristically is expressed in the form of mathematical models. Because in the use of game theory the rules define the game, contextual factors (or rules) of the type presented in Chapter 1 are automatically part of the game. As Brams emphasizes, the tension between more formal (and abstract) models and the multiplicity of real-life factors remains. Nonetheless, as Aldrich and especially Page demonstrate, the approach can connect campaign decisions with voter — and pre-sumably policy-maker — decisions. While the problems of precise measurement of many of the factors foreclose firm and handy conclusions, the basic logic of the formal connections clarifies such things as the electoral mandate a president might have, and numerous hypotheses about the effects of rules, candidates, issues, resources, and strategies on electoral success or failure.[29]

Not all of these conclusions are based on equally high levels of applied theory, not only because of the differences between the books, but also because of variations within the books of Aldrich and Page. As I have indicated, they frequently shift from formal to metaphorical use of rational decision theory as they deal with combinations of factors. Consequently, the capacity of this approach for integration with others is mixed, depending on whether their particular elements can be reformulated in terms of strategic choices. For example, within the approach a campaign is treated as a single decision-maker, in which case problems of interpersonal relationships or collective decision-making simply disappear. In the case of some applications of game theory, the campaign itself is reduced to a series of strategic decisions, a price that many of those preferring to study campaigns more concretely would feel is too high to pay for powerful theory.

Strategies of Electoral Coalition Building

A second variant of the strategies of election approach moves away from the mathematical rigor of rational choice theory while retaining the emphasis on strategic decisions. In terms familiar to students of American political parties, elections are conceived as a coming together of opposing coalitions of interest of "issue" groups.[30] Perhaps the most notable example of this approach is the work of John Kessel, and specifically his most recent study, *Presidential Campaign Politics: Coalition Strategies and Citizen Response*, which covers presidential elections since 1964.[31]

Kessel concentrates his analysis on how candidates can gain support from coalitions of issue groups given what is known about voter attitudes, information, interests, and the type of factors that were reviewed in Chapter 1. He does not slight campaigns themselves, but they are not subjected to the same systematic analysis as the electorate, and indeed are often treated in terms of a conventional version of the management and organization approach. Thus the study becomes very much a mixture of coalition strategy analysis and descriptions of campaign operations and events in almost atheoretical terms. At all points, Kessel utilizes a rich variety of empirical data to support his analysis.

The result is that while Kessel's coalition approach exhibits only an incremental advance in theory development — and is far behind the formal theory of the first version — its contextual linkages are excellent. Because the approach focuses on voter attitudes and responses, there is an explicit effort to link strategic choices of candidates with the electoral structure of coalitions. Inevitably, these linkages are not always very tight; and the connections between features of campaign organization, and so on, and electoral consequences are especially loose. Nonetheless, Kessel brings an abundance of information about presidential campaigns to bear, giving the reader a good review of what is known about the subject.

This version of the strategies of election approach sacrifices a good deal of the theory-building potential of the rational choice version to achieve greater "realism" about the campaigns themselves. The capacity of the coalition approach to be integrated with others seems to me quite high, which essentially is demonstrated by Kessel. Yet the basis of this integration tends to be not theoretical compatibility but the adaptability of the electoral findings to other approaches.

As a whole, the strategies of election approach have achieved a relatively high level of theoretical development, and the potential is strong. The approach ranges from formal game theory, in which strategic choices can be derived mathematically, to fairly conventional analyses having a mixture of loose theoretical bases. The approach's ability to relate campaigns to their contextual environments — for example, through "rules of the game" — and to electoral consequences is generally excellent. Because strategies usually involve policy issue positions, there is no reason to doubt that policy consequences cannot also be incorporated. In emphasizing the decisions the campaign should make with regard to groups of voters, the approach tends to be theoretically and analytically weaker in terms of the internal workings of campaigns themselves. It is this aspect of campaign strategy that is in the greatest need of improvement.

The Campaign Resources Approach

The idea that campaigns need resources, and that they may be evaluated according to their effectiveness in acquiring and using resources, is not only self-evident, but also familiar in the literature. Most of the time this idea is not pushed very far conceptually. Resources are usually taken to denote money, and perhaps volunteer workers and staff, and the usual assumption is that more resources produce larger and better campaigns. Improved analysis, even when the concept is limited to money, quickly shows that more does not necessarily mean better, at least not if better means more successful.[32]

However, in a study of congressional campaigns in 1962 in ten California districts, David A. Leuthold went considerably farther with the concept, defining the candidate, political parties, interest groups, finances, and workers as "resources that can secure votes."[33] This more rigorous conceptualization enabled Leuthold to deal with most of the factors found in descriptions of campaigns by comparing how candidates acquired and used them as resources in getting votes. Leuthold's most compelling finding was that still another resource, incumbency, so powerfully affected the collection and deployment of other resources that challengers were systematically disadvantaged, and electoral competition was significantly reduced.

That same year, Huckshorn and Spencer, whose work we considered earlier under the management and organization approach, studied all congressional campaigns and reached essentially the same conclusion:

> It is true that an occasional candidate can win a particularly difficult race by employing interesting and unique campaign strategies. But it is also true that the largest percentage of contested seats are decided with little regard for campaign styles or political tactics....
>
> Our central and prevailing thesis has been that the incumbent congressman has the advantage over the nonincumbent....[34]

I reintroduce Huckshorn and Spencer because throughout their study, as they take up candidate backgrounds, recruitment, campaign organizations, issues, and so on, they find that the resources of incumbents are *cumulative* — seldom to be overcome by other elements of the campaign. At this late date the fact that incumbent office-holders usually have campaign advantages over nonincumbents is hardly news; but Leuthold's sharpened conceptualization of what resources are, and how they are related to each other, other political factors, and electoral outcomes, deepens our understanding both of campaigns and of elections as a whole. His findings enable him to relate campaigns to aspects of democratic theory, in particular the need for political competition.[35] This in turn points to policy implications for the importance of evening out campaign resources available to incumbents and nonincumbents alike.

Since Leuthold's *Electioneering in a Democracy* was published in 1968, little has been done to elaborate and refine the nature of campaign resources so that their theoretical significance is developed. The resource approach makes good connections with the contextual factors previously mentioned, since a number of these are directly tied to resources. Its capacity for integration with other approaches is excellent. Indeed, references to specific resources are common in other approaches, and these now take on added significance. The inherent logic of associating resources with the decisions and strategies needed to collect and deploy them seems compelling. We can conclude, however, that despite the ubiquity of concrete resources, the potential of this approach for conceptual and theoretical development remains to be fulfilled.

The Candidate Beliefs (and other characteristics) Approach

Since candidates are an integral part of any campaign for public office, every analytic approach must deal with them in some fashion, whether as organizers, decision-makers, strategists, resources, or some combination. The candidate beliefs approach comes to grips with this need by viewing the entire campaign from the perspective of the candidate — candidates being bundles of attitudes, opinions, experiences, and so on, that affect perceptions of their constituencies, of their roles, and of themselves, all of which serve to establish and reinforce patterns of action. It is a simple matter to add other figures within the campaign — such as chief aides of the candidates — to the focus of analysis.

Two basic examples of this approach are John W. Kingdon's *Candidates for Office: Beliefs and Strategies*,[36] and Marjorie Randon Hershey's, *The Making of Campaign Strategy*.[37] From comparative data on Wisconsin congressional and state legislative candidates in 1964, Kingdon finds that candidate beliefs about their political environment vary according to such factors as party, office, area of the state, and past election returns. Moreover, how a candidate "sees" his situation not only reflects a combination of personal attitudes, campaign conditions, and direct experiences, but also has a major impact on campaign organization and strategy.

Hershey's study of campaigns for Congress and five statewide offices (also in Wisconsin) in 1970 takes this approach farther. She elaborates three types of influence on campaigners — personality, position in the organization, and chances of winning — and constructs a series of general propositions (formulated and tested systematically) covering campaign strategies and organization and the implications for democratic politics. Both Kingdon and Hershey demonstrate that approaching campaigns from the perspective of the candidate certainly does not stand in the way of analyzing organizational, decision-making, strategic, or contextual factors; and many of their results appear to be of substantial use to other approaches. Hershey's detailed empirical findings about the relationships between candidates and their campaign managers, for example, are immediately relevant to our knowledge of campaign decision-making and organization. Both authors show how much distance lies between the assumptions of rational choice theories and what actually goes on in campaigns.

The development of theory is of central importance in each study, with both authors leaving no doubt about their commitments in this respect. They draw upon theories of attitude formation, personality, information (particularly uncertainty), decision-making, social psychology, and organization in formulating their own approaches. Of course, this theoretical diversity leads to some dispersion of thrust — but not for long. For example, at the end of *The Making of Campaign Strategy*, Hershey introduces "a learning approach to campaign strategy" — an approach that she subsequently refines into a "social learning theory of campaign behavior" in a later paper.[38]

In this significant variant of the overall approach, Hershey draws upon an established and specific body of theory from social psychology both to reanalyze her 1970 data and to apply to a selected group of 1980 senatorial campaigns. Using three "laws" derived from the theory, she finds a host of relationships, such as that election results are extremely blunt feedback mechanisms, causing candidates to rely on close advisers, their own learning histories, and other candidates in similar situations. Furthermore, inexperienced candidates are the principal source of campaign innovations, since those who have run before tend to learn and repeat campaign practices that they think (on the basis of crude packages) worked for them before. It turns out that political parties continue to be major conduits of information among campaigners.[39]

Hershey's successful application of a general theory constructed in other disciplines marks an important advance in this approach. A great variety of what is known about campaigns seems to fit smoothly into the explanatory structure of this theory; it produces empirically testable hypotheses; and it is widely applicable in other political arenas, such as legislatures, for purposes of comparative analysis. Thus we see here the classic functioning of theory to expand and deepen our understanding of the fundamental nature of political campaigns given the "rules" of American politics.

Still another version of this overall approach gives less emphasis to candidate beliefs and presents congressional campaigns as essentially continuous activities. Congressmen are conceived simultaneously as law-makers and candidates, whether or not they are playing their campaign roles formally. Good examples of this approach are the studies of Richard F. Fenno, Jr., *Home Style: House Members and Their Districts*,[40] and, again, John W. Kingdon, *Congressmen's Voting Decisions*.[41] While these scholars also analyze campaigns from the perspectives of the candidates — their attitudes, perceptions, styles, and so on — they are primarily interested in the seamless nature of campaign concern and activity on the part of congressmen, and not campaigns as such. Consequently, this variant helps explain the already-mentioned incumbent advantage in congressional elections, but it does not go as far as the previous versions of the approach in adding to campaign theory.

The explication of the sources and campaign consequences of candidate beliefs (a rather all-inclusive term as used here) has produced in this approach a substantial body of empirical findings and theory-based explanations. This is especially true of Hershey's social learning theory, the application of which has been an excellent example of the function of theory in generating testable hypotheses and new ways of looking at old phenomena. As I have already indicated, the contextual linkages within this approach, and its capacity to be integrated with other approaches, are also very strong, while electoral outcomes are treated as one of the factors influencing the perceptions and actions of campaigners. (Otherwise, the impact of campaigns on voters is usually slighted.) In the same way, this approach clarifies the connection between campaign beliefs and public policy decisions by candidates who are or will be public officials. Therefore, the approach is unusually useful in tying campaigns to their policy consequences.

Mixed Approaches

Numerous works deal with campaigns under the general rubric of "campaigns and elections." I have mentioned a few of these in the management and organization category, but there are others that make an explicit effort to draw upon a mixture of approaches in presenting a comprehensive picture of the electoral system. Probably the most familiar of these is the discursive but informative book by Nelson W. Polsby and Aaron Wildavsky, *Presidential Elections*, now in its fifth edition and likely to go to many more.[42] Although books of this type vary considerably in the amount of attention given to campaigns,[43] they are intended to bring together material about a rather large topic. Generally they are not designed to be reports of original research or analysis. One that does adopt a rather distinctive analysis is by Stephen Hess.[44] Dealing with presidential campaigns, Hess also says a good deal about the presidency and combines an "insider's" view with diverse other studies.

In the case of congressional campaigns, the most useful recent example of this mixed approach is Alan L. Clem's collection of seven original case studies of 1974 congressional campaigns in different parts of the nation.[45] While Clem provides a common framework of 14 "campaign variables" that each study is supposed to address, there is considerable variation among the individual cases. Nevertheless, taken together they constitute a rich set of raw materials that probably can be used for some time to come. The 14 variables (incumbency, marginality, resources, political insight, and so on) are distilled from various sources, including some of those we have reviewed, and do not express a particular approach. Clem summarizes the different theoretical perspectives that are used,[46] and his concluding analysis, a "comparative perspective," also provides a good summary of what the studies can tell us about each of the variables. Although theory is lacking, Clem's theme throughout is the extent to which the campaigns served to hold congressmen accountable to their constituents.[47]

In their way, the mixed approaches partially represented by the works of Polsby and Wildavsky, and Clem, demonstrate the costs and benefits of adopting a single theoretical approach and pushing it as far as it can productively go. Loaded with information about campaigns though they are, these mixtures make it difficult to advance our understanding very far. On the other hand, nothing restricts their ability to look at campaigns from various sides, which is particularly helpful to someone trying to get an initial overview of the subject. In general, however, books on "elections" cannot be counted on to single out campaigns for specialized treatment.

These mixed approaches remind us of another point about the individual approaches we have examined: Most of them are mixtures. Only occasionally does an author adhere so closely to a particular conceptual or theoretical approach that it is a simple matter to assign the work to a single category. In large measure, therefore, studies of campaigns tend to use a variety of perspectives, even while emphasizing a particular one.

Summary and Conclusions

Taken together, the foregoing approaches to the study of election campaigns reflect a conceptual discipline, vigor, and diversity that was not present two decades — or even one — ago. Of course, labeling different modes of analyses as "approaches," and then applying these labels to specific studies, is a tricky business, especially given the internal variety in many of the works that I have mentioned above. And there remain a goodly number of books about elections that simply do not analyze campaigns as such.

Yet the uncertainties about placing specific studies into categories of analysis do not detract from the importance of taking the measure of the conceptualization and theorizing that has been going on. In this respect there are several conclusions.

First, by far the most activity and theoretical progress has occurred in studies of congressional campaigns — progress challenged only by analyses of presidential campaigns using formal models of decision. One reason for the accomplishments of congressional studies lies in the advantages of comparative research conducted on a relatively large scale. The availability of hundreds of campaigns, carried on simultaneously every two years, in districts having important common and divergent characteristics, invites the collection of quantitative data to test comparative hypotheses — with the results yielding more secure generalizations than are possible with the smaller number of presidential elections.

At the same time it is worth noting what is missing. There are obvious differences between campaigns at different "levels" of the electorate.[48] Yet with only a few exceptions, there has been a dearth of theory-directed research ranging across campaigns at different levels of government, much less across nations.[49] Some differences between such campaigns — in budgets, candidate backgrounds, use of media, and so on — are easily observed, but systematic research has not kept pace.

Second, election campaigns are now a distinct subject of rigorous analysis *in themselves*. Of course they also continue to be treated as adjuncts in some studies that deal with the electoral process as a whole. Nevertheless, campaigning is now recognized as a distinguishable activity worthy of serious research both because of its functions within democratic political systems and of the knowledge it can provide about varieties of political action.

Third, scholars interested in political campaigns no longer must contend with a literature dominated by journalistic descriptions, anecdotes, and untested assumptions. Instead, there is a respectable set of reasonably well-defined analytic approaches from which to choose, add, and contribute to. As in other areas of political science, there is an expressed sense that research should be as systematic as possible and contribute to the development of theory. While admittedly untidy, the current variety of approaches is also healthy to the extent that it generates new ways of thinking about campaigns and preventing premature closure in what is, after all, a young field of study.

On the other hand, there is also a certain lack of "building," with scholars tending to strike off on their own rather than adding to the contributions of others. Some of this can be expected to continue; yet as research goes forward, an already discernible process of "natural selection" can also be anticipated. Which approaches are likely to be favored? Presumably those with high capacities for integration with others, for making linkages with both causes and consequences, and for development into formal theory. These qualities mark the advance of scientific understanding.

A CYBERNETIC MODEL

Consciously or not, how we think about election campaigns strongly affects what we see in them. Our mental images and our perceptions mutually reinforce each other. This is true for any observer, but some make greater efforts to be "objective" − to guard against being swept along by distorted images of reality. The purpose of observation is, of course, to determine what "reality" is. Yet we saw in Chapter 1 that this is not a simple matter. A disciplined journalist follows a set of procedures designed to get "all sides" of a story; but the story will nevertheless be different when expressed by a columnist who places it in a larger context, suggests nonapparent relationships, and makes judgments. Needless to say it is rare for such commentators to agree on what the story "means."

The different approaches we have been discussing are, to a greater or lesser extent, more formal versions of these mental images that shape what is seen and reported.[50] Since formality means more explicit boundaries and internal structures, if we know that an analyst is taking a particular conceptual approach to a given campaign event, the ensuing report should embody much less uncertainty about meaning than the comparable story of a political columnist, whose conceptual biases we can only guess. A conceptual approach tells us not only how an event should be interpreted, but also what should be included and not included in its observation. As the approach becomes more formal, fewer exceptions are allowed; that is, earlier evidence that "seemed" to be applicable within the approach now might not pass muster − with the general result that data need to be "purer," or the analysis must become more abstract.

I reemphasize these points from Chapter 1 because they bear directly on the conceptual approach I shall be taking to the 1980 campaign. In choosing the approach − actually a model − it was clear near the start that the decision-making approach that Karl Lamb and I used in our study of the 1964 presidential campaign was not well-suited to the major campaigns of 1980. The "comprehensive" and "incremental" models of decision that worked so well in 1964 did not appear to fit the 1980 cases with much precision. True, the models could have been modified, but it seemed likely at the cost of explanatory power.

If the decision-making approach was not to be used, it nevertheless included a number of specific elements, such as how campaign strategies were formulated under conditions of more or less uncertainty, that should not be disregarded. The considerations of generality, rigor, linkage, and integration also needed to be met. The approach that has been chosen does not satisfy all the sometimes contradictory values that we have discussed, but it rejects none. Drawn from information theory, it is able to encompass major elements of a number of the other approaches without losing its own theoretical structure.

Let us then consider the 1980 presidential campaigns as *systems of communication and control* and analyze them through the use of a cybernetic model.[51]

Information, Organization, and Entropy

As a system of communication and control, a model cybernetic campaign collects information about those parts of the political environment that can affect the outcome of the election, "processes" this information through internal communications and decisions, and then communicates information to the political environment in order to maximize electoral support for its candidate. Thus the ultimate purpose of the campaign is the election of its candidate.* For this purpose the campaign selects from the infinite set of possible information that subset which will improve decisions, which in turn are used to exert as much control as possible over the

---

*It is true that some campaigns, including presidential campaigns, might have other purposes, such as gaining visibility for an ideology or issue position, facilitating the organization of a new political party, and so on. Even though the cybernetic model can easily be adapted to such alternative goals, I shall not do this without making the change explicit.

external political world in order to maximize votes. This incoming and outgoing information is sometimes called *input* and *output*.[52]

Information is itself a form or pattern of organization, its opposite being disorganization or *noise*.[53] Information is communicated through units or "bits" that comprise messages. However, messages, like any other organization, are subject to decay in accordance with the second law of thermodynamics. The measure of this disorganization is *entropy*.[54] Entropy can be resisted, even reversed, by drawing energy (information) from outside the system, but *in any closed system entropy will increase*.[55] The cybernetic campaign therefore will be organized and run to maximize its exchange of information with the outside political world.

Communication takes place in steps. First, messages are *coded* (given a particular pattern or form of organization) by the sender. Second, they are transmitted to the receivers. During transmission they are of course subject to entropy; that is, they may lose some of their organization. For example, a shouted order can become indistinct at a crowded airport stop; a telephone conversation can be garbled by interference on the line; radio signals can be weakened by loss of power; and so forth. Time itself is a factor if the lapse between sending and receiving the message makes its content less relevant because circumstances have changed. Third, messages are *decoded* by the receivers. Obviously, if the sender and receiver are not using the same code, the message is more or less lost. We are not speaking here of supersecret codes employed by national intelligence operations, although these are examples of this step. Instructions passed from person to person, as experiments have long shown, invariably suffer an information loss from coding-decoding, in addition to noise in transmission. Simple difference in language usage between sections of the country can affect the meaning of messages. If the sender uses a different style of speech than the receiver, or words the receiver does not understand, there is a coding breakdown. Information is lost and entropy increases.

There are two additional points. First, these communication steps are not confined to communication between human beings. They are universal. Thus they also take place between man and machines and machines and machines. Second, the laws of entropy are *probabilistic*, with the chances favoring noise over information.[56] Therefore, unless greater efforts (energy) are made to maintain organization, more information loss will occur in large

systems than in small systems. The significance of these two characteristics is apparent when we recall the increasing use of computers
and machine processing of information in larger campaign organizations mentioned earlier. This is not to say that data processing
machines contribute to entropy, because if used correctly just the
opposite is the case. The point is that entropy occurs in these electronic and mechanical machines as well as human machines and that
larger systems provide more opportunity for breakdowns than
smaller systems.

The Critical Role of Feedback

To cope with disorganization, and specifically the need to
adapt to changing conditions and circumstances, and to correct
mistakes, communication systems employ feedback.* This is the
"control of a machine on the basis of its *actual* performance rather
than its *expected* performance."[57] In other words, it is the process
whereby information about how the system is actually operating
is returned to decision-makers who make any corrections that are
needed to keep the system on its intended course. Usually illustrations of this concept refer to antiaircraft guns tracking enemy planes,
but let us take a political example.

Suppose that in order to gain increased support from American
farmers the presidential candidate announces that he favors the
sale of more wheat to the Soviet Union in order to bolster wheat
prices. However, when both opinion surveys and field staff report
sharp opposition to this position not only from consumer groups
(some of which was expected), but also from cotton and dairy
farmers, campaign decision-makers quickly have the candidate
make a further announcement to the effect that his position has
been "misunderstood" and that any actual sales will take place
only "after a full review so that consumer and other farm prices
will not be negatively affected."

---

*Technically, the type of feedback I am describing here is "negative feed-
back"; that is, it serves to restrain and correct actions that deviate from the
system's purposes or goals. However, "positive feedback" is also quite possible,
in which case messages about deviating actions are interpreted as "let's have
more of the same," causing the system to go increasingly off course. We shall
see cases of this in the 1980 campaign. Only negative feedback is "good."

This example points up several additional elements of feedback that are important to keep in mind. The first is time. No response can be instantaneous, but the more time that elapses between the detection of a "mistake" and the system's response the more damage can occur. This time lapse is called *lag*. The second element comprises the extent and speed of changes in the target's position. This is called *load*. In the case of our example this is the opinion change of the agricultural population. Notice, however, that the opinions of other segments of the electorate are also relevant. Election campaigns face the difficulty of multiple targets with differing loads, combinations of which are far more complex than a single moving airplane. These two elements obviously can work together, and the greater lag is in relation to load, the less able the campaign to achieve its goals.[58]

The third element is the amount of corrective action taken. This is called *gain*. Ideally, feedback will bring the system perfectly in line with its goal, but even under the best of circumstances there is a good chance that the correction will be too little or too much. A high rate of gain is often seen as desirable; yet it can easily lead to "oversteering," with the system swerving back and forth. In our example the candidate is attempting to avoid this by taking a presumably reassuring "further study" position, thus *damping* overcorrection. Obviously, optimal gain requires quick and precise measurements of effects, something that faces inherent difficulties in campaign politics.

The last element of the feedback process involves looking ahead; the ability to "predict the position of a moving target" in the future and take action to "lead" it. *Lead* is thus the use of knowledge of past behavior to anticipate future behavior, thereby enabling the system to minimize the distance between its expected and actual performance. In our example this might have been achieved by drawing upon past experiences with similar issues, and past and current opinion polls, to anticipate the farmer responses and make the candidate's first announcement more like the "correction." A good illustration of an effort to develop the capacity for lead was the *simulmatics* project in the 1960 Kennedy campaign, and we shall see it again in 1980.[59]

The Advantage of Memory

The need to draw on past experience in order to better adapt to current and future circumstances calls attention to the vital role of a system's memory. Using the machine metaphor, memory is essentially a "tape" (storage) of the system's past input and output, coded in such a way that it can be drawn upon selectively.[60] Depending on its size and accessibility, memory is thus a resource of information that adds (meaning) to current input. When integrated with current information, messages from memory can multiply a system's information enormously because of the almost infinite capacity for combinations and permutations.[61] In the case of political campaigns, however — even cybernetic ones — this potential is not quite so glorious. Because campaigns are short-lived systems, not only is their memory base relatively modest, but also their decision-makers, knowing this, tend to allocate few resources to storing information. Nevertheless, the workings of memory suggest a number of hypotheses. For example, candidates who have run before have resources of decision-making superior to those who have not; experienced personnel are a campaign advantage; and how campaigners (as cybernetic systems) code their experiences makes a big difference in the information their memories hold.[62]

Learning

The type of feedback we have been discussing so far is "simple." That is, it involves direct adjustments to keep the campaign on its intended course. However, when the system responds by changing whole "policies" of operation, "higher-order" feedback or *learning* occurs.[63] This involves structural changes in the system. Using our preceding example, if the campaign is reorganized so the mechanisms for appraising public attitudes (upon which policy positions of the candidate are based) are modified and the better information reduces the probability of a similar mistake, learning has taken place. Such structural changes can be triggered by the same type of information used in simple feedback, but these messages are combined with others, including memory, to make more generalized adaptations. Even subgoals of the campaign may be altered.[64] Although higher-order feedback covers a range of structural modifications, any such change requires significantly more flexibility and resources of decision than simple feedback. Thus any rigidities within the campaign will, to that extent, limit the system's capacity for learning and growth.

Some specific implications for campaign "management" are suggested by Norbert Wiener in the following, even though he is referring to other organizations:

> The businessman who separates himself from his employees by a shield of yes-men, or the head of a big laboratory who assigns each subordinate a particular problem, and begrudges him the privilege of thinking for himself so that he can move beyond his immediate problem and perceive its general relevance . . . is a degradation of man's very nature, and economically a waste of the great human values which man possesses.[65]

Wiener's argument is that the structure of systems — in this case of human beings — is an index of their potential performance, which should not be restricted by their "use" in larger systems. It is evident, therefore, that the cybernetic model applies to individual campaigners, including the candidate, as well as the collective organization itself, and that the two systems are intimately related. The effectiveness of both is determined by their ability to use information to accomplish their purposes, and this is determined primarily by their mechanisms of feedback. The candidate whose attitudes and beliefs (structural characteristics) cause him to ignore or misinterpret (decoding errors) certain messages impairs not only his own performance but also that of the campaign.

Conversely, a campaign that does not accurately transmit messages to and from the candidate, whether because of a lack of resources or of rules of organization, limits the candidate's ability to think and decide and to have decisions expressed as influential action. In short, a campaign is comprised of individual, collective, and usually mechanical systems, all governed by the same laws of information. The performance of each will affect the performance of the others, and the effectiveness of the campaign.

The Danger of Overload

This brings us to another important consideration. All channels of communication have limited capacities. (Visualize the different amounts of electric power [information] lines of different sizes can carry.) Overloading a channel simply reduces its messages to noise, and of course the same is true for message processing. Thus the cybernetic campaign must limit the number of incoming messages (input) so system *overload* does not occur. This is a major problem for political campaigns, since the amount of potential information is so vast and resources of decision, record-keeping (memory), and so on, are often modest. When decision-makers become overloaded with messages, their capacity for converting input into output is sharply diminished, if not destroyed.[66] Obviously, this explains the need for resources of staff, with appropriate delegations of authority and specialized functions within the campaign organization.

It is evident, therefore, that more than an open-minded and quick-witted candidate is needed for a cybernetic campaign. Substantial resources of information selection, processing, and communication are essential, with their nature and amounts being governed by the input-output demands of the particular system. The demands imposed by a local city council election will be very different from those of a presidential campaign. In the case of the latter, information-collecting devices must include such things as a national polling organization with means of information processing (for example, computers) that will convert survey data into properly coded messages that are intelligible to campaign decision-makers; facilities to construct and transmit output messages to large populations (for example, through television advertising); mechanisms of transportation to get the candidate (as a message) from one part of the country to another; and an organization to collect money and other resources (which can be converted into varying forms of information), and to cope with the federal election campaign rules we have discussed before.

While not able to include such details, an overall picture of the cybernetic presidential campaign is presented in Figures 2.1 and 2.2. Although they are abstract two-dimensional models, they call attention to several additional points. Even in this simplified form, the system's exchange of information with its environment is formidable, both in scope and amount. Of course some of this information, such as national and local party structures and political cultures, will presumably be brought into the system through staff members and their personal networks of communication. In other words, some of this information might be relatively "free."[67] Nevertheless, the models suggest that a major problem for the system will be how to reduce its information *costs* (this is quite different from the problem

FIGURE 2.1
The Cybernetic Campaign and Its Environment

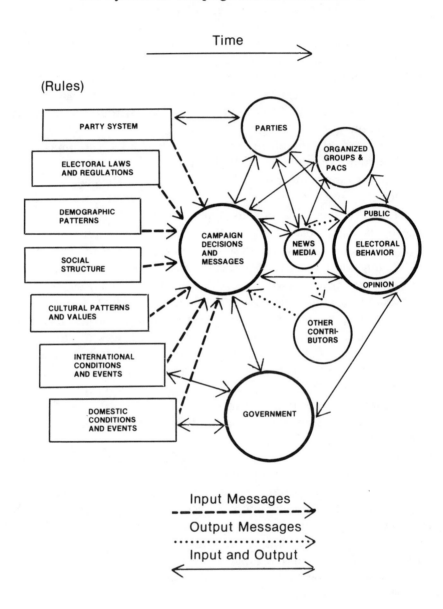

Source: Compiled by the author.

FIGURE 2.2
Inside the Cybernetic Campaign

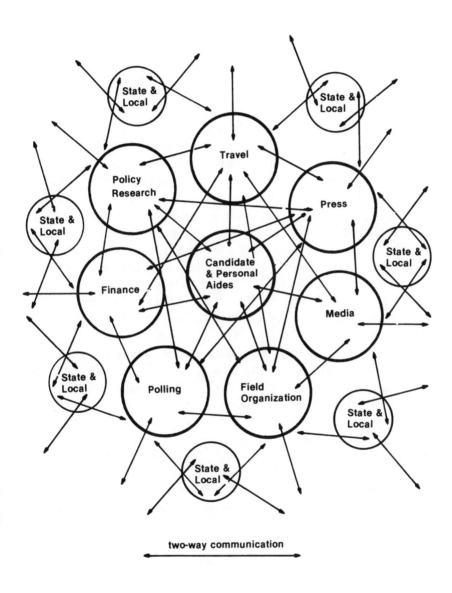

two-way communication

Source: Compiled by the author.

of limiting input to prevent overload). Since messages of control are more directly related to votes, it is likely that this economizing will be greater on the "side" of input than that of output. It is not obvious that this is supported by information theory.[68]

Another point that is emphasized in Figure 2.1 is that the campaign is not exchanging information with an unformed environment, but with one comprised of other systems. One of the most important of these is what we have called the mass media. The model makes it clear that a segment of these, the news media, serves vital communication functions for the campaign — first by transmitting messages that inform other key systems (for example, voters, sources of money and other resources, and other campaigns) about the campaign's performance, and, second, by providing the campaign with similar information about other key systems in its environment. Furthermore, the news media are not merely information conduits. They are separate systems that collect, process, and transmit information for their *own* purposes.* To the extent that its own resources of information collection are limited, the campaign must thus use information provided by the media, but after decoding and translating it to "correct" for what has been added or removed.[69] Similarly, the campaign must be sensitive to how the media are likely to alter their own output, since this determines the messages that voters and other systems actually receive about the campaign.[70]

What I have said about the importance of the news media in presidential election campaigns is surely not surprising. Yet because information *is* the cybernetic campaign, any elements in the environment that affect communication demand even greater attention than would be the case if we were conceptualizing the campaign in some other fashion. Incidentally, keep in mind that my references here are *only* to the news media, not to media as a whole, which obviously include a variety of vehicles and types of information. Furthermore, a certain part of the media will be an extension of the campaign itself — in the form of paid advertisements. These carry the system's output messages, and essentially they are used because news coverage of these messages is not considered adequate. The logical implication is clear: One of the most vital tactics of the cybernetic campaign is to so shape its output (including multiple

---

*Which means that campaigns cannot count on the news media to serve campaign purposes, even though the media to a large extent do.

types of influence) so as to make maximum use of the news media. To the extent that stable patterns of information flow are established, these media may be thought of as actually *incorporated* within the cybernetic system.

Crossing the Boundaries

Another significant point about the models in Figures 2.1 and 2.2 concerns system *boundaries*. The broken lines encircling the campaign and particular functional units within the campaign are meant to show these as networks of specialized information and decision that are pervious and dynamic, not closed and firm.* At every level the system is to be exchanging information with its environment. What is more, the exchanges between units of the campaign organization — media advertising and finance, for example — consist not only of spoken and written words but also of campaign staff. Thus organizational divisions are highly permeable both to ideas and people. Particularly for decisions affecting the performance of the campaign as a whole, the "crossing over" of staff to participate in decision-making in some other unit is a common occurrence.

This is not another way of stating the familiar procedure of corporate executives calling in lower-level specialists to provide them with expert information for their decision-making in the boardroom. Not only is the cybernetic campaign much less hierarchic, but also boundary permeability extends through most of the hierarchy there is. Because the purposes of the campaign system are so highly concentrated on an extraordinarily complex series of events and relationships, few output decisions can confidently be divorced from a wide range of "considerations" — that is, information. As sources of information, including those involving feedback, become more specialized and sophisticated, the cybernetic campaign faces inevitable tensions between the need to exploit this information within functional units (networks of specialized information) and the need to incorporate additional information in output decision-making.

---

*Norbert Wiener makes this point in striking terms as he describes human beings as cybernetic machines: ". . . the individuality of the body is that of a flame rather than that of a stone, of a form rather than of a bit of substance."

The basic mechanism for easing tensions is through maximum interchange between staff members (also cybernetic systems). This requires personal compatibility between these individuals, which eases the problems inherent in specialized coding and decoding of messages. Common goals and procedures of decision are inherent in this compatibility. The foregoing carries significant implications for campaign recruitment. In more permanent organizations the personal relationships that foster communication can be built up over extended periods of time — a continuity of organization (system) that campaigns lack, at least formally. Realizing that the organizational life of a campaign is short, its architects try to recruit personnel whose common values and experiences work to shorten the time it takes their patterns of interpersonal communication to fuse into a cybernetic system. Obviously, those candidates who have run before, and are able to sustain close relationships among key campaign staff between election periods, have a strong head start in forming each "new" campaign. Those who, as incumbents, are able to achieve this by placing campaign aides in closely associated governmental positions, from which they can be drawn for the new campaign, are in an even better position. Other things being equal, therefore, incumbent officeholders have a considerable advantage in constructing a cybernetic campaign.

Relating the Cybernetic Model to Other Approaches

From the basic ingredients of information theory I have formed a simple model of a political campaign — a cybernetic campaign. This model can be in turn elaborated into detailed prescriptions for campaign organization and action, since the theory is not limited in its reach. As a system of communication and control, the cybernetic campaign collects and uses information to achieve the election of its candidate. The system's effectiveness is measured by its capacity to identify and interpret those elements of the political environment that have most to do with the outcome of elections; to take action on the basis of this information; and to monitor and adjust its performance so that unforeseen circumstances and events do not distract it from its goal. Each of these operations involves the reception, processing, and sending of messages, and the campaign succeeds to the extent that the information in these messages is maximized.

Translated into more conventional terms, the cybernetic campaign of a presidential candidate will have effective means for "reading" the multiple "rules of the game" that were indicated in our earlier review; for detecting relevant public attitudes and opinions; for making and implementing strategic decisions; for discovering how well these strategies are working; and for making both internal and external changes in these strategies as new information is received. Obviously this is a tall order, and the cybernetic model presupposes that breakdowns will occur: that messages will lose their meaning; that information will be lost. In this world of uncertainty, campaigns will thus be assessed according to their ability to *approximate* the model in the real world of politics.

While the effectiveness of this cybernetic model as an explanatory tool remains to be determined in the ensuing application to the 1980 presidential campaigns, our earlier review of alternative approaches to campaign analysis invites a word about how the model can be integrated with these various approaches. In general, the integrating capacity of cybernetics is high. Several other approaches can be translated directly into the cybernetic model. Since cybernetics refers to "steering,"* or control through the use of information,[71] it is a very short step to the analysis of decision-making. Indeed, it must be evident, given the frequent references to decision-making in the cybernetic campaign, that these two approaches are closely compatible. As for the two models of decision applied by Lamb and Smith, if translated into cybernetic terms, they would appear to come out as they did in 1964, with the comprehensive model being troubled by too little feedback and too much rigidity — the strengths of the incremental model being the reverse. Although the use of large collections of empirical data and computerized analysis in current presidential campaigns suggests that elements of the comprehensive model might fit quite nicely into a cybernetic system, this point merely affirms that it is easy to move from the decision-making to the cybernetic approach.

Similarly, the candidate beliefs approach, and especially social learning theory, readily lend themselves to reinterpretation in cybernetic terms. For example, the analytic concept of higher-order feedback, or learning, can comfortably explain the findings that

---

*Wiener derived the term "cybernetics" from the Greek word for "steersman," from which the word "governor" also originates.

certain candidate beliefs and experiences sharply affect the ability of campaigns to make appropriate adaptations to new circumstances.

Although different versions of the campaign management and organization approach often seem to have little in common, all are susceptible to reanalysis in terms of communication and control. In fact, there is a substantial literature on applications of information theory to organizations.[72] These, of course, tend to be formal analyses, as do those that integrate cybernetics with the strategies of election approach. Rational decision theories, such as game theory, share some of the same mathematical foundations as information theory, and Wiener makes frequent references to the work of John Von Neumann and Oskar Morgenstern in his study of cybernetics.[73] This is not to suggest that these two bodies of theory – game theory and information theory – are essentially the same, for they are not;[74] but cybernetics is able to interpret the findings of decision theory, even though both of these would be at a more formal level than I shall use here.

In sum, while a cybernetic approach to political campaigns certainly cannot be all things to all analysts, it combines a strong theoretical foundation with an unusual degree of flexibility in relating to other modes of analysis. This should make it easier for other scholars to compare their findings with those in the chapters that follow.

In applying the cybernetic model to the various presidential campaigns of 1980, I shall proceed by describing those aspects of the respective campaigns that provide a sufficient empirical basis for analysis. This analysis will be interspersed with the descriptions, hopefully affording a reasonably coherent "story" of what happened in the 1980 election. In no sense should my descriptions be taken as complete, for this is not my purpose. Moreover, I shall not treat *all* the presidential campaigns, even though some, such as those of the Citizens and Libertarian parties, may have considerable inherent interest for other reasons. On the other hand, I shall cover all those candidates that began as "serious" contenders for the Democratic and Republican party nominations, even though there will be cases that add little to our understanding of a cybernetic campaign. Admittedly, this might seem a bit arbitrary; yet in the end it provides a reasonable sample of the presidential campaigns that took place in 1980.

NOTES

1. Karl A. Lamb and Paul A. Smith, *Campaign Decision-Making: The Presidential Election of 1964* (Belmont, Calif.: Wadsworth, 1968), pp. 7-13.

2. The best of the series was the first, *The Making of the President 1960* (New York: Atheneum, 1961). It won a Pulitzer Prize and was made into a movie that is still shown in colleges and universities.

3. Lamb and Smith, *Campaign Decision-Making*, Chapter 14.

4. Gerald M. Pomper, "Campaigning: The Art and Science of Politics," *Polity* 2 (Summer 1970):533-39.

5. Still one of the best expositions of this point is Anatol Rapoport, "Various Meanings of 'Theory,' " *American Political Science Review* 52 (December 1958):972-88.

6. There are too many of these works to list. Good examples covering the period since 1960 are Stephen Shaddeg, *The New How to Win an Election* (New York: Daniel McKay, 1964); Hank Parkinson, *Winning Your Campaign* (Englewood Cliffs, N.J.: Prentice-Hall, 1970); Daniel M. Gaby and Mark H. Treusch, *Election Campaign Handbook* (Englewood Cliffs, N.J.: Prentice-Hall, 1976); and S. J. Guezzetta, *The Campaign Manual* (Alexandria, Va.: Campaign Publishing, 1981). Both Democratic and Republican National Committees (Washington) issue a *Campaign Manual* every two years, sometimes with additional separates on special topics.

7. Guezzetta, *The Campaign Manual*, Table of Contents.

8. Robert Agranoff, *The Management of Election Campaigns* (Boston: Holbrook Press, 1976). An earlier volume taking the same approach was *The New Style in Election Campaigns* (Boston: Holbrook, 1972).

9. For example, see Chapter 16 in Agranoff, *Management of Election Campaigns*. Also see James I. Lengle and Byron E. Shafer, eds., *Presidential Politics: Nominations and Elections* (New York: St. Martin's Press, 1980), esp. Chapter 5.

10. Xandra Kayden, *Campaign Organization* (Lexington, Mass.: D. C. Heath, 1978).

11. Burdett A. Loomis, "Campaign Organization in Competitive 1972 House Races," Ph.D. dissertation, University of Wisconsin, Madison, 1974.

12. Robert J. Huckshorn and Robert C. Spencer, *The Politics of Defeat* (Amherst: University of Massachusetts Press, 1971).

13. Ibid., Chapter 8.

14. James Q. Wilson deals with various types of organizational motives and structures in different party contexts in his *Political Organizations* (New York: Basic Books, 1973), Chapter 6.

15. Agranoff, *Management of Election Campaigns*, pp. 182-83.

16. Especially David Braybrooke and Charles E. Lindblom, *A Strategy of Decision* (New York: The Free Press, 1963).

17. Lamb and Smith, *Campaign Decision-Making*, Chapter 14.

18. For example, Graham Allison, *Essence of Decision: Explaining the Cuban Missile Crisis* (Boston: Little, Brown, 1971); Richard M. Cyert and

James G. March, *A Behavioral Theory of the Firm* (Englewood Cliffs, N.J.: Prentice-Hall, 1963); John W. Kingdon, *Congressmen's Voting Decisions* (New York: Harper and Row, 1973); Charles E. Lindblom, *The Policy-Making Process* (Englewood Cliffs, N.J.: Prentice-Hall, 1968); Donald W. Tayler, "Decision-Making and Problem Solving," in *Handbook of Organizations*, ed. James G. March (Chicago: Rand McNally, 1965), pp. 48-86; Herbert A. Simon, "Political Research: The Decision-Making Framework," in *Varieties of Political Theory*, ed. David Easton (Englewood Cliffs, N.J.: Prentice-Hall, 1966).

19. Morton H. Halperin, *Bureaucratic Politics and Foreign Policy* (Washington, D.C.: Brookings Institution, 1974); Charles O. Jones, *An Introduction to the Study of Public Policy*, 2d ed. (North Scituate, Mass.: Duxbury, 1977), esp. Chapters 1, 4, 6, and 9; Anthony Downs, *Inside Bureaucracy* (Boston: Little, Brown, 1967); Richard C. Snyder and Glenn D. Paige, "The United States Decision to Resist Aggression in Korea: The Application of an Analytic Scheme," *Administrative Science Quarterly* 3 (December 1958):341-78.

20. Marjorie Randon Hershey, "A Social Learning Theory of Innovation and Change in Political Campaigning," paper delivered at the Annual Meeting of the American Political Science Association, Washington, D.C., September 1-4, 1977, p. 4.

21. Lamb and Smith, *Campaign Decision-Making*, p. 18.

22. William R. Keech and Donald R. Matthews, *The Party's Choice* (Washington, D.C.: Brookings Institution, 1976).

23. Anthony Downs, *An Economic Theory of Democracy* (New York: Harper & Bros., 1957).

24. William H. Riker, *The Theory of Political Coalitions* (New Haven, Conn.: Yale University Press, 1962).

25. Steven J. Brams, *The Presidential Election Game* (New Haven, Conn.: Yale University Press, 1978).

26. John Aldrich, *Before the Convention: Strategies and Choices in Presidential Nomination Campaigns* (Chicago: University of Chicago Press, 1980); and Benjamin I. Page, *Choices and Echoes in Presidential Elections: Rational Man and Electoral Democracy* (Chicago: University of Chicago Press, 1978).

27. Denis G. Sullivan, Jeffrey L. Pressman, and F. Christopher Arterton, *Explorations in Convention Decision Making* (San Francisco: W. H. Freeman, 1976).

28. Brams, *The Presidential Election Game*, p. xviii.

29. See Aldrich, *Before the Convention*, Chapter 8; and Page, *Choices and Echoes*, Chapter 10.

30. For example, Robert Axelrod, "Where the Votes Come From: An Analysis of Electoral Coalitions," *American Political Science Review* 66 (March 1972):11-20, and his "1976 Update," *American Political Science Review* 72 (June 1978):622-24.

31. John Kessel, *Presidential Campaign Politics: Coalition Strategies and Citizen Response* (Homewood, Ill.: Dorsey, 1980). Kessel uses a similar approach in an earlier study, *The Goldwater Coalition: Republican Strategies in 1964* (Indianapolis: Bobbs-Merrill, 1968).

32. Gary C. Jacobson, *Money in Congressional Elections* (New Haven, Conn.: Yale University Press, 1980), esp. Chapter 5.

33. David A. Leuthold, *Electioneering in a Democracy* (New York: John Wiley, 1968).

34. Huckshorn and Spencer, *The Politics of Defeat*, p. 227.

35. Leuthold, *Electioneering in a Democracy*, Chapter 10.

36. John W. Kingdon, *Candidates for Office: Beliefs and Strategies* (New York: Random House, 1968).

37. Marjorie Randon Hershey, *The Making of Campaign Strategy* (Lexington, Mass.: D. C. Heath, 1974).

38. Hershey, "A Social Learning Theory."

39. Marjorie R. Hershey and Darrell M. West, "Single-Issue Groups and Political Campaigns: Six Senatorial Races and the Pro-Life Challenge in 1980," paper presented at the Annual Meeting of the Midwest Political Science Association, Cincinnati, April 15-18, 1981, p. 50.

40. Richard F. Fenno, Jr., *Home Style: House Members and Their Districts* (Boston: Little, Brown, 1978).

41. John W. Kingdon, *Congressmen's Voting Decision's*, 2d ed. (New York: Harper & Row, 1981), esp. Chapter 2. Also see the earlier studies by Lewis A. Froman, Jr., *Congressmen and Their Constituencies* (Chicago: Rand McNally, 1963); and David Mayhew, *Congress: The Electoral Connection* (New Haven, Conn.: Yale University Press, 1974).

42. Nelson W. Polsby and Aaron Wildavsky, *Presidential Elections: Strategies of American Electoral Politics*, 5th ed. (New York: Charles Scribner's Sons, 1980).

43. Of the others published in conjunction with the 1980 presidential election, that by Stephen J. Wayne, *The Road to the White House* (New York: St. Martin's Press, 1980), includes an unusual amount on campaigns and campaigning.

44. Stephen Hess, *The Presidential Campaign*, rev. ed. (Washington, D.C.: Brookings Institution, 1978).

45. Alan L. Clem, *The Making of Congressmen: Seven Campaigns of 1974* (North Scituate, Mass.: Duxbury, 1976).

46. Ibid., pp. 4-6.

47. Ibid., pp. 251-53.

48. For example, see Jerome M. Mileur and George T. Salzner, *Campaigning for the Massachusetts Senate: Electioneering Outside the Political Limelight* (Amherst: University of Massachusetts Press, 1974).

49. A collection of widely varied studies, some embodying comparative perspectives, is Louis Maisel, ed., *Changing Campaign Techniques* (Beverly Hills, Calif.: Sage Publications, 1976).

50. Kenneth Boulding, *The Image* (Ann Arbor: University of Michigan Press, 1956).

51. Most of what follows is based on the ground-breaking and still exciting little book by Norbert Wiener, *The Human Use of Human Beings* (Garden City, N.Y.: Doubleday Anchor, 1954). More complex and less accessible here is his *Cybernetics*, 2d ed. (Cambridge, Mass.: M.I.T. Press, 1961).

52. Wiener, *The Human Use*, p. 23. These concepts have been elaborated and applied in sometimes loose, but usually more detailed, forms of systems analysis. See, for example, David Easton, *A Systems Analysis of Political Life* (New York: John Wiley, 1956); and "An Approach to the Analysis of Political Systems," *World Politics* 9 (April 1957):383-400.

53. "Information is a name for the content of what is exchanged with the outer world as we adjust to it, and make our adjustment felt upon it." Wiener, *The Human Use*, p. 17. For the definition in terms of organization, see p. 21.

54. Ibid.

55. Ibid., pp. 28-31.

56. Ibid., pp. 7-12. The most probable state of the universe is one of complete entropy or disorganization. Wiener points out that "it is possible to interpret the information carried by a message as essentially the negative logarithm of its probability" (p. 21).

57. Ibid., p. 24. Also see Karl W. Deutsch, *The Nerves of Government* (New York: The Free Press, 1966), pp. 80-91.

58. Deutsch, *The Nerves of Government*, pp. 187-89. All four elements of the feedback process are summarized in these pages.

59. Ithiel de Sola Pool, Robert P. Abelson, and Samuel Popkin, *Candidates, Issues and Strategies* (Cambridge, Mass.: M.I.T. Press, 1964).

60. Deutsch, *Nerves of Government*, pp. 85-86; Wiener, *The Human Use*, pp. 23-24.

61. Deutsch, *Nerves of Government*, pp. 206-8, sees this as an essential element of individual freedom and identity.

62. The findings of the candidate beliefs approach provide support for this hypothesis. See Hershey, "A Social Learning Theory."

63. Wiener, *The Human Use*, pp. 33 and 49-63; Wiener, *Cybernetics*, pp. 69-80; and W. Ross Ashby, *Design for a Brain*, 2d ed. (New York: John Wiley, 1960), pp. 113 and 234.

64. Deutsch, *Nerves of Government*, pp. 91-97.

65. Wiener, *The Human Use*, p. 51.

66. Deutsch, *Nerves of Government*, pp. 161-62.

67. Downs, *An Economic Theory of Democracy*, Chapters 11-13, shows how different types of information are more or less expensive.

68. Since input messages are the "raw material" from which decision-makers "construct" their output messages, economizing on the input side will presumably be more costly (in terms of feedback) in the long run.

69. Doris A. Graber, *Mass Media and American Politics* (Washington, D.C.: Congressional Quarterly Press, 1980), Chapter 3; and Hess, *The Presidential Campaign*, Chapter 7.

70. Graber, *Mass Media and American Politics*, pp. 157-89; and Hess, *The Presidential Campaign*.

71. Wiener, *The Human Use*, p. 15. Deutsch refers to steering and decision-making repeatedly in his exposition of cybernetics and political life. *Nerves of Government*, Chapters 5-7.

72. For a summary, see Harold Guetzkow, "Communications in Organizations," in *Handbook of Organizations*, Chapter 12.

73. For example, Wiener, *The Human Use*, pp. 181-82.

74. Deutsch, *Nerves of Government*, Chapter 4.

3

The Prenomination
Campaigns:
The Democrats

The campaigns for the 1980 presidential election began well before 1980. By this I am referring to both the patterns of purposive action — or systems of communication — that are the campaigns themselves, and the personal backgrounds of the candidates. The latter can produce separate patterns of public recognition, expectations, and (dis)approval that stretch back a long time. Sometimes these patterns fade into obscurity, but at other times they persist — to be activated by the flow of information occasioned by the new campaign. They are collective memories that are triggered by relevant events.

As an electoral factor this is enormously complex — simplified over years of political research and experience into categories of candidate experiences that are likely to be embedded in public memory: the "public record," for example, or even more simply, "incumbency." To some extent such categories have worked; that is, they provide generalizations about expected increments of public support. But these generalizations served poorly in 1980, and the campaign playing field was littered with failures to cope with public images of candidate pasts. The campaigns of Carter, Connally, and Kennedy were notable examples, but in other cases the lack of difficulty seemed more a matter of luck than calculation.

In another respect, however, the memory of past events comprised a lesson that was definitely learned by 1980. It was drawn from the campaigns of 1972 and especially 1976, and it was simple and peremptory: Start early! Exactly how early was early proved less a matter of definition than of strategy and logistics, and some campaigns started much earlier than others. Moreover, because few campaigns were able, like Athena, to spring fully armed from the head of some political Zeus, there remains the usual empirical uncertainty about just when it is accurate to say certain campaigns began. Such uncertainties are most pronounced in the cases of the two eventual nominees, Jimmy Carter and Ronald Reagan.

As an operating guide to when campaigns should make their first moves according to the new rules of the game (reviewed in Chapter 1), "start early" was effective. For 1980 it was a lesson well learned. Yet in practice it did not seem to aid campaigns either to exploit or protect (and especially the latter) themselves from the public memory factor — the legacy of past performances of the candidates.

CARTER

Nowhere was the eagerness to get an early start stronger or more revealing than in the Carter White House — raising again the conceptual, normative, and practical question: When during a President's first term does his reelection campaign actually begin?[1] Although the Carter administration was not immune from the "normal" partisan accusations that public policy was a hostage of electoral designs, the particular qualities of the President's top staff add a distinct element of personal background and taste to the factors that affected the amount of electoral intervention. As a member of Carter's White House staff during its first two years, James Fallows found a disturbing lack of intense concern for public policy on the part of the "President's men." On the other hand,

> the one subject that did engage their passions was the one in which they had all proven expert: politics in the horse-race sense, winning elections. This made legislation and administration marginally interesting, but only to the extent that they affected the prospects for the next election. Flying back on Air Force One from a series of political appearances shortly before I left, I heard one of the Georgians say to several others, "You know, there really ought to be a place for people like us between elections, someplace we could rest up and get ready for the next one." This reminded me all too clearly of the conversation

I had had two days before with one of the more highly respected members of the White House press corps. I heard his lament about the tedium of the White House beat; there was only one solution he saw, and that was for the fun and excitement of the 1980 campaign to begin.[2]

Fallows' points mesh with innumerable other commentaries of the time that emphasized the inexperience and general ineptness of the White House staff in dealing with policy making, and particularly with relationships with Congress. Usually the President's tendency to surround himself with long-time friends and associates from Georgia, and specifically from his 1976 campaign, was also singled out. This last in itself is hardly unusual in American politics; but the inexperience of these individuals in the ways of Washington was uncommon. Thus we see a White House staff that for various reasons was inclined to think in terms of electoral rather than governmental consequences long before 1980.

On January 17, 1979, Hamilton Jordan, Carter's chief of staff, and one of the "Georgians" referred to above, wrote a comprehensive memorandum to the President setting forth the basic strategies for the 1980 campaign.[3] Among Jordan's recommendations, several are noteworthy: The President should utilize the advantages of incumbency; efforts should be made to influence (especially Southern) states to hold early caucuses or primaries in order to balance possible losses in such areas as the northeast; and the President should raise the bulk of his campaign funds by December 1979, but "remain in a non-candidate posture for as long as possible." Jordan further observed that "we will be re-elected or not re-elected based largely on your performance as President."[4]

Jordan's memorandum served to signal other administration officials that it was time to keep their eyes on the electoral ball; that concern for public responses to Carter's presidential performance, and for maneuvers by potential challengers, was now approved at the top. Not only were these obvious messages of control, but also it must be reemphasized that such political considerations did not come suddenly to life with Jordan's memorandum. Patrick Caddell, the President's pollster, and also a member of the 1976 campaign, had been writing memos to Carter about his public support problems since 1977. The Democratic party's midterm convention in 1978 had been the scene of various campaign-like sallies between supporters of the President and of Senator Edward Kennedy.[5] In October 1978, Caddell, Jordan, Jody Powell (the President's press secretary, and also from the 1976 campaign), and Tim Kraft (Carter's first appointments secretary, and then, as Jordan's assistant, White House liaison with party leaders around the country) met at Caddell's and Kraft's apartment to start serious planning for the 1980 reelection effort. In accordance with Jordan's design, explicit organizing moves were kept at a low level of visibility. A Carter/Mondale Reelection Committee was formally established in March 1979, and, significantly, by April 11 it had qualified for Federal Election Commission matching funds — thus indicating a substantial level of organization for such an early period.

Meanwhile, other actions were being taken. In January 1978 the President began attempts to strengthen his notoriously weak ties with the "regular" Democratic party organization, both by bringing in a more vigorous national chairman (John C. White) and by committing himself to more party activities, such as fund raising.[6] By 1979 the White House was being more specific, moving to shore up the Democratic National Committee (DNC) staff, and getting it to increase its fund-raising efforts, to improve its state-level contacts, and to get busy on the project to change the timing of various state primaries.[7] Clearly, the DNC* was being converted, insofar as politically possible, into an arm of the White House for the ensuing campaign.

The campaign organization itself, as a distinct system, cannot be understood apart from those members of the White House staff who dominated it. Foremost among these was Hamilton Jordan, whose January memorandum essentially marked its beginning in the form of the Committee for the Reelection of the President. The first chairman of this committee was Evan Dobelle, treasurer of the DNC, young, competent, inexperienced, and completely loyal to Jordan. Dobelle's ability to run the expanding organization depended

---

*Unless otherwise indicated, references to the Democratic or Republican National Committees will denote not the committees themsleves but their staffs. Although these staffs are formally neutral in prenomination politics, they are usually tied through appointment and policy agreement to the incumbent president. The best that presidential challengers can hope for is to have their supporters on the National Committee, and, in the states, to make enough of a fuss to prevent the president from using the committee staff too aggressively and overtly.

on close and continuing guidance from Jordan. As events unfolded, however, and Jordan's White House responsibilities remained unrelieved (not to mention his temporary preoccupation with allegations that he had used cocaine a year before), this guidance became hard to get when needed.

Late in August, therefore, Jordan replaced Dobelle with Tim Kraft, with Dobelle becoming the campaign's chief fund raiser.[8] Kraft was a strong organizer but uncomfortable in the role of campaign spokesman; so in November Robert Strauss took over as chairman (and spokesman) and Kraft became the operating manager of the campaign.[9] (This arrangement continued until September 1980, when Kraft was forced to resign, also because of cocaine allegations.) Strauss was a veteran Democratic politician who had worn many hats both in politics and government. He was a master of political judgment and articulation. Throughout, however, it was Hamilton Jordan who, for want of a better word, ran the campaign — although this does not capture the element of collective decisions and mutual understanding that was present.

From a cybernetic perspective, the prenomination Carter organization, both early and late, had advantages over all others. The most important of these by far was incumbency — the presidency itself. This constituted an unrivaled mechanism for gathering information, internal communication and decision-making, and sending messages of control. For input, the President could call upon unmatched resources of data, including a very large memory, and analysis concerning both campaign issues and rules — the economy, the population, the budget, other nations, and so on. Much of this was "inside" information, unavailable to other candidates, even if they could marshal the analytic resources needed to process the data. Much of it also could be campaign feedback, because wide-ranging monitors were available to find out how programs were working, how the public was responding to both statements and governmental action, and how other decision-makers (including those abroad) were reacting to Carter's performance.

Then there was the campaign's output, its messages of control. Not only was the candidate the President, who could act authoritatively, but also it was understood throughout the apparatus of government that the President's top aides could speak authoritatively, and they too were members of the campaign. Similarly, the candidate could put pressure on Democratic officials in the states, both directly and through the DNC. These state and local connections further could be reinforced through the President's second advantage, his *personal* supporters still in place from the 1976 campaign. To be sure, all the Carter "troops" from the 1976 primaries and general election were not prepared to return to the trenches, but some were, and they constituted a significant resource of communication and control.

Using these output resources, the Carter campaign moved in 1979 to implement Jordan's recommendation that certain state primaries and caucuses be rescheduled. Its success was limited but interesting. Connecticut moved its primary from March 4 (where it was paired with Massachusetts) to March 25 (pairing it with New York). Georgia and Alabama were moved to March 11, where they could join Florida in giving Carter an early big day. And the Missouri caucuses were shifted to April 22, where they could blunt an expected Kennedy win in Pennsylvania. Of course there were a number of other states that Carter's forces tried but failed to move.[10] Yet it is worth noting that in a number of cases Jordan's expectations about how states would vote turned out to be far off the mark, suggesting limitations in this effort to cybernetically *lead* the target. This effort also is interesting because it is essentially an example of one player in a game being able to change the rules. Naturally, other candidates could use their supporters in selected states to attempt the same thing, as Kennedy did in New York, for example; but it is clear that a candidate as President and party leader is able to deal with more states, earlier, and with greater resources.

Turning to the campaign's use of government as an output vehicle during the prenomination period, Jordan's prescription was carried out with a grasp of detail that was unrivaled by past presidential candidates. One of the most competent presidential assistants, Jack Watson, was responsible for White House liaison with the states. In this position he developed a comprehensive list of federal programs able to render various types of aid to states and localities. This list was long, including everything from highway and mass transportation funds to outright grants for innumerable projects. In 1979 these resources were used to persuade governors, mayors, and congressmen of note to endorse the Carter candidacy. In the 1980 caucuses and primaries it was used for the purpose of gaining direct electoral support.[11] For the key Illinois primary, for example, a vast number of specific grants were distributed to help local politicians in the state to see their way to endorse Carter and work for Carter support. As a cybernetic system, the campaign was thus able to increase the influential power of its output.

Directly related to these uses of party, incumbency, and the organizational remnants from 1976 was a particular type of input mentioned earlier in passing. From the very start the campaign's development was based upon a programmatic analysis of past events; in short, the incorporation of memory into decision-making. This was Jordan's January memorandum that was essentially a strategic plan. Far from accurate in all its appraisals, the memorandum was nevertheless masterful in capturing the *basic* elements of what the 1980 campaign needed to be and do. Relevant history was mostly the campaign of 1976, and of that, primarily President Ford's. It was Ford's ignorance of campaign laws, failure to exploit every resource of incumbency, lack of self-assessment, and delay in preparing for Reagan's challenge that Jordan drew upon for the strategies of 1980.[12] As for the opposition, Jordan was convinced it would include Governor Jerry Brown and, depending on the President's level of support late in the summer, Senator Edward Kennedy, of whom Kennedy was far more dangerous — and who should be met with public confidence and careful preparation. Thus in addition to its other resources, the Carter campaign began and grew with a strong sense of direction, and what turned out to be effective anticipations of its major challenger.

Given these formidable attributes, what were the cybernetic problems of the prenomination Carter campaign? There were two, one of which was its major source of strength: incumbency. This led to what can be called the "responsibility problem." A substantial number of citizens picture the President as responsible for all national government actions and consequences. This image is not uniform or inflexible, but when combined with the tendency to feel more intensely about policies that fail than those that succeed,[13] the result can be a growing negative appraisal of the President as minorities angered over different failures coalesce into larger and larger proportions of the electorate.[14]

However, we need not reach as far as this "coalition of minorities" hypothesis to appreciate Carter's level of public support as the prenomination campaign was getting under way. By midsummer 1979 overall public approval of the President's performance had sunk to 30 percent, and, perhaps more significantly, approval among Democrats was little better at 35 percent.[15] With rising inflation, continuing unemployment, energy shortages, and nagging reports of presidential ineptness in world affairs, the Carter campaign was faced with finding either dramatic policy solutions or a new image for the President, who was widely seen as ineffectual.

But these solutions required a decision system in the administration that was not available — the second problem. Both the President and his chief associates had qualities that undermined governmental communication and feedback in the White House. One of these qualities was inexperience. Dominated by the previously mentioned "Georgians" (for example, Jordan, Powell, Kraft, Frank Moore, Stuart Eizenstat, Robert Lipshutz, and Gerald Rafshoon), the president's top aides came into the administration untrained in running the federal government, including managing the bureaucracy and working with Congress. They had to learn, and this learning was impeded by their shared conviction that the Washington establishment was against them. There was a feeling of defensiveness, and an unwillingness to seek out old Washington hands for guidance and advice.[16]

At the core of the communication and learning problem was Carter himself — who did not stimulate his associates to better performances, practice to improve his speech-making, meet effectively with large groups, and delegate responsibilities. By initially attempting to make an exhaustive range of decisions (such as who would use the tennis court) personally, the President was subject to information and decision overload. He coupled this with a penchant for highly compartmentalized relationships that restricted communication that was vital for a cybernetic system. Here, again, is how James Fallows saw it from the inside:

> After a few months of sending memos to the President, Powell, Jordan, and Eizenstat on subjects unrelated to my stated functions — on the volunteer army, the tricks of monitoring bureaucracies, different gestures Carter might make — I learned to stop. It was not that my superiors disagreed with me . . . but rather that I was out of my place. . . . [T]his was a bureaucratic organization, in the sense Max Weber defined: interchangeable people performing strictly limited tasks. Everyone was safe within the confines of his organizational box; few were welcomed outside. Run like a bureaucracy, the White House took on the spirit of a bureaucracy, drained of zeal, obsessed with form. . . .[17]

Carter emerges from this and numerous other commentaries as a "true loner — not a lonely neurotic afraid of the outside world but a man at ease with himself and what is inside his head."[18] Personally close to only a small number of people in Washington — especially his wife, Rosalynn, Jordan, Powell, and Vice-President Walter Mondale — the President was not comfortable with the small talk and jocularity of politics. This limited his exchanges with congressmen, cabinet officers, party leaders, and even much of the White House staff, such as Fallows. Carter also shrank from disciplining his subordinates, especially his staff, and few were fired.* Even notable cases of men who performed badly, sometimes to the public embarrassment of the President, were long tolerated — thus slowing organizational adaptation (learning).

As we shall see, the composite character of the candidate is absolutely vital to the functioning of a campaign, and this is explicitly true for a cybernetic system. Jimmy Carter's complex and subtle presidential style of action is hardly exhausted by the preceding points, and we shall return to these and other aspects of his character as they affected the subsequent campaign. For the moment, however, the points that have been made about the characteristics of Carter and his aides show that for purposes of governance, communication and decision-making in the White House were far different from the cybernetic model. As Jordan said from the start, the President would win or lose based on the *performance* of his government, not the *promises* of his campaign.

The shortcomings of the White House as a cybernetic system explain why an otherwise impressive campaign was saddled with such negative images of its candidate as it was getting under way. Of course formal efforts were made to separate the campaign, by establishing a headquarters, phone numbers, and so forth, separate from the White House, but since the intersection of White House and campaign de facto leadership was virtually complete, the two cybernetic systems were largely integrated.

A striking demonstration of this was the famous "Camp David Domestic Summit" of July 1979. Patrick Caddell, after repeated

---

*Of the eight original members of Carter's top staff, six were still present at the end of his term. Noteworthy cases of shoddy performance include Bert Lance, director of the Office of Management and Budget (resigned), Dr. Peter Bourne, Carter's health adviser (resigned), and Frank Moore, congressional relations (continued).

vain attempts to focus Carter's attention on the electoral implications of his worsening public image, was able to do so by pressing his findings on Rosalynn Carter. Caddell conceived a public "malaise," with Americans caught in a feeling of frustration and unease, and perceiving Carter as a very weak leader. It was a crisis of confidence. The President, impressed by James MacGregor Burns' recent book on leadership,[19] responded by holding a series of intensive meetings with virtually all the top officials of his administration (plus various other knowledgeables) at Camp David. In the style of a retreat, the general question was posed by Caddell: What could be done to restore public confidence (and particularly confidence in Carter)? There was no doubt that the reelection of the President in 1980 was the most important consideration in the minds of Carter and his aides.

The resulting action – a nationwide television address on July 15 and a call for the formal resignations of the President's entire cabinet and senior staff, of which five were accepted – was decided on only after vigorous debate among Carter's top political associates. (Another action was the formal appointment of Hamilton Jordan as the President's chief of staff, making his governmental responsibilities more constraining.) The ten days of meetings at Camp David were cybernetically stronger than the normal White House routine. Approximately 130 prominent individuals participated at one time or another and brought a variety of input. Feedback was relatively, but not entirely, unrestricted, and some learning occurred in the form of the new cabinet appointments and guidelines.

Although obviously not advertised as such, the Camp David "summit" was a major event in the early prenomination campaign. Its electoral effects are impossible to determine. Most public commentaries were negative about the sweeping demand for resignations, which was apparently contrived to enable Carter to make the needed dismissals with less pain[20] – a restriction on feedback. More significantly, it was a clear signal to the entire administration that adherence to campaign purposes was henceforth of first priority. For campaign decision-makers, the experience showed how difficult it was to control output messages affecting, simultaneously, the complex systems of government, the media, and the electorate.

Closely following the summit came a major campaign meeting on August 19 and 20. Arranged by Jordan, and attended by all the leaders of the campaign,* the meeting reviewed the progress of the organization so far and made decisions about money and such tactical moves as making a major effort to win the Florida "caucus" later in the fall. By this time the operating form of the campaign was basically set. Tim Kraft, a veteran of 1976, replaced Evan Dobelle as chairman and manager of the organization. Regular meetings were held weekly in the White House to review developing events and to make both strategic and tactical decisions. Usually attended by both Jimmy and Rosalynn Carter, Mondale, Caddell, Rafshoon, Strauss, Powell, and Kraft, they were formally chaired by Carter, but actually led or "expedited" by Jordan, who was recognized by everyone as the chief strategist.†

As a cybernetic system, the campaign was in very good shape. Resources of money and personnel were abundant, as were those of information and memory, in the form of experience. Caddell's highly refined polling techniques produced a continuing flow of information about public attitudes and opinions that was both explanatory and predictive. With decision-makers so close at hand, internal communication was generally excellent and decisions could quickly be converted into output. Judgments to seek additional information in the field, or use the mass media in a particular way, could be converted into action (output) by Caddell (polls), Rafshoon (public relations and television), or Powell (statements to the press). Such decisions as to keep the President in the White House after the American Embassy was seized in Tehran and the campaign was officially begun, and to make a negative issue of Kennedy, were made with a high level of system input and output.

Higher-order feedback, or learning, was also apparent and effective, at least within the formal system. The already-mentioned shifts from Dobelle, to Kraft, to Strauss were made with a minimum of friction and gains in operational effectiveness. At lower levels, modifications in both the Washington and field organizations also were carried out smoothly. In the field itself, feedback, such as in the October caucuses and the November convention in Florida where

---

*For example, Caddell, Jordan, Powell, Rafshoon, Dobelle, Kraft, Richard Moe (for Mondale), Tom Donilon, Tim Smith, Phil Wise, and Sarah Waddington.

†These meetings became daily during the primaries, when they were joined by afternoon meetings of a "reaction committee" having different members.

Carter defeated Kennedy almost two to one, was impressive.* It was evident that the Carter campaign was fully prepared to compete in the grass-roots operations of identifying supporters and getting them to the polls or caucuses. In many respects the Carter campaign attained levels of communication and control during this early period that approached those of the cybernetic model.

Yet even a cybernetic model could not overcome problems in other and related systems. Events in Iran, beginning with the embassy takeover, could not be effectively anticipated or controlled by the campaign. Domestic economic conditions, particularly with respect to energy and inflation, proved intractable, and administrative actions, such as the "anti-Israel" vote in the UN Security Council — and the subsequent contradictory statements by the State Department shortly before the New York primary on March 25 — worked to confirm deep-seated public images of the President unable to manage his government. Although I have emphasized that with few exceptions (such as domestic affairs advisor Stuart Eizenstat and national security advisor Zbigniew Brzezinski) the President's chief White House advisors were indistinguishable from the leadership of his campaign, they were in fact members of different systems of action, obviously related but not the same.

Based on early and systematic preparation, in the fall of 1979 the Carter campaign demonstrated a significant superiority over that of Edward Kennedy — a superiority that became manifest as the formal campaign period opened with the Iowa caucuses in January 1980. The campaign of course expanded into a larger and more active system of communication as it entered every caucus and primary.[21] Having committed himself at the time of his formal December 4 announcement to stay at his desk in order to devote his full attention to the hostage situation in Iran, Carter's was a classic "Rose Garden" posture. Nevertheless, at the White House, campaign activities accelerated apace. The leadership meetings were now held daily, and the exchange of messages to and from the Washington headquarters and various field operations, and with the White House

---

*The Florida caucuses and subsequent convention are hard to categorize. The state holds caucuses in October to select delegates to party conventions in November, where state party platforms are constructed and straw polls of presidential preferences taken. None of these actions are connected to the regular presidential primary, which takes place the following March, and which selects the delegates to the national convention.

press corps, increased. The media recognized that the White House was the authoritative source of campaign information. For field appearances (a form of output) in the primaries, Carter's place was taken by "surrogates" — various cabinet officers; family members (especially Rosalynn Carter); Vice-President Mondale; and such others as Muriel Humphrey.

In terms of direct electoral results, the preconvention campaign was a distinct success, with Carter winning 24 of the 34 primaries, and a commanding majority of convention delegates (see Appendix A).* It did this against a major candidate, bearing a distinguished name in Democratic politics, who began the race decisively ahead of the President in the polls. The campaign's analysis of Kennedy's strengths and weaknesses, and its use of this information to win votes, was cybernetically impressive. Interestingly enough, however, the key elements of this success also became sources of subsequent weakness. These elements were the systematic use of governmental resources, the negative campaign against Kennedy, and the "hostage factor." As we shall see, each of these elements eventually contributed to further tarnishing the President's image, first in the media and then the electorate. This raises the question of how far ahead — how much lead — the cybernetic campaign must calculate in order to maintain control.

KENNEDY

If his public image reduced Carter's ability to draw the maximum benefits from an effective preconvention campaign, the public memories that bedeviled Ted Kennedy's campaign were much worse. A productive and widely respected third-term senator from Massachusetts, Kennedy was able to use his position in the Senate and his family legacy in the Democratic party to gain continuing publicity for his public policy positions. In important respects these were different from the President's, with Kennedy pressing for more

---

*The total number of primaries and caucuses is not a simple matter, but depends on what is counted. Some states have both, others have a primary for only one party, and others have different types for the two parties. Then there is Puerto Rico with two primaries. And so on. This can produce totals ranging from 34 to 39. In any case, Kennedy definitely won 10 and Carter 24 distinct primaries. Carter virtually swept the caucuses.

liberal policies — and doing this aggressively, such as at the 1978 midterm party convention.

Kennedy had been frequently "mentioned" as a potential presidential candidate in 1972 and 1976, but he consistently declined to run, usually citing family responsibilities.* Partly because of his family's political history, and partly because of his own political activities and assertiveness, Kennedy was a well-known public figure — sufficiently so that during most of the 1970s, in numerous states, large numbers of Democrats were convinced that he would be a very strong candidate and stood ready to support a Kennedy campaign.

There was, however, another side to the Kennedy legacy. Various episodes in Ted Kennedy's personal history, capped by the Chappaquiddick incident in 1969,† and including the current painful status of his marriage, made up an image of a man who was unreliable, and perhaps frivolous and even sexist. This negative perception was especially strong among women. Yet by the late 1970s it seemed quite possible that Kennedy's steady, generally admired performance in the Senate would work to displace the other view.[22] It is obvious that this movement in public opinion was not only gradual but also bolstered by Kennedy's ability to project a favorable image compared to Carter's. In any case, by July 1979 Gallup surveys found that among Democratic identifiers, 54 percent preferred Kennedy, compared to 21 percent for Carter. Moreover, "if the election were held today" polls during the same period showed Carter being defeated by Gerald Ford and running neck-and-neck with Ronald Reagan, while Kennedy won handily over both.[23] Perhaps even more important, several different surveys found that the electoral impact of the Chappaquiddick incident had declined substantially, although a CBS/New York *Times* poll still showed that of those who remembered Chappaquiddick (80 percent), 24 percent still thought they were less likely to vote for Kennedy because of it.[24]

---

*These evidently involved both the family's children, especially those of his brother Robert, and the feelings of his mother, who, after losing her oldest son, Joseph, in World War II, saw first John (1963) and then Robert (1968) assassinated. Of her sons, only Ted remained, and there were mixed feelings within the large family about the dangers he faced as a presidential candidate.

†In July 1969 a car driven by Kennedy ran off a bridge, drowning a young woman who was with the Senator. Delays in reporting the accident, and other circumstances surrounding it, left widespread suspicions that Kennedy's responsibilities had not been fully reported.

As this survey information about comparative public support held through the spring and summer of 1979 (note that Caddell's polls for the Carter campaign contained more information about the "softness" of Kennedy's support), Democratic leaders turned increasingly to Kennedy as a viable salvation from the looming Carter electoral "drag." Indeed, by July 1979 some accounts had the senator virtually beseiged by Democratic House and Senate colleagues who were apprehensive about being pulled under by a Carter-led ticket. While these politicos realized that Kennedy had weaknesses of image (character) and ideology (his liberal policy positions), they also knew that Chappaquiddick had not prevented him from standing at the top of the opinion polls for a long time — *and* that he would be a strong campaigner. The Kennedy campaigns of 1960 and 1968 were immortalized in political lore, and there was an "understanding" that if Ted decided to run, all the famous names, with their connections and panache, would be with him again.

I am not sure there was an exact moment when Ted Kennedy decided to challenge Carter for the nomination. The decision was made incrementally as he was drawn forward by the urgings of his staff and other politicians, the attentions of journalists, and the continuing evidence of Carter's weaknesses as a policy maker and public leader. By mid-August 1979 the die was cast. Early in September Carter was privately informed, and then, unofficially, the press. In terms of numbers and experience the early campaign staff was strong. Some were drawn from the classic earlier campaigns of Kennedy's brothers. Others came from the McCarthy and McGovern campaigns of 1968 and 1972, and even the Carter campaign of 1976. The largest number were current or past members of the senator's staff.[25] In addition, a variety of political friends, such as former Senator Dick Clark of Iowa, would help where they could.*

But creating a working organization out of these human resources proved more difficult than most had anticipated. The veterans of various Camelots were a disparate collection of individualists who

---

*Some of the leaders, and their positions, as of January 1980, were: Rich Burke (administrative assistant), Morris Dees (fund-raising), Dick Drayne (press and special assistant), Peter Edelman, Carey Parker, Charles Palmer, and Steven Schlesinger (issues), Paul Kirk (political director), Tony Podesta, Stephen Robbins, and Liz Stevens (scheduling), Robert Shrum (speech writing), Steven Smith (campaign manager), Tom Southwick (press secretary), Richard Sterns and Carl Wagner (strategy), John Gage and Larry Windsor (campaign plane).

had gotten their experience at earlier times.* There were internal conflicts over leading roles as the staff "shook down" and established working relationships. Setting up effective operations in the early primary states, raising money, dealing with the Federal Election Campaign Act regulations, producing television commercials – all were matters demanding detailed attention, and often there was at least a temporary shortage of expertise. Coping with all this in the teeth of a tough and prepared incumbent's countercampaign was more difficult than even the veterans had experienced before.

Consequently, well before the November 4 occupation of the U.S. Embassy in Iran, and the Soviet invasion of Afghanistan in December, the pressure of deadlines – and especially of unexpected events – was intense. The campaign was not ready for the Roger Mudd "60 Minutes" television interview in August,† the field effort required in the Florida caucus on October 13, or the Iowa caucus coming up on January 21. As in other states, reliance initially had been placed on the volunteer "Draft Kennedy" organization in Florida. Operating semiindependently, and fueled by enthusiasm and high expectations, the Kennedy effort drew press attention to an event that otherwise might have been irrelevant to the preconvention campaign. Once the issue was joined, Kennedy's forces could not match the resources and organization of the determined and carefully planned Carter effort.

The television interview was an hour long on prime time, on November 4, the day of the embassy takeover. It had been vigorously advertised by CBS, and with the long build-up of interest in Kennedy's possible, then probable, then actual candidacy, it captured a large and expectant national audience. Washington *Post* reporter T. R. Reed describes what happened:

> The result – a stumbling, vacuous performance that showed Kennedy as a man with no coherent explanation for Chappaquiddick and no

---

*Some of the more notable from the 1960 and 1968 campaigns were now tied to careers and did not have the same close relationships with Ted they had had with John or Robert. Thus a number of the campaign veterans that journalists had expected to join the 1980 campaign did not make themselves available.

†This entire episode was a fascinating example of the role of the media in political campaigns. This interview was filmed in August before Kennedy had decided, firmly, to run. But it was aired on November 4, with no indication on the part of CBS of the two and a half month gap.

clear reason for seeking the Presidency — was a disaster from which the campaign never recovered. [Tom] Southwick (Kennedy's press secretary) never did either. The dedicated young aide took personal blame for the Mudd fiasco, and eventually quit his job. . . .[26]

Cybernetically, the campaign began in a condition of information overload, with more messages coming in than could be converted into meaningful output. Some of these messages were in the form of new staff, entering without well-defined roles or relationships, many of whom had not worked together before. Furthermore, many brought memories (experience) of past campaigns that did not fit smoothly into the needs of the new organization. Other messages were from volunteer field units around the country asking for resources and guidance. Still other messages were from the various news media seeking output to satisfy the public's pressing curiosity about the progress of the Kennedy challenge.

It is important to keep in mind at this point that in terms of ordinary comparisons, the informational resources inherent in these input messages were generous. The number of experienced staff, the attentions of the press, the self-creation of volunteer field organizations — all would have delighted many other campaigns. What is more, not only were the opening problems of role definition and interpersonal relationships to be expected; it would be unbelievable had they not occurred. In short, the organizational problems faced by the campaign during September and October were hardly out of the ordinary.

The trouble was that Kennedy was not in an "ordinary" situation. He was challenging a highly developed cybernetic campaign, the core of which had existed at least since 1976. Kennedy needed to mold the aforementioned resources into a working *system* of information and control, and to do it quickly. It was clear that during the spring and summer period of active speculation about his candidacy, the senator had not made serious preparations for his campaign. As the system emerged, decision-making took an extreme form of disjointed incrementalism. This produced plenty of decisions and considerable action (output), but it meant that much of this action was uncoordinated, and a number of other actions — such as preparing the candidate for the Mudd interview and controlling expenditures (internal output) were not taken at all. It also meant that feedback was often interrupted and erratic.

All of this was at a time when decision pressures on the system were very high. As already indicated, field organizations for the early caucuses and primaries, testing and correcting the candidate's issue positions and style, and the organization of internal functions and authority needed to be accomplished.

In part, this problem of system construction was caused by a shortage of aides who were old enough, experienced enough, and close enough to the candidate to tell him when things were not going well. And in part the Kennedy campaign myth — that with a candidate so rich in political ability and popularity, with gifted family and friends, success would just happen — served to encourage positive rather than negative feedback. Thus the candidate initially received too little training and correction on how to speak, answer questions, pace himself, and so on. Other internal monitoring also was weak, with expenditures being a prime example. Through the whole of 1979 the Carter campaign spent $2.8 million, while Kennedy spent $2.4 million in November and December alone.[27] Worse than the unnecessary extravagances, such as overly plush offices and inefficient use of chartered aircraft, this heavy spending left the campaign critically short of funds during the early primaries.

In the meantime, the effects of both campaign and noncampaign events, including the "60 Minutes" interview and the takeover of the embassy in Iran, were being felt; and the realities of Kennedy's lost and the President's found public approval, along with the senator's personal difficulties, quickly caught up with the campaign. In one of her early reports, Elizabeth Drew described what was happening on the inside:

> In December, the anxiety at the Kennedy headquarters was apparent — not just over what Iran was doing to the campaign but also over what Kennedy himself was doing to it. There was a morale problem: people who had joined up thinking they were about to ride the crest of a wave were adrift. They found themselves not being greeted triumphantly but having to explain, defend. Kennedy himself seemed to have been thrown off stride. . . . He was not performing up to his capacity on the campaign trail. And each failure to live up to his billing was given great significance. A man who had become accustomed during his entire career to . . . praise for his political acumen and ability suddenly, according to press reports, could do nothing right. . . . Each slip of the tongue was reported, which made him more self-conscious, which led to further slips. . . , which increased the reporting on such

incidents. Whereupon, at the urging of his staff, he began to read his speeches, which led to wooden delivery. . . . Even a candidate who starts out confident can be shaken by such things. And virtually each day Kennedy was faced with what was probably the most painful criticism of all: that he was not as good as his brothers.[28]

Drew's description lets us see the effects of the Kennedy myth, particularly on Kennedy himself, and how difficult campaign feedback actually can be. The idea that the willing candidate can easily use staff criticism to make perfect adjustments is not the way feedback works in the uncertainty of political campaigns. It is more a matter of trial and error, abetted by staff diversity and experiences, as the candidate *learns* to make specific adjustments to specific campaign situations, with initial adjustments being primarily intuitive — and, if successful, being ascribed to a "natural politician."

The same principle holds for external feedback, which also was inadequate during the early months of the Kennedy campaign. Without frequent and systematic public opinion polling (as Caddell was doing for Carter), the campaign had difficulty perceiving and quickly adapting to the great shifts in how the American people were viewing the candidates that occurred in November and December. Yet even had such polling been done, would it have prevented Kennedy from making a remark critical of the Shah of Iran on December 2? Here is how the Washington *Post* reported what took place after Kennedy, at the end of a 14-hour campaign day, completed a television interview in San Francisco:

> The producers of KRON saw nothing particularly striking about Kennedy's remarks on the Shah, and they left them on the cutting room floor that night when brief passages of the interview were broadcast. . . . Kennedy's traveling press corps . . . concluded that this had been just one more uneventful interview. . . . But the reporter from the UPI . . . wandered down to the press room and found a transcript. . . . In the pre-dawn quiet of the news rooms of the major eastern newspapers, warning bells began to ring. . . . The first major furor of the 1980 campaign had been born. In a time when most other candidates had effectively taken a vow of silence on Iran, Kennedy's eruption became big news. Now the questions people already had about his character and his political views had to make way for doubts about his judgment.[29]

This episode was but one example of the special problems faced by a candidate who enters a campaign bearing deeply set public images and expectations – including *press* expectations. Both Kennedy and his campaign were subjected to intensive scrutiny. On-the-stump lapses that might be ignored or forgiven on the part of other candidates were magnified in the case of Kennedy, who was measured against what were, by 1980, primarily *imagined* performances of his brothers. The Carter strategy of making Kennedy the issue with "negative" advertising and comments succeeded not because of Kennedy's performance in early 1980, but because of Kennedy's past – emphasizing the extent to which basic public images of a candidate can interact with events of the campaign period to form an attitudinal context easy to manipulate but hard to control. This point would come home to Carter later in the year.

Ted Kennedy's prenomination campaign suffered serious break-downs of feedback and control in its opening months, but by the Iowa caucus it was not cybernetically decrepit. It was, in fact, a comparatively strong cybernetic system that sustained itself in the face of defeats that probably would have destroyed a less resilient system. Kennedy entered every primary and every state and territorial caucus. He lost 24 of 34 primaries, and 20 of 25 caucuses (see Appendix A). He lost more elections in 1980 than any other candidate.[30] Yet he scored impressive victories in major states* and ended up with 40 percent of the delegates to the national convention. His campaign persisted as an effective system until the last possible moment when he was defeated in the convention.

Consistent with his December 4 statement that the international situation required his undivided attention, Carter, in late December, withdrew from a scheduled debate with Kennedy in Iowa. In field appearances throughout the caucus and primary states Kennedy struggled to find ways of criticizing Carter's policies and conduct without activating the public's attitude that in times of international crisis the nation's President must not be undermined. Carter's White House spokesmen and campaign surrogates were quick to imply that Kennedy's attacks on the Shah and Carter's embargo of grain shipments to the Soviet Union, for example, were unpatriotic.[31]

---

*Kennedy won the primaries in the District of Columbia, California, Connecticut, Massachusetts, Michigan, New Jersey, New York, Pennsylvania, Rhode Island, and South Dakota.

This exploitation of underlying public attitudes worked to constrain Kennedy's natural speaking style, thus reducing the effectiveness of his performance in the field. As she traveled with Kennedy in the Iowa campaign, Drew observed that with his advisers — after reading poll results — shying away from attacks on Carter or policy issues,

> he's being advised not to try to stir the excitement that he in his own way can, and he is following that advice. The reputedly most natural and experienced politician of the Kennedy brothers is being programmed and reprogrammed. When he's at his best, he goes with his instincts, speaks from his gut, and can also be very funny. Now he seems battened down and unnatural.[32]

However, Kennedy did, in his stump speeches, attack Carter's refusal to leave the White House and debate him, as well as the President's use of government programs to influence local politicians.* Indeed, Carter's refusal to debate became one of the most common themes in Kennedy's campaign. From Carter's perspective, the Rose Garden strategy was not only working (Carter had pulled ahead of Kennedy in public support by January), but also could not be reversed because it was tied to the American hostages in Iran. As for the use-of-grants-to-get-endorsements strategy, which had been formulated at the August meeting, it was initially intended to show that all Democratic politicians, in the words of a Carter aide, "didn't believe that if the President was nominated the party would take a bath."[33]

There was some inherent plausibility in this reasoning, but the "two-step" communication flow whereby federal largesse convinced local politicians, who then convinced local voters, to support the President in caucuses or primaries is another matter. There were cases pointing each way, and net effects in a competitive environment

---

*This was usually done through the use of humor. Both attacks can be seen in the joint appearance in Waterloo, Iowa, of Brown, Kennedy, and Mondale about a week before the Iowa caucus. After making fun of Carter's use of surrogates, such as Mondale, and his refusal to debate, Kennedy went on: "I've been getting along pretty well with the Administration (pause) lately. All I have to do is talk about a particular problem or an issue and the Administration comes in the area and awards those grants. (Pause) And if you haven't gotten plenty here in Waterloo, you ought to make your applications now . . . before next week" (Drew, *The New Yorker*, February 4, 1980, pp. 89-90).

are far from certain. The Carter strategists were aiming primarily at state and local politicians directly, and there is no doubt that they used these "rewards" to the hilt.[34]

Fundamentally, however, it was not Carter's grants or refusal to debate that troubled the Kennedy campaign. As a cybernetic system it faced the enormous difficulty of overcoming the changes in public attitudes and opinions occasioned by the series of dramatic fall events — the Mudd interview, the embassy takeover, and the invasion of Afghanistan. Campaign responses (feedback) to these changes were not as swift as Carter's, partly because the problem (of hitting the target) was more intractable for Kennedy. For the campaign's major difficulty was not feedback *lag*, but rather *load*. The amount and speed of opinion change had been very large with respect to Kennedy. In response, the system's feedback initially overcorrected its candidate, causing him to be less effective in field appearances (or output). Yet this overly large *gain* was rather quickly reduced, and Kennedy generally adjusted to a performance up to capacity through the many primaries and caucuses. What must be kept in mind is the enormous load that the system had to deal with, especially during the early primaries and caucuses.

At the more mundane level of these individual state contests, a host of contextual variables rather than substantial changes in the campaign system affected the differing outcomes. Noncampaign differences between the states of Georgia and Massachusetts, for example, explain why Kennedy did so poorly in the first and well in the second. But to say that predispositions of the party's rank and file affected outcomes in the states is not to say that the performance of the campaigns was irrelevant. Certainly then as now the overall fluidity of electoral opinion, and specific changes in opinions following campaign events in particular states, was ample reason for campaigns to do their best. I have emphasized that despite unusual difficulties the Kennedy campaign achieved high levels of system effectiveness. Yet, as we have seen, it was competing against a campaign that had field organizations in many states months before Kennedy even decided to run, and had resources of communication and control that Kennedy could not match. Carter's early start and careful preparations paid off in the spring of 1980.

It produced a very strong financial base that was sustained through the most important caucuses and primaries. This enabled the campaign to have paid staff — a "presence" — early in every contested state, thus aiding and impressing the local activists. Modest amounts of money were thus converted into messages that the Carter campaign was there and meant business. Kennedy's "draft" committees in the different states were important but variable and erratic until they were linked with the national system. Both Carter and Kennedy had sizable (100-150 paid and volunteer) headquarters staffs in Washington, but Carter's paid forces in the field were considerably larger, numbering over 300 by the middle of the primaries. Often Kennedy's volunteers were impressive, such as in Maine, yet the paid people were more reliable and easier to move from place to place. In the Illinois primary, for example, Carter had about 60 paid staff to help organize, build crowds, get-out-the-vote, and so on whereas Kennedy relied almost entirely on local volunteers.

Kennedy's financial resources, in total, were competitive, but they came in unevenly. In the opening period of his campaign — when Carter's poll ratings were reaching record lows — money flowed in, only to trickle off in December.[35] By January the originally loose controls over expenditures were tightened, and income remained strong through the primaries (about $150,000 a week). However, because of the early lapses, including the initially unsystematic collection of federal matching funds, Kennedy's budget was smaller and less stable than Carter's. Perhaps the most notable cybernetic effect of this was a cutback in professional polling for the early caucuses and primaries — leaving the campaign with less information than Carter had about the shifting basis of public opinion. Interestingly, the decision to reduce polling was made on the assumption that because Kennedy's themes were set, detecting small variations in opinion would not be as cost effective as moving the campaign into the field more aggressively. However plausible the decision was at the time, denying feedback in this manner obviously was not cybernetically benign.

Both the Carter and Kennedy campaigns made explicit provisions for feedback, but Carter's were more numerous and refined — in part because the resources of the government were involved. A good example of an explicit feedback mechanism that also involved government resources was Carter's "reaction committee" mentioned earlier in passing. Led by Richard Moe, Mondale's chief of staff, and composed mainly of deputies,* the group met late every afternoon to decide how to respond to Kennedy's latest charges — often made that same day — and then assigned the response to some surrogate speaker in the field. This new organization (learning) resulted from the felt need to respond to media questions (reporters traveling with the Kennedy campaign would communicate with colleagues in the White House Press Corps, who would, in turn, question Carter spokesmen, such as Jody Powell), yet to do so on the basis of a relatively wide review of program information and with the benefit of collective judgments.

Although similar in basic structure, the Kennedy campaign's feedback and decision mechanisms were less specialized and abundant than Carter's. It too had a Washington headquarters where the campaign manager was located, and it too had provisions for communication and decision-making in consultation with the campaign in the field. Key decisions were made by the candidate closely in touch with aides not only on the campaign plane but also in Washington. Decision-making in both campaigns took the form of centrally oriented disjointed incrementalism, with the Kennedy campaign at times being considerably more disjointed because of the greater independence of the "draft" committees in the states and the candidate being in the field. This last point, although rather obvious in the sense that Carter, Jordan, Powell, and others were together in the White House, had more subtle effects. Compared to Kennedy and his traveling staff, for example, Carter and his top aides were less subject to personal exhaustion and the immediate pressures of inquiring reporters.

This brings us to interesting differences between the two campaign systems in their forms of output. Some forms, such as television advertising, were virtually the same (but, again, with both Caddell and Rafshoon [polls and media] operating together in the White House, television advertising feedback was faster and more precise in the Carter campaign) for the two campaigns. In terms of media expenditures, Kennedy was definitely competitive.[36] In

---

*Bert Carp, one of Stuart Eizenstat's deputies; Martin Franks, in charge of research for the Carter/Mondale Presidential Committee; Rex Gramen, deputy press secretary; Gail Harrison, Mondale's domestic policy assistant; David Rubenstein, another deputy of Stuart Eizenstat; and sometimes Jody Powell and other persons with specific areas of expertise.

other respects, however, the forms of output were quite different. A very large portion of Kennedy's output took the form of traditional stump speeches and associated interviews with national and local reporters. As we have seen, the national news media covered these events quite closely, more closely than they did the field appearances of Carter's surrogates.

Where Carter broke through was in his use of personal telephone calls to local citizens. Often using updated information about families he had visited during the 1976 campaign, the President made countless direct calls during which he would chat with the individuals for a few moments and ask for their support. This was done throughout the prenomination period and on a very large scale. Many times it was supplemented by invitations to visit the White House. Needless to say, when a "family next door" in Iowa, or Maine, or Illinois, received a personal phone call from the President of the United States, news of the call would surely reach the local newspaper and radio and television stations — the basic information of this action thus reaching a much wider audience.* The irony of this form of campaign output, especially during the early months of 1980, was that it absorbed many hours of the President's time — a President too tied to his busy routine of foreign negotations to leave the White House! This "personal courtship" of voters represented an interesting cybernetic tactic through which the Carter campaign exploited the prestige of the Presidency to multiply the impact of simple messages to carefully selected members of the electorate. In this fashion the campaign was able to *use* local media to spread its message in a manner that was very difficult for the Kennedy campaign to match or counter.

A NOTE ABOUT THE MEDIA AS A SYSTEM

Earlier I pointed out that the media was in itself a system within the cybernetic model. It is difficult to overemphasize the importance

---

*Elizabeth Drew describes a case in Iowa: "The President has been assiduously phoning Iowans in recent weeks. This morning's Des Moines *Register* has a story headlined "FROM THE BLUE, CARTER PHONES IOWA TRUCKER," which tells of Carter's calling Thomas Pelham, of Marshalltown, Iowa. . . . (Pelham is quoted as saying, "We had a nice chat, I guess. No big deal, though. . . . It's kind of funny. He knew all about me. He asked me about being a truck driver and things like that.")

of this system — even if it is broken down into subsystems — to political campaigns in general, and to the Carter and Kennedy campaigns in particular. Television and the other media were more than technologies for which campaign uses could be found. They were systems of communication and control, with decision-makers focusing on the goals of their media, not (necessarily) of the campaigns. In most cases the goals of the media and those of the campaigns partly intersect, but this intersection is by no means perfect — often leading campaigners to suspect that certain newsmen are incompetent or unfriendly (which quite possibly is true).

Of course, the media perform a communication function, linking the campaigns to larger audiences, including voters, interest groups, contributors, and other campaigns. Idealized models show the media transmitting information with perfect accuracy, with no noise or entropy. Yet this is impossible, both theoretically and practically. Whether print, radio, or television, the media must *select* from a larger amount of information that which is to be transmitted. Also, as explained in Chapter 2, in the steps of transmission and reception noise will invariably occur — sometimes more, sometimes less. Without thinking in these cybernetic terms, experienced campaigners know that since perfectly accurate information about their candidate is not attainable, and probably not desirable, their major purpose is to have *favorable* information about their candidate transmitted. Campaigns thus may go to great lengths to present their candidates so that reporters, cameramen, and so on, perceive the "right" aspects that then can be transmitted to their listeners, readers, or viewers.

If this selective process is considered negatively biased or unreliable, the campaign will attempt to influence the media to be "fairer," and, if there are sufficient resources, to have the candidate "speak directly to the people."[37] Commonly, this takes the form of the candidate addressing a national audience over purchased transmission channels. A considerable amount of this was done in the latter part of the 1980 campaign.

Yet efforts to control how the media see the candidate can become not only expensive but also risky. News reporters and commentators are sensitive to this and are likely to call attention to the candidate being "overprotected" or "packaged," or to the campaign being "afraid" to expose the candidate to the challenges of the media — thus projecting a negative image of the entire campaign.

Conceptualizing the media as a system also calls attention to their internal complexity. The reporter may choose what part of a candidate's speech to cover or record, but the editor back in the central newsroom decides what parts of this will be transmitted to the public. The significant 30-minute television evening news broadcasts rarely use more than 15 to 20 seconds of a candidate's speech to capture the entire event. Obviously, therefore, within the media system numerous decisions intervene between the event itself and the messages about the event that are finally communicated to the larger population. If this is the case, what criteria or standards of selection and interpretation are followed? In his study of news coverage of the 1976 presidential campaign, Thomas E. Patterson found that while the media adhered to a standard of neutrality in presenting the candidates, certain aspects of the campaign were strongly favored. These in particular included the campaign as a "horse race," as a conflict between two personalities, and a series of colorful lapses. "The press's version of election politics elevates competition over substance, outcomes over process, and the immediate over the enduring. While these favored aspects are not an insignificant part of the election, focus on them represents an unquestionably limited perspective."[38]

Finally, while there is intense internal competition within the media system, there is also a "herd" tendency — a process of group influence. Reporters and editors are reluctant to ignore an approach that others are taking — the result being a type of serial concentration on certain aspects of the campaign at the expense of others. This phenomena was depicted vividly by Timothy Crouse in *The Boys on the Bus*, and it frequently has been mentioned since.[39] We have already noted it in the 1980 campaign and will have several occasions to do so again.

Both the Carter and Kennedy campaigns probably devoted more attention to exchanges with the media than with each other. This is hardly surprising, since a cybernetic system must deal with the media virtually as an extension of itself. Kennedy earlier and Carter later felt the effects of the media's own judgments of their candidacies and campaigns. Apart from such conventional mechanisms as press secretaries, provisions for media to accompany the traveling campaign, press conferences, and so on, the Kennedy campaign did not make special efforts to analyze and exploit the media. Carter strategists, on the other hand, did do this, sometimes with distinct success, but always with the threat of negative reactions as journalists judged these efforts according to the norms of their own system (in which the model reporter rejects exploitation or being taken in by others). In complex and subtle ways this threat eventually materialized for Carter.

As a cybernetic system, the Kennedy campaign gets relatively high marks. Although its input, output, and feedback were not as refined as Carter's, they were carried out with little loss of information. Formulating messages of control was inherently difficult because public (and media) attitudes toward both its candidate and the presidency were deeply ingrained. Yet the campaign continued to adjust to information about its performance in the media and Peter Hart's* polls. We have seen that sometimes this feedback overcorrected; nevertheless, it stayed on target, often with marked success. For example, after criticisms that Kennedy was not articulating the purposes of his campaign, the candidate delivered a major address at Georgetown University near the end of January – which impressed the media and revived the spirits of campaign workers.[40] It thus constituted both internal and external feedback.

This reminds us that the internal communications and control sustaining the system are not to be forgotten. This was a very large campaign comprised of diverse individuals needing coordination. For most of the prenomination period, the traveling entourage was larger than that of any other candidate – often numbering 150 staff, media, security agents, and so forth. This imposed not only a logistic burden upon the campaign system but also a burden on the candidate, whose freedom of movement and decision were impaired.[41] These elements of noise, reducing the cybernetic quality of the system, were present, more or less, throughout the campaign. They were consequential for campaign operations. Yet what is striking is that the system endured, bolstered by the humor and determination of the candidate himself.

---

*Kennedy's pollster, who specialized in statewide polls for Democratic candidates. He did not, however, poll regularly and exclusively for Kennedy as Caddell and Wirthlin did for Carter and Reagan. This is an important point, since Kennedy was thus without the continued monitoring of public opinion that the other two candidates had.

BROWN

The campaign of Jerry Brown, governor of California, was interesting for its effort to be distinctive in the face of adversity. If the Kennedy campaign was set back by its candidate's late decision to run, Brown, who decided to run in 1976, and began organizing after he was decisively reelected governor in 1978, continually found that Kennedy captured most of his party's anti-Carter interest. Certainly there was no doubt about his intention to run. Although not entering the 1976 campaign until May, he defeated Carter not only in California but also in Nevada and New Jersey, and he made a very strong showing in Oregon as a write-in candidate. It was impressive, and Brown made no secret of his 1980 ambitions. As early as April 1979 he visited New Hampshire, and in September he made a campaign swing through the state, having registered as a candidate with the FEC on July 25.

In New Hampshire as elsewhere, however, Brown had great difficulty finding local organizers, and his early fund-raising efforts were not even successful in California.[42] Lacking funds and local activists, Brown, while making selected appearances in Iowa (such as at the "debate" in Iowa with Kennedy and Mondale), dropped out of contention in the Iowa caucuses, entered the primary in New Hampshire, where he came in a distant third (Carter 49 percent, Kennedy 38 percent, Brown 10 percent). Then, ten primaries later, he made a major effort in Wisconsin, where, after defeat, he withdrew from the campaign.

The primary factor that had encouraged Brown, before he confronted the overwhelmingly negative response in 1980, was his success against Carter in the concluding primaries of 1976. This convinced him that an image of a "new" politician, willing to upset the conventional political wisdom by being unpredictable and innovative on issues, would appeal to the American electorate generally, and the Democratic primary voters in particular. His issue strategy was summarized in his formal campaign announcement on November 8, 1979: "My principles are simple. Protect the earth, serve the people, and explore the universe."[43] By the Wisconsin primary, Brown was being referred to as "governor moonbeam." Consistent with his issues and style, Brown ended his Wisconsin campaign with a statewide television spectacular produced by Francis Ford Coppola (the movie director of "Apocalypse Now" fame), featuring strobe lights, helicopters, and complex sound effects. Bad weather and failed electronics prevented this space-age extravaganza from achieving its technological potential, and it actually generated more humor and disparagement than political support.*

The Brown campaign was a cybernetic curiosity. Combining calculation and conviction, Brown raised issues that others did not, and that served to integrate conservatism (for example, a constitutional amendment requiring a balanced federal budget) and innovation (solar, cogenerated, and geothermal energy production). They also tended to break out of the conventional conservative-liberal categories. Within the Democratic party, his uncertain positions regarding the role of government alienated liberals and convinced old-line political leaders that he could not be trusted, while his futuristic ideas about energy and space and the environment had intense meaning for only a limited segment of the rank and file.

Although Brown's "fresh" ideas and "vision" impressed a few editorial writers,[44] his actions and ideas embodied messages that were difficult to decode by the politicians and voters with whom he needed to communicate. They were essentially noisy. His campaign included imaginative, almost experimental efforts to create a positive image of its candidate as distinct from both Carter and Kennedy, and Brown could be personally effective on the stump. However, the mixed messages referred to above produced a shifting image that was badly blurred and lacking in credibility.

As a functioning system, Brown's campaign was centralized around a small staff led by campaign chairman Thomas Quinn and finance chairman Anthony Daugherty and drawn almost entirely from people who worked in his gubernatorial campaign.[45] The lack of personal experience in nationwide presidential campaigns and the specific failure to achieve the financial support needed to pay for polls, media, and organization and to meet the continuing requirements of the FECA, resulted in a system unable to sustain itself.

In particular, there were insufficient resources of both input and output for the campaign to employ feedback. Decisions were made

*Brown was also associated with a flip-flop (from against to for) position on the conservative tax cut sponsored by Howard Jarvis in California; philosophic speculations; and a romance with rock star Linda Ronstadt, who appeared with him in the campaign. It was an unusually ambiguous political image.

by the candidate and a small number of aides with too little current information about public attitudes, electoral rules, and the actions of other campaigns. On the output side, the campaign did not have the resources to convince the media that it was competitive. Thus the interesting substance of Brown's issue positions received little publicity from media that were focusing on the "horse race" — and hence, for Brown, negative — aspects of the election.[46] Finding it impossible to mount substantial operations in more than an occasional primary, the campaign could not begin to match Carter and Kennedy in the collection of delegates, therefore in media attention, and hence in voter credibility.* It may be likened to a ballistic missile, built with some innovative features, but at such low cost that it lacked the guidance mechanisms needed to identify and reach its target.

---

*Interestingly enough, during the early (December-January) period of the campaign, Brown was respected as a very dangerous opponent, particularly in debate, by both the Kennedy and Carter campaigns.

NOTES

1. This question applies to many incumbent officials, but especially to those with short terms, such as congressmen. There is ample evidence that the campaigning of a growing number of congressmen may wax and wane but does not stop. See Richard F. Fenno, Jr., *Home Style: House Members and Their Districts* (Boston: Little, Brown, 1978).

2. James Fallows, "The Passionless Presidency II," *The Atlantic Monthly*, June 1979, p. 77.

3. David Broder et al. (reporters and staff of the Washington *Post*), *The Pursuit of the Presidency 1980*, (New York: Berkley, 1980), pp. 87-98. (Hereafter referred to as Broder, *Pursuit*.)

4. Ibid., p. 97.

5. Held ostensibly for the purpose of adjusting the party's public policy positions between presidential elections, the 1978 convention was in fact a precurser of the Democratic 1980 prenomination campaign. Kennedy vigorously proposed more expanded social welfare programs, while Carter forces worked quite effectively to limit delegate responses to these Kennedy overtures. The competition for party leadership was obvious.

6. Terence Smith, "Carter, Apologizing for Neglect, Makes Up With Party Committee," New York *Times*, January 28, 1979, p. A6.

7. Broder, *Pursuit*, p. 92.

8. A somewhat earlier staff list is given in "The Carter Campaign," *Congressional Quarterly Weekly Report*, October 13, 1979, pp. 2267-74.

9. Broder, *Pursuit*, pp. 90-91; and "Shake-ups in Presidential Campaign Staff," *Congressional Quarterly Weekly Report*, December 15, 1979, p. 2879. The latter suggests more discontinuity and conflict in the campaign than I found. Nonetheless, the resignation of Political Director Jack Walsh, a veteran of 1976, on grounds that he "could not function effectively," shows that there was indeed competition for leadership positions in the campaign.

10. Broder, *Pursuit*, pp. 92-93.

11. There were numerous references to this in the press. For example, Timothy D. Schellhardt, "Carter Who Railed Against Pork-Barrel Politics in 1976, Now Exploits Them for Illinois Primary," *Wall Street Journal*, March 6, 1980, p. 48.

12. Broder, *Pursuit*, pp. 83-90.

13. Anthony Downs, *An Economic Theory of Democracy* (New York: Harper & Brothers, 1951), pp. 55-60.

14. John E. Mueller, *War, Presidents and Public Opinion* (New York: Wiley, 1973), esp. pp. 205-8 and 247-49.

15. These figures are from surveys by the Gallup organization, reported in *Public Opinion*, October/November 1979, p. 21.

16. This was widely commented on even after the 1977-78 period. James Fallows provides an "insider's" view in "The Passionless Presidency," *The Atlantic Monthly*, May 1979, p. 45; and the reactions of the Georgians are indicated in Steven R. Weisman, "The Power of the Press Secretary," New York *Times Magazine*, October 26, 1980, pp. 32 ff.

17. Fallows, "The Passionless Presidency II." There were many similar appraisals, especially commenting on Carter as a "loner." See Broder, *Pursuit*, pp. 235-52.

18. Broder, *Pursuit*, p. 248. Also see Austin Ranney, ed., *The American Elections of 1980* (Washington, D.C.: American Enterprise Institute, 1981), Chapter 1, esp. pp. 4-10.

19. James MacGregor Burns, *Leadership* (New York: Harper and Row, 1978).

20. Broder, *Pursuit*, p. 100.

21. The Carter campaign's superiority was overwhelming in the caucus states, the diverse procedures of which were extremely complex. See the *Congressional Quarterly Weekly Report*, December 29, 1979, pp. 2957-65, and May 5, 1980, pp. 1242-43. The effectiveness of the Carter caucus effort continued through the last caucuses late in June.

22. Originally elected in 1962 at age 30, Kennedy has been an unusually productive senator. He has shown the ability to work with Republicans and others of divergent views to pass legislation. In the Senate he is known as "a very hard worker who masters details and outargues the opposition." Michael Barone and Grant Ujifusa, *The Almanac of American Politics 1982* (Washington, D.C.: Barone and Co., 1981), p. 485.

23. *Public Opinion*, October/November 1979, pp. 22-23.

24. Ibid., p. 24.

25. Elizabeth Drew, "Kennedy: 1980," *The New Yorker*, February 4, 1980, pp. 67-68; and *Congressional Quarterly Weekly Report*, October 27, 1979, pp. 2397-2404. A somewhat different staff is listed on p. 2402.

26. Broder, *Pursuit*, p. 69.

27. Martin Schram gives examples of this and the lack of internal campaign coordination in Broder, *Pursuit*, p. 103.

28. Elizabeth Drew, "1980: Diversion," *The New Yorker*, January 7, 1980, p. 47.

29. Broder, *Pursuit*, p. 71. Responding to Reagan's defense of the shah, Kennedy said the shah had run "one of the most violent regimes in the history of mankind," and had "stolen . . . umpteen billions of dollars" from the Iranian people.

30. Ibid., p. 68.

31. Elizabeth Drew, *The New Yorker*, April 14, 1980, p. 121.

32. Drew, "Kennedy, 1980," p. 57. Drew details repeated instances of this (and of Kennedy's success in overcoming these restraints) in the Iowa campaign.

33. Drew, April 14, 1980, p. 124.

34. For example, see Timothy D. Schellhardt, *Wall Street Journal*, March 6, 1980, p. 48. Drew relates the case of the Loring Air Force Base in Maine, where Carter lost. April 14, 1980, p. 128.

35. The power of Kennedy's early fund raising was shown on October 25, when 100 supporters gave $150,000 to the campaign. *Congressional Quarterly Weekly Report*, October 27, 1979, p. 2397.

36. In fact, in some states, such as Iowa, Kennedy outspent Carter on radio and television, though not significantly. New York *Times*, January 21, 1980, p. A13.

37. The image that is sent directly, however, may be a carefully constructed one. See Joe McGinniss, *The Selling of the President 1968* (New York: Pocket Books, 1970), Chapter 2.

38. Thomas E. Patterson, *The Mass Media Election* (New York: Praeger, 1980), p. 53.

39. Timothy Crouse, *The Boys on the Bus* (New York: Ballantine Books, 1973). There are now many examples of this, with the Nixon 1968 campaign generally seen as innovative in producing events that appear natural. See McGinniss, *The Selling of the President 1968*. However, Haynes Johnson emphasizes the "herd instinct" of the press in its treatment of Kennedy following the Roger Mudd television interview. Broder, *Pursuit*, pp. 44-45. Michael J. Robinson finds the media attempting to adjust to their electoral role in 1980 in "The Media in 1980: Was the Message the Message?" in Ranney, *The American Elections of 1980*, Chapter 6, pp. 206-10.

40. Broder, *Pursuit*, p. 77.

41. Many journalists commented on how at many of his appearances Kennedy would be overwhelmed by persons attempting to gain access. Ibid., pp. 72-75; and *Congressional Quarterly Weekly Report*, February 9, 1980, p. 355 (which contrasts the large Kennedy and the small Bush entourages).

42. Tom DeVries, *The New Republic*, April 15, 1979.

43. Broder, *Pursuit*, p. 79. Also see Nelson W. Polsby, "The Democratic Nomination," in Ranney, *The American Elections of 1980*, Chapter 2, pp. 42-43.

44. For example, *The New Republic*, December 15, 1979. However, Brown did not receive a "good press" in general. See Michael Robinson, et al., "The Media at Mid-Year: A Bad Year for McLuhanites?" *Public Opinion*, June/July 1980, pp. 42-44.

45. *Congressional Quarterly Weekly Report*, October 20, 1979, pp. 2329-34.

46. Robinson et al., "The Media at Mid-Year," p. 43.

4

The Prenomination Campaigns: The Republicans

The Republican candidates — John B. Anderson, Howard H. Baker, George Bush, John B. Connally, Philip M. Crane, Robert Dole, and Ronald Reagan — can be classified in numerous ways, but from the start of their campaigns the other six saw Reagan as the man to beat. During 1979, while media attention was focused primarily on the problems of the Democratic President and the intentions of his Democratic challenger, the Republicans were hard at work building their organizations and becoming familiar with the territories of key states — at least most of them were. Their basic approach to the campaign was remarkably similar: Begin by recruiting *professional* (that is, paid and experienced) aides to handle four or five key functions — polling, finance, media, and field organization — and make subsequent decisions collectively with these persons.

In view of their diverse backgrounds and electoral experiences, the Republicans also used a strikingly similar set of electoral events from which their initial campaign lessons were drawn: the 1976 Presidential campaign, and, in particular, Jimmy Carter's prenomination effort. There were variations, of course, with Reagan paying more attention to his prenomination contest with Gerald Ford, yet every candidate was at least sensitive to the lessons taught by Carter's success in defeating, first, better-known Democrats, and then an incumbent Republican President.

One reason why Carter's case was so relevant was that Reagan in 1980 had significant characteristics of an incumbent. He had been a major political figure since 1964, and by 1979 had managed not only to define many of the nation's political issues but also to shape the dominant ideology of Republican voters. He also had a very high public recognition level among Americans as a whole — over 90 percent of the electorate was familiar with his name. Finally, Reagan had been active in presidential election campaigns since 1968, and during most of this period had also been a frequent and popular speaker at party dinners and meetings around the country. He thus had strong local contacts that were much like those of an incumbent president.

In short, the other Republican candidates looked upon Ronald Reagan as the front runner not only because he ranked at the top in the early straw polls, but also because he had the personal experience, skills, sources of money and staff, and resources of local support that would make him a very tough competitor. All of this was well known from the very beginnings of the preconvention campaign. What was not known was whether Reagan would run at his age (he would be 69 in 1980), and, even more uncertain, whether Gerald Ford — the man who had defeated Reagan in 1976, and whose qualifications to be president were stronger — would run. On October 19, 1979, Ford announced he would not be a candidate in 1980.

REAGAN

Ronald Reagan formally announced his candidacy on November 13, 1979, a timing close to that of the major Democratic candidates. By then his campaign was well underway, led by John Sears, the same man who had managed his 1976 challenge to Ford. With them were experienced assistants in charge of each major campaign function, such as Bay Buchanin (treasurer), Charles Black (national director), Michael Deaver (public relations), Lyn Nofziger (press), Paul Laxalt (campaign chairman), Edwin Meese (chief of staff), Richard Wirthlin (polling), and Daniel Terra (finance).[1] Not only did these top aides have previous campaign experience, but also most of them were personally familiar with the candidate and would remain with him into the White House.

From the beginning, however, there were differences over campaign tactics and authority, generally precipitated by Sears.[2] In 1976, because of Reagan's very conservative image, Sears had pressed him to move in the moderate direction (for example, with the selection of Richard Schweiker, an almost liberal senator from Pennsylvania, as his vice-presidential running mate). The 1976 experience had also convinced Sears of the importance of the Northeast because of the region's early primaries. Reagan himself could not forget his narrow defeat in New Hampshire, which he believed had cost him the nomination. Together, these two "lessons" from four years before helped divert the campaign from what in 1980 was the first major event, the Iowa caucus.

Two other factors contributed more directly to a downplaying of Iowa. The first comprised some immediate experiences with the candidate. Reagan was 69 years old. Would he have the stamina and acumen to be president? This question, posed repeatedly, if idly, by the media, haunted some members of the campaign, since the wrong answer could undermine the entire candidacy; and the wrong answer seemed to threaten. On NBC's "Today" show on the morning of November 13, the candidate appeared not to recognize the name of Valéry Giscard d'Estaing, President of France. Matters were not improved when the campaign's press secretary explained that Reagan had not heard the question. Later in New York City he seemed ignorant of the federal loan guarantees the city was receiving, just as still later, in Grand Rapids, Michigan, he was not aware of federal legislation designed to help the Chrysler Corporation.[3]

In view of these lapses, which served to confirm that Reagan no longer had the intellectual grasp to handle the presidency, campaign strategists decided to minimize his exposure to direct questions from the press. This tactic was consistent with Sears' thinking that with Reagan so far ahead, risks should be avoided. Therefore, while the candidate did a lot of moving from state to state during December and January (to give the impression of vigorous activity), he was generally shielded from the press and specifically kept out of the Iowa debate. This was a major television event in which every Republican candidate except Reagan took part. Predictably, since he was the man to beat, each of the other candidates made a point of Reagan's absence. They also made quite impressive presentations of their own, with the result that the event was judged by the media to be a loss for Reagan — a judgment that was confirmed by subsequent poll ratings and the victory of George Bush in the caucuses.

The loss of Iowa to Bush led to immediate feedback and then learning in the Reagan campaign. All the campaign leaders now agreed that the candidate had to get out on the New Hampshire hustings. For the first time, the polls showed Bush leading in the state. For the campaign, the leisurely schedule preceding Iowa was replaced by virtual barnstorming. The age issue was diffused by Reagan himself making fun of it, and it was decided to have the candidate debate at every opportunity.

Two debates were held in New Hampshire. At the second, in Nashua, Reagan made his often-quoted remark, "I paid for this microphone, Mr. Green," as the debate's pro-Bush managers were striving to limit the event to Bush and Reagan.* Although this episode received wide publicity, and was assessed by participants and accompanying journalists alike as a major Reagan coup, Wirthlin's polls showed that it was the *first* debate, held earlier at Manchester, that appeared to turn the tide of public opinion.[4] That event, scarcely reported outside New Hampshire, and rated by attending journalists as a dull no-win affair, was the first demonstration in 1980 of Reagan's

---

*It was a dramatic moment arising out of complex preliminaries. Reagan's New Hampshire chairman, understanding that Bush was leading in the state, proposed a two-candidate debate, which Bush accepted on the condition that it be held in Nashua, where he had strong support. The debate was originally to be sponsored (and paid for) by the Nashua *Telegraph*, which endorsed Bush. A week before the event, however, the Federal Election Commission ruled that such sponsorship might be an illegal contribution by the paper to the Bush and Reagan campaigns. When the Bush campaign objected to paying any of the $3,500 expenses, the Reagan campaign opted to pay the entire bill — thus justifying Reagan's statement about the microphone. It probably did not justify Sears' invitation to the other candidates (Anderson, Baker, Crane, and Dole) without telling Bush. Upon learning of this on the evening of the debate, an irritated Bush refused to proceed on grounds that only the *Telegraph* could decide. When the other candidates appeared, *Telegraph* editor Jon Breen (not *G*reen), still trying to maintain the original format, ruled that they would not be allowed to speak. Reagan's statement occurred after he had argued that the others were being silenced unfairly, and they came onto the stage waving to the crowd. At this point Breen threatened to cut off Reagan's microphone. During all this, Bush simply sat with a stony expression on his face, refusing even to recognize the others, who then walked off to hold press conferences attacking Bush. And it all was played out before the television cameras.

effectiveness over television, even when contradicted by on-the-scenes appraisals.* Bush's apparent rigidity, in contrast to Reagan's openness and panache, cast him in a very unfavorable light and doubtless cost him a number of votes in the primary three days later — not to mention the delayed effects in other states.

Reagan's satisfying and decisive victory in New Hampshire was not celebrated by everyone in his campaign. The simmering friction between John Sears and the so-called California group (comparatively conservative men mostly associated with Reagan's governorship) had pushed the candidate too far. When Sears called for the dismissal of Ed Meese, Reagan decided that Sears and his allies must leave instead. He chose the moment of victory to soften the public effect. Sears (campaign manager), Charles Black (political director), and James Lake (press secretary) were fired. It was a major upheaval.

Although inside accounts assign ample blame for earlier campaign mistakes to all sides, it appears that the conflicts leading to the separation were essentially neither ideological nor strategic, but matters of style and authority. Sears saw the position of campaign manager as one of comprehensive authority, especially over decisions of strategy and the candidate's "presentation." This insistence on hegemony produced inevitable disagreement with others, and by Christmas Sears had fired Nofziger, Deaver, and Martin Anderson. Now, with Sears gone, these men returned, and those who had been close to Reagan for years in California were not challenged again. Reagan lost a widely respected strategist but gained more mutual compatibility and understanding among his aides. William J. Casey was brought in to replace Sears as campaign manager.†

This higher-order feedback came none too soon, for the campaign was approaching financial exigency. Spending had been very high during the preceding months. By March, $12 million had been

---

*The difference was striking. While those present saw the first debate as virtually of no consequence, Wirthlin found Reagan a point behind Bush before the event and 20 points ahead afterward. The famous second debate merely marked a continuing gain in public support.

†The differences between the old and new managers were revealing. Sears was 39 years old, Casey 67. A former chairman of the Securities Exchange Commission, Casey had business and management experience but lacked the political knowledge of Sears. He was also more conservative both in manner and strategy.

spent — two-thirds of the approximately $18 million allowed by the FEC regulations; and 30 states and the national convention remained. Therefore, under the new leadership, travel and staff expenditures were sharply curtailed. Sears' basic strategy of winning early and often, and spending to do it, worked sufficiently well to drive all the other candidates except Bush out of contention by early April. Yet by then remaining funds were too few to match the strong media effort that Bush mounted in Pennsylvania and Texas.

By the Illinois primary the Reagan prenomination campaign had shaken down to a relatively permanent organization. From the first, its feedback mechanisms had been good, though not excellent. Before the "public" campaign had begun in the fall of 1979, Sears's personal appraisals of the rules that were reviewed in Chapter 1, and shifting public attitudes, were careful and insightful. Aided by some polling by Wirthlin, his conclusion that Republicans in the Northeastern states had moved toward Reagan's policy positions proved basically correct, but he was insensitive to messages indicating the importance of Iowa and the effects of opposing campaigns. Perhaps more important, he was insensitive to the intense internal dynamics of the campaign system. Sears's reaction to the campaign's financial condition in terms of federal expenditure limitations is more difficult to evaluate. Whether they constituted a breakdown in feedback, a tendency to risk-taking, or sophisticated planning depends on complex calculations of basic electoral predispositions and the strength of opposing candidates in future primaries. In any case, the common internal assessment was that the campaign had been unwisely profligate in its early months. Certainly the campaign learned from its initial loss in Iowa and was able to go through a major staff shakeup without apparent loss of effectiveness in the field, even with Charles Black leaving.

The campaign's monitoring of public attitudes and opinions through Wirthlin's polling was of a very high order. While these polls were not at first as frequent or sophisticated as Caddell's for Carter, they were by far the best among the Republican campaigns, and they steadily improved. Wirthlin's subtle measures of voter value systems, for example, enabled him to identify those elements of Reagan's conservative ideology that appealed to working-class segments of the electorate — information that was useful in the Illinois primary and subsequent general election. Reagan's ability to respond to these data was limited by his personal beliefs and those of his aides, thus limiting feedback based on the polls. Yet the candidate had an innate ability to adapt to different types of audiences by "manufacturing" factual-type illustrations or stories to make rather bitter policy medicine more palatable.

As the Reagan campaign moved through the primaries it demonstrated an impressive capacity to get information from and exercise control over its field organizations. In large measure this was based on the existence of long-time Reagan loyalists who had been previously identified in various states. These people were often deeply involved in local party organizations, this giving them additional influence. Because their ties to Reagan were long-standing — many had been active in previous campaigns — they were quick to grasp the need for tactical adjustments and hard work; and they knew how to get things done in their communities. To be sure, there were the inevitable cases of these local organizations taking imperfect actions on their own, but as a whole central guidance was both flexible and strong.

New Hampshire confirmed Wirthlin's findings that among Republicans Reagan began the campaign with deep-seated support throughout the country. The formidable difficulties he presented to his Republican opponents were summarized by Bush's campaign manager, David Keene, after the first New Hampshire debate:

> On camera, Bush looked pretty much like a guy that puts his pants on one leg at a time like everyone else. And Reagan had started with the strongest base in the Republican Party, with the only question being, "Was he up to it?" If he looked as good as anyone else, and he did, why not vote for him?[5]

Reagan obviously had weaknesses, but the campaign's ability to finesse these so that they were of little use to opposing candidates soon became evident. The candidate's age and his tendency to make inaccurate statements are cases in point.

Reagan became 69 on February 6, while campaigning in New Hampshire, Florida, and South Carolina. Over the course of days, wherever he went, he found cakes, balloons, and "Happy Birthday Ron" signs. In Greenville, South Carolina, he fell into an enormous cake, providing even more mirth for the accompanying media. The issue was diffused by the simple expedient of celebrating and making fun of it. The problem of factual inaccuracies and outright misinformation (sometimes contained in the stories mentioned above) would remain with the campaign virtually until the November election, but the candidate's ability to avoid negative consequences of these slips, often with little more than a smile or shrug, was remarkable.*

Decision-making in the Reagan campaign was fundamentally collegial. In terms of earlier models, it was incremental but not sharply disjointed. There was strong central direction on the part of Reagan's top aides. The collegiality, however, required not only agreement about ideology, but also about the bounds of power. Sears's personal conflicts with others close to Reagan abused those bounds during the early months, with the eventual "corrections" in the campaign that we have observed. With Sears's departure, the acute conflicts of personality and status generally ended. Since mutual compatibility and trust were quite high, and campaign experience substantial, internal communications were open and effective. Following Iowa, campaign events (and electoral outcomes) were sufficiently consistent with the prevailing strategies that incremental decisions, with small adjustments to new circumstances, could be and were the pattern.

There was little inclination in the campaign to distort information about the electorate to make it consistent with the prevailing ideology. This made it easier for Wirthlin's polls to be the very useful instrument for input and decisions that they were. The ideological beliefs, however, were definitely to the right, and they were accompanied by attitudes of suspicion toward other Republicans who had not demonstrated their ideological purity. Essentially these attitudes biased the decoding of messages about other political leaders, leading to a certain amount of misperception. Fortunately for the campaign, the potential conflicts between these conservative perceptions and the actual political world were eased by the predominant conservatism among the Republican electorate in the primaries.[6]

As a system of communication and control, the preconvention Reagan campaign lacked the efficiency of Carter's, but it was

---

*An example of this occurred in one of the New Hampshire debates when Reagan was asked by a hostile questioner about an anti-Italian ethnic joke that he had in fact told. Reagan's stern reply that he was opposed to such jokes and had been "stiffed" by a reporter who had not understood that he told the joke to illustrate what should *not* be told so impressed the television audience that, according to Wirthlin's polls, it considered the question unfair.

nonetheless quite effective. In resources of input, decision, and output, it was robust. There are indications that the memory of the 1976 primaries, and some indifference to the expenditure limitations of the FECA, led to a misallocation of resources so that output was severely limited in the later primaries. Throughout, lower-level feedback tended to be excellent and field operations were impressive. Furthermore, the system's ability to make major organizational adjustments (learning) was also evident. The Illinois primary on March 18 probably showed the campaign at its best. As a source of output, the candidate was not entirely susceptible to feedback. He could only partially be controlled. Yet as a message Ronald Reagan clearly had a greater impact on his party's primary electorate than any other candidate. While other campaigns, on occasion, could mobilize more output resources in the form of television ads, and so forth, they were never able to produce a stronger message than Reagan himself.

BUSH

George Bush began his campaign earlier, conducted it with greater preparation, and carried it on with more persistence than any other Republican candidate. Using the 1973-76 Carter campaign as an explicit model, Bush began organizing in the fall of 1977. James Baker, Ford's manager in 1976, was the first of the top staff to be recruited and became Bush's campaign manager. A political action committee was established to finance the early efforts, and by 1978 the candidate was in the field proceeding to visit 42 states.[7] Bush's strategy was to exploit his abundant resources of time to build organizations in as many states as possible *before* the immediate pressure of the preconvention began,* and to do this while building a highly professional and nonideological staff. By 1979 he had organizations in over 40 states and experienced aides in charge of the major campaign functions, including David Keene on political organization and Robert Goodman on media.[8]

---

*As a Texas businessman who had made a fortune in oil, Bush was unencumbered by a position that demanded his attention, such as a member of Congress or the Senate. Bush had had an unusually rich political career, having been a congressman, chairman of the Republican National Committee, director of the CIA, ambassador to the United Nations, and chief of the U.S. Liaison Office in China.

Bush was careful to connect his campaign to the regular party organization wherever possible, and this was facilitated by one of his past positions as chairman of the Republican National Committee (RNC). This same strategy was pursued in the formation of a national steering committee, composed of approximately 350 notables, including congressmen, former congressmen, governors, cabinet officers, industrialists, entertainers, and so on — big names to give the campaign credibility.[9] Furthermore, the committee was targeted, with the Iowa component alone numbering 70 prominent GOP leaders. By April 1979 Bush, with the help of Mary Louise Smith, cochairman of the RNC when Bush was chairman, and John McDonald, a national committeeman from Iowa, presented a campaign in the state with very respectable leadership and a full-time director. Intense grass-roots organization, supported by frequent visits by the candidate, continued until the caucuses in January 1980. Similar if less extensive efforts took place in many other states.

The Bush organization was classic in form and efficient in operation. An inner group of aides, with the candidate, made decisions collectively, and state organizations were given general themes and strategies around which they had considerable leeway. In addition to conventional means of communication, central and state operations were tied together by visits of Bush himself. Most of the early resources of money and personnel also were collected by the candidate directly, and then by a network of supporters that originated from those initial contacts. All of these diverse components were coordinated through very fine staff work and a complex process of mutual adjustment that produced a good deal of action with very little friction. In terms of decision-making, the campaign came close to a model of disjointed incrementalism.

Cybernetically, the campaign was not perfection, yet it was an impressive accomplishment. Internal feedback was excellent, with the flow of information generally unimpeded by ideological or personality conflicts, and facilitated by resources of experience and management. (In a number of state organizations, however, such resources were not as strong).* Information about public

---

*In New York, for example, about a week before the New Hampshire primary, almost half of Bush's delegates were ruled off New York City ballots following challenges by Reagan's organization. The Bush organization had not mastered the strict requirements of the State Election Law and had not

attitudes, party organization, FECA regulations, and so on, was analyzed exhaustively during the formulation of the campaign's basic strategy, and the collection and expenditure of financial resources were carefully controlled to maximize federal matching funds and to sustain the campaign through the primaries. Polling was less extensive than in the Reagan campaign, limiting feedback somewhat. Feedback based on local field contacts was swift but sometimes inadequate because of shortcomings in state organizations. In New Hampshire, for example, Bush's state manager (Hugh Gregg) did not detect the Reagan "trap" at Nashua or respond effectively afterward.[10] There and elsewhere some analysts believed that in certain instances Bush and his central staff should have asserted more local control. Yet had this been the general practice, central decision-makers would have suffered from overload.

Given the many positive cybernetic qualities of the Bush campaign, why did it not win more delegates? The answer lies in its inability to modify the predispositions of rank-and-file Republicans. This can be reduced to the function and use of the candidates's image. In contrast to Crane and Dole, Bush decided that he could not win by projecting himself as a younger and more vigorous Reagan; that he must distinguish himself from Reagan, yet not reject Reagan's conservative ideology that now mirrored the ideological distribution of Republican voters. The result was a complex mixture of positions designed to have some appeal for all Republicans.[11] Bush and his media chief, Goodman, fashioned an image of a vigorous, optimistic, can-do candidate who was experienced, mature, and conservative. Bush's personal style, however, and his avoidance of sharp (offensive) issue positions seemed to project an image of a nice guy — softer, malleable, and bland.

Adjusting to this response (feedback), Goodman's commercials began emphasizing Bush's "toughness," an image that was also designed to present a positive alternative to Carter. The candidate began giving sharper answers to questions in the field, and by the Illinois primary he was emphasizing definite policy positions. Bush, however, was not a strong "natural" speaker, and when he adopted voice inflections and body movements to overcome this weakness it led to occasional awkwardness on the stump.[12] Here is Drew's

---

anticipated Reagan's decision to file a slate of his own, contrary to the state party organization's wish to run "uncommitted" slates.

description from the New Hampshire primary:

> Bush does not give the impression that he has given hard thought to hard questions. He is a handsome man, and he comes across as likeable, reasonable. It is an American likeableness, the American regular guy. At fifty-five, he is youthful-looking. . . . His voice is a bit high, and he talks loud and very fast, conveying a sense of urgency. . . . He seems eager, and his eagerness conveys a certain weakness. . . . The gestures seem unnatural; the clear impression is that he has been told he is too bland, and is working to overcome the problem.[13]

I conclude with this element of the candidate's style not because Bush or his campaign were weak, for they were not. (Drew and other reporters generally found Bush's style to be variable, and quite strong "when he talks naturally, as he does when he is not on stage.") As a candidate, Bush made very favorable impressions on those he met in small meetings during 1978 and 1979, and his campaign, organized early and well, was an effective cybernetic system — a system that did not break down under the impact of multiple defeats; for after Iowa, Bush did not win again until Massachusetts, and then so narrowly as to not gain in the delegate count.

We have seen that Bush attempted to improve his style, and in so doing — at least at first — might have done himself more harm than good. (Note the parallel with Kennedy.) Yet feedback continued in the campaign, and by the later primaries Bush was not only making sharp policy criticisms of Reagan but also had developed a more successful style of presentation. At this point, by targeting his resources Bush was able to fight toe-to-toe with Reagan in Pennsylvania, Texas, and Michigan. It was too late. After a victory in Michigan, Bush was rewarded by the media emphasizing that Reagan had just won a majority of all national convention delegates. Contributions virtually ceased and the candidate ended his campaign.

It is easy to speculate that had George Bush done this or that differently in New Hampshire or Florida or Illinois, the outcome could have been different; but the campaign had to deal with other systems over which it had little control. In the matters of style and Republican voters, Bush was running against a man who was a master of style and who had a long-standing policy attachment to conservative Republicans. After Iowa, Bush received a burst of publicity that enhanced his campaign's output. Yet in the end the media that provided this "Big Mo"* also reduced the campaign's message of victory and competence to noise, undermining its credibility to contributors and voters. Carefully constructed and vigorously maintained, the Bush campaign was a good example of how the performance of a very respectable cybernetic system can be limited by its competition and its environment. It is worth remembering that the campaign did overcome five other candidates.

CONNALLY

If George Bush lacked a "commanding presence," this was precisely what John Connally had, and Connally's campaign was notable for how this and other major candidate resources failed. Former governor, cabinet member, and presidential adviser, John B. Connally of Texas was a self-made millionaire and a converted Democrat. He also had been indicted for taking a bribe while serving in the Nixon administration but had been found not guilty. He was recognized on all sides as a man of great ability and assertiveness.

Connally's campaign was distinctive in strategy and, consequently, organization. His analysis of Carter's weaknesses was similar to that of the other candidates but less restrained. He saw Carter as a weak, inept President — so much so that he was confident that the Democrats would not renominate him. Similarly, he saw the American people yearning for a strong leader. This perception led Connally and his staff to design a campaign that would project a candidate of great personal strength and command. In their view, such a candidate would appear most able to take on their expected Democratic rival: Senator Edward Kennedy.

Such an image, however, seemed out of place in countless small living rooms and town halls — the arenas favored in the Bush and Carter approaches — across the country.[14] So Connally opted for more formal addresses to larger groups and the use of nationwide

---

*Bush's original plan was to come in second in Iowa and then win in New Hampshire and Massachusetts, thus appearing to have electoral momentum. With his surprising success in Iowa, he asserted that he had "Big Mo" that would help him undercut Reagan's credibility before the southern primaries on March 11. Unfortunately, "Big Mo" deserted him in New Hampshire.

television commercials as the best means to reach the rank and file. Connally agreed that Ronald Reagan was the Republican to beat, and this approach held the promise of drawing closer to Reagan in public recognition and support (the polls) before the campaign formally began. Connally also agreed that Reagan must be confronted in virtually every state because past campaigns had lent him broad support. All of this meant a campaign that started early and spent large amounts of money.

Connally announced his candidacy at the beginning of 1979. His sources of financial support were plenteous, being found mainly in corporate boardrooms of the Southwest. With excellent access to large contributions, but no grass-roots organization, the candidate recruited a staff led by Eddie Mahe, Jr. (campaign director) and Charles Keating, Jr. (fund raiser) and spent most of 1979 traveling across the country, raising funds and building an organization in all the 50 states.[15] Given the premises mentioned above, there was a plausibility to Connally's strategy, and a serious effort was made to think it out. The more specific plan was to begin large-scale commercials in the fall, while Connally continued his wide-ranging personal appearances to present himself to the country and to keep money flowing in. Whether or not the candidate would enter the initial caucuses and primaries would depend on the progress of the national recognition effort, but in any case the hope was that the large media campaign would enable the candidacy to catch fire early in 1980.

The first problem that occurred was virtually decisive. With the taking of the American hostages in Tehran, not only was public attention monopolized by this crisis, but also the television networks refused to sell candidates any appreciable amounts of time (since the formal campaign period had not begun). Thus the campaign was forced to abandon a major part of its strategy and to restructure its organization. Early in December Keating took on the role of campaign administrator. The campaign headquarters in Arlington, Virginia, with a staff of 160 people, was cut back to about 130, and resources were reassigned to Iowa and the early primary states, such as New Hampshire, South Carolina, and Florida.[16]

But now it was late. Comparatively centralized as it was, the state organizing effort had been superficial. This meant that the adjustment to early state contests would require a concentration of resources. Since Connally had good access to private wealth, the campaign decided to eschew federal matching funds, thereby freeing it from state-by-state (and overall) spending limits. It was thus able to target record-breaking expenditures in those states where he chose to compete. For the early prenomination period, these expenditures were enormous. By mid-December, with the strategic changes having been made, the campaign had already spent almost $8 million. Half a million dollars, more than that of any other candidate — except perhaps Kennedy — was spent in Iowa.[17] By the South Carolina primary, expenditures had reached $11 million.

All to no avail. Connally came in fourth in Iowa, passed up the primaries in New Hampshire, Massachusetts, and Vermont, and made his stand in South Carolina on March 8.* Earlier, Connally and his aides had calculated that Reagan would have trouble with the other contenders in the New England primaries, and thus if defeated in South Carolina would also be vulnerable to Connally in the Florida, Alabama, and Georgia primaries that followed. Connally won the support of major political leaders in South Carolina, most notably former governor James B. Edwards and the extremely popular Senator Strom Thurmond. Thurmond and Connally campaigned back and forth across the state for weeks, with Connally making rousing speeches that stressed conservative positions and the promise of a strong presidency. The crowds seemed to love it, but on primary day Connally was trounced by Reagan, coming in 24 points behind. It was a clear demonstration of what money and endorsements could not buy. With the campaign now almost out of money (contributions dropped off after Iowa and New Hampshire), and having gained only one delegate (in Arkansas), John Connally withdrew from the race on March 9.

Perhaps more than any other campaign, Connally's reflected the character of its candidate. Very large sums of money were raised from wealthy individuals and political action committees, and these funds were spent with little apparent impact on either local organizations or voters. Connally could and did campaign on the state level, such as in Iowa and South Carolina, but these efforts were not associated with vigorous local volunteer organizations. As he traveled

---

*Although both the original and adjusted strategy had included a possible run in New Hampshire, polls made it increasingly evident by January that voter dispositions in all the Northeastern states were too negative toward Connally to justify major assignments of campaign resources.

around the country in 1979, Connally often made strong impressions on the Republican leaders that he met. He was an impressive person. Moreover, his public "reputation index" was quite respectable during that year, trailing only Kennedy's and Reagan's in November.[18] The trouble was that in direct competition for votes, Connally's campaign could not match those of Bush, Reagan, or even Anderson.

Cybernetically, this meant a lack of both information about and control over grass-roots operations. Connally's use of polls as a mechanism for feedback was marginal. Such feedback occurred in the strategic and organizational readjustments to the public opinion effects of the hostage situation, but it was always limited by the candidate's attachment to particular policies and images. Connally promised a presidency of strong, almost bellicose, action. When the Iowa caucuses did not respond to this message, the campaign could not modify the candidate's image in New England. True, it did not expect to do well in that region anyway, but given what is known about the role of these primaries in the nomination process, there is an evident question about how open the Connally strategists were to this information.

Then there were other attributes of Connally's public image. By January 1980 he was bedeviled more than Kennedy by perceptions that he was untrustworthy, reckless, even dishonest. He had what pollsters called a "high negative." Every national survey that probed the public's support for the various presidential contenders found that about one-third of the electorate declared they would not vote for Connally under any circumstances.* Yet Connally chose to deal with this information by projecting himself in a manner bound to activate fears that he would be a reckless commander-in-chief. What is more, in selecting South Carolina as the ground upon which he would fight his decisive battle against Reagan, he selected a state where both the 1976 primary and recent polls showed Reagan with more support than in any other state but California. Of course

---

*An instance of this occurred during the Iowa campaign when Connally was on a T.V. call-in show. A Connally supporter called, asking for the candidate's help in dealing with the man's wife, who "thinks you're a crook." Connally was prepared for this and gave a lengthy explanation of how he had been acquitted of federal bribery charges, concluding, "I'm the only certified nonguilty political figure in the country!" "I've told my wife all that," the man responded. "What did she say?" asked Connally. "She still thinks you're a crook." Broder, *The Pursuit of the Presidency 1980*, p. 145.

there were contrary arguments based on Connally's local endorsements and his need to knock Reagan out in a convincing arena, but these bring us back to the question of how such a major campaign found itself able to compete in only one primary and one caucus.*

The internal communication within the central portion of the campaign system was strong, as were resources of staff, facilities, and travel — all generated by an ample supply of early money. These resources, however, were not used effectively to incorporate state and local operations within the working system. Essentially, the candidate was linked to the electorate through mass media and major personal appearances without much intervention by field operatives.[19] This linkage obviously suffered when the image of the candidate was not tailored to the attitudes and perceptions of the voters. In the end, Connally's was a noncybernetic campaign based on the assumption that, with sufficient exposure, the candidate would be able to sell himself to an electorate hungering for assertive and powerful leadership.

BAKER, CRANE, AND DOLE

The campaigns of these two senators and one representative (Crane) have basic similarities, although the candidates themselves were quite different. Of the three, Howard Baker of Tennessee (minority leader of the Senate) was viewed by many politicians, including Carter and Reagan, as potentially the most formidable competitor. The Carter campaign of 1976 had also impressed Baker, who decided to run in 1980 immediately after that election. His campaign was delayed, however, by his need to be reelected to the Senate in 1978 and then by repeated interruptions by Senate business due to his leadership position.[20] In contrast to most other candidates, Baker's announcement on November 1, 1979, marked the actual beginning of his organizational efforts (except for some fund raising). Baker had calculated that he could "campaign from the Senate." This turned out to be generally correct with respect to other political leaders and even fund-raising efforts, but not for

---

*Connally did compete in the Arkansas congressional district meetings, which received little publicity, and in which he came in last, winning one delegate.

the voters in the states. Reality quickly became clear to Baker in a shocking defeat by Bush in a straw vote in Maine on November 3. A major campaign shake-up followed and helped produce a vigorous try in Iowa. But the campaign, perhaps too heavily dependent on Senate staff and Tennessee friends, had begun too late.[21] The potential of a highly respected candidate could not be exploited.

Philip Crane of Illinois, on the other hand, began very early, making his announcement on August 2, 1978. He was into Iowa no later than Bush, and was much less constrained by his duties in the House of Representatives than was Baker in the Senate. However, Crane was not only virtually unknown outside his congressional district but also a very firm conservative. Consequently, although he was personally articulate and attractive, as long as Reagan was in the field (and not decrepit), Crane lacked a rationale for running that would attract contributors and volunteers. He was dependent on Reagan's age and infirmity even more than were the other conservatives, Connally and Dole.

In the beginning Crane was able to use conservative groups to aid his campaign, and to appeal to conservative-minded contributors on the possibility that Reagan would not run, or might be physically unable to meet the demands of a vigorous campaign. This, his initial strategy, had some success. Halfway through 1979 Crane had collected almost $2.5 million — more than any other candidate.* However, early in May issues of internal control led to the loss of much of the campaign staff, including fund raiser Richard Viguerie, who left to join John Connally.[22] Worse, as news of Reagan's positive intentions filtered out, major conservatives turned against Crane, seeing in him the threat of a split conservative vote. In the case of extremists, this reaction could be very severe. The Manchester *Guardian*, for example, carried on a series of attacks on the personal lives of both the candidate and his wife during the New Hampshire primary. Needless to say, this did not help the campaign, which by then was suffering badly from a lack of funds.

While it started early, was carefully planned, and was carried out with great persistence, the campaign as a whole was a very modest operation. Repeatedly it was prevented by a shortage of

---

*Unfortunately for Crane, his case illustrated the treacherous costs of direct-mail operations and professional consultants. The bulk of the money that was collected was paid to Richard Viguerie.

money and staff from taking full advantage of federal matching funds, and it was thus unable to employ sufficient polling, media, and travel to become competitive. Crane withdrew on April 17, having won three delegates (in Illinois).

Senator Robert Dole of Kansas was in a similar position. Better known and more experienced than Crane because of his 1976 vice-presidential campaign with Gerald Ford and his greater visibility in the Senate, Dole suffered from the image of a "hatchet man" that developed in 1976. In 1979 his campaign raised less money than that of any other candidate, except Anderson, and he had difficulty establishing early credibility with either voters or political leaders in the states.[23] More than others, his campaign organization was beset by staffing problems.[24] Also conservative (but with a better sense of humor than Crane), Dole was explicit about his dependence on Reagan. In the famous Iowa debate where Reagan was not present, Dole said: "If you want a younger Ronald Reagan with experience, I'm here." Yet competing with several others, including Reagan himself, for the conservative vote, Dole came in last with 3 percent of the vote in Iowa. Lacking the resources to continue, Dole did not campaign in New England and formally withdrew from contention on March 15.

These three campaigns, though with different candidates, shared common problems. The most fundamental was an inability to carve out a large enough proportion of the Republican electorate in the early contests to achieve credibility. Related to this was a severe shortage of organizational resources, including money, field workers, and professional staff. Of the three, Baker was by far in the best position to overcome these problems. At the start, his fund raising was quite successful, and although his field organization lagged badly, he recruited a professional staff, including the veteran team of Douglas Bailey and John Deardourff to handle his media efforts. Baker's television commercials in Iowa were considered very effective and were well-financed.* Their effects were limited, however, by a field organization that was outclassed by those of Bush and Reagan. His third-place showing, coupled with Bush's victory, lost

---

*In Iowa, Connally spent $200,000 on media; Baker $140,000; Bush $80,000; Kennedy $60,000; Dole $55,000; and Carter $50,000. All these figures are approximate, but indicative. Total campaign expenditures were about $2.8 million.

him media attention in New England and crippled his subsequent fund-raising efforts. He withdrew on March 5 after poor finishes in New Hampshire, Vermont, and Massachusetts, and heavily in debt.

These three cases demonstrate that a cybernetic campaign cannot be cheap. Apart from collecting accurate information about the electorate and the opposition, the resources needed to transmit messages about the candidate to the electorate are substantial. These can be resources of time, with which the candidate speaks to audiences personally; of money and volunteers, which make it possible to organize meetings for the candidate and to carry the candidate's message by door-to-door canvassing; and of money and technology, through which the messages can be sent through the mass media. The media costs of the Iowa campaign hamstrung every candidate who was not well prepared. They were at least ten times more than in 1976 and effectively changed the accepted rule that radio and television advertising were of little use in a caucus state. Internal messages of control through which local campaign workers identify supporters and get them to the polls or caucuses are also costly, whether these costs are paid with money, professional time, or volunteers.

Looming over these candidates, whatever their success in building and operating a cybernetic campaign, was the vital importance of the messages the mass media transmitted about them and their competitors. Such messages were interpreted by voters, financial contributors, other campaigns, *and the people in their own campaigns* as true indicators of who were still viable candidates, and who were not.

These costs of information and control, that is, of a cybernetic campaign, were illustrated by the Iowa caucuses and the New Hampshire primary, both of which were abolutely critical for these three candidates, as well as others. The use of mass media to inform and persuade the electorate was not the norm in Iowa, but it became so in 1980. In 1976 all candidates spent about $35,000 on advertising; in 1980 over $700,000. Of course, John Connally's media expenditures show that the volume of messages does not guarantee their effectiveness. Mismatched coding by the campaign and decoding by the electorate simply produces noise. Nevertheless, in view of the Reagan campaign's total expenditures of over $500,000 on the Iowa caucuses, where does that leave a candidate such as Robert Dole, whose total 1979 receipts were only about $800,000?

ANDERSON

The campaign of Congressman John B. Anderson of Illinois was significant for many reasons. It comprised a unique mixture of similarities with and dissimilarities from the other campaigns we have reviewed. To begin with, Anderson came into the campaign after a decision to retire from the House of Representatives in 1980. A bright, independent-minded, "maverick" representative, whose ability and tenure earned him the chairmanship of the Republican Conference, and whose independence (on social and civil rights issues especially) produced increasing friction with his party's conservative majority, Anderson was leaving the House out of frustration. His 1978 renomination had been won with difficulty against a well-financed right-wing challenger. It galled him to think that after 18 years in the House, and as the third-ranking officer of his party, he should be subjected to this. Yet he had realized for some time that the growing conservatism of House Republicans made his prospects for influencing public policy increasingly remote.

Although the possibility of running for president was discussed with a small group of confidants in the summer of 1978, and a "decision" to run was made in November of that year, Anderson had hesitated, and for good reason. He had no experience in presidential campaigns. Initial explorations were negative, since he had no promising sources of funds, almost no staff, and low public recognition. Moreover, Anderson did not like "politicians" or "politicking," and he did not want to use public opinion polls to help shape his issue positions.[25] Yet he began. From January through April 1979 his exploratory efforts dogged along — until Jim Nowland, the political consultant who was heading it, decided it was fruitless and withdrew, leaving a useful set of strategic ideas in case Anderson decided to go ahead anyway.

Anderson announced his candidacy on June 8, 1979, and began traveling around the country, often alone, speaking wherever he could find an opportunity, but with virtually no measureable effects. It was during this period that he developed — drawn from his congressional experience — the basic issues he would carry through most of the campaign: the 50 cent tax on gasoline, the cut in social security taxes, the opposition to the MX missile, and others. But there still was no media consultant, no pollster, no field coordinator; in short, no respectable campaign organization. In the fall Anderson's wife, Keke, moved to New Hampshire to build up a field organization. She and Michael MacLeod, Anderson's administrative assistant in the House, and now his campaign manager,[26] were his chief "aides."* As for money, Anderson raised $506,000 and spent $476,000 — less than any other candidate in 1979. Then and earlier, Anderson was well received by the press. Reporters and editors complimented his intelligence, articulateness, and sense of national needs; but none saw him as a viable candidate, just as when, in March, he had sought support from friends in the Illinois congressional delegation, only to be advised not to run.

On the eve of the 1980 campaign, therefore, the Anderson campaign was virtually nothing and had gone virtually nowhere. Campaign decision-making was disjointed and generally incremental, and it involved a very small group of persons, almost always including MacLeod and Keke. Close friends in Congress, such as Morris Udall, were consulted about "big" decisions (such as whether to run), but many tactical decisions were left to other staff members. As a result, the invitation to participate in the Iowa debate was initially declined because Anderson was not running in the caucuses. Had this mistake not been caught, Anderson would have missed the very event in which his campaign became consequential. Expressing the campaign's initial strategic ideas, Anderson's performance in the debate showed him to be a smart, articulate, principled, and *different* candidate compared to the other Republicans on the platform. His positions were often opposed to theirs, including Reagan's (who, of course, was not there). For example, when asked how one cut taxes, spent more for defense, and balanced the budget, Anderson replied, "You do it with mirrors" — a phrase that would be used against Reagan for the rest of the campaign.

The television image of Anderson appealed to an audience, and a constituency, that Anderson had not anticipated or sought — liberals and independents, including those with money. From New York to Beverly Hills donations flowed in to the campaign. Persons such as philanthropist Stewart Mott (who was to become a major

---

*Ironically, as it turned out, at the beginning of September, Anderson found time to come to the Annual Meetings of the American Political Science Association being held in Washington. There he met with a modest panel and accepted the cochairmanship of a new Committee on Party Renewal, whose purpose was to strengthen party organizations in the United States.

fund raiser), television producer Norman Lear, and authors Gore Vidal and Irving Wallace were among those responding. Anderson was "discovered," not by conventional Republicans, but by affluent and well-established liberals of weak political allegiance. Tom Mathews of the direct-mail firm of Graver, Mathews and Smith (whom Nowland had contacted almost a year before without result) now contacted Anderson and essentially joined Anderson's campaign. The result was the first of a long series of direct-mail solicitations, which were to finance Anderson through the entire election period.

Meanwhile the candidate campaigned through New Hampshire, Massachusetts, and Vermont, with his organization now larger and fleshed out with volunteers, especially from the area's colleges, where Anderson also had been discovered. The campaign also was being covered by the media. Its decision-making, however, remained disjointed as, once again, an invitation was first refused, and then accepted only at the last minute. It was to an ideal forum from which to project the candidate's image of courage and integrity: a meeting of New Hampshire gun owners on February 18. Millions of American television viewers saw Anderson being shouted down as he defiantly argued for gun licensing. The electorate responding to Anderson now was becoming quite clear as he came in a distant fourth in the New Hampshire primary, but a close second in Massachusetts and Vermont, those states benefiting from Democratic and Independent cross-overs. Indeed, in Massachusetts more than half of Anderson's support came from voters not registered as Republicans.[27]

Tom Mathews had foreseen this vote on the basis of the response to his direct-mail solicitation for Anderson, and he took the initiative to explain its electoral meaning to the campaign leaders immediately after the New Hampshire primary. The overriding point was that Anderson's message was appealing not to regular Republicans, but to a scattering of voters who were predominantly liberal and not tied to either party. Mathews argued that Anderson's campaign had promise only if it would adopt a strategy that reflected this analysis. The next logical step was an independent candidacy; but Anderson and most of his staff were still hopeful of winning the Republican nomination – a prospect that was destroyed by the outcomes in Anderson's home state of Illinois, and in Wisconsin, where the primary was entirely open to cross-overs, and where it was apparent that the campaign was not able to compete among Republican voters alone.[28]

Meanwhile, Mathews helped arrange a second meeting on March 25, attended by almost all the campaign leadership, plus such familiar outsiders as Norman Lear, Stanley Scheinbaum, and political consultant David Garth.[29] The question was, Should Anderson go independent? Anderson and most of his staff continued to be resistant or uncertain, but after Wisconsin, Mathews took it upon himself to contact first Garth, and then Arnold and Porter (a Washington law firm that could deal with the legal problems of getting Anderson on state ballots) about their willingness to take part in an independent Anderson campaign, and at what price. Both Garth and the law firm were forthcoming, and on April 6 Mathews presented the package to the candidate while he was vacationing in California. On April 24, in Washington, John Anderson announced that he was running for president as an Independent. His primary campaign was over. It can hardly be called a success, yet in less than three months it had achieved a national visibility and collected significant resources of money, expertise, and volunteers — and a new status and strategy.

Cybernetically, the Anderson prenomination campaign suffered from entropy and benefited from improbable communication successes. Even more than usual, the candidate was the key element; he was almost the only element that distinguished the campaign from those of other Republican candidates who had given up. Being pushed to the fringe of his party in Congress, Anderson decided to seek command of that party as president. Early negative messages from his congressional colleagues, his exploratory committee, his fund-raising failures, and his lack of endorsements were largely ignored, and needed information from professional surveys was not sought. Lacking resources, the campaign could scarcely communicate with the voters. What is more, when — almost by accident — it did in the Iowa debate, the Republican population Anderson was aiming at was not the one that responded. Feedback from this experience was sluggish, so afflicted with lag that when it occurred it was through persons outside the campaign who saw meaning in the messages that Anderson had not intended and was slow to accept. As far as its goal was concerned (that is, getting the Republican nomination), Anderson's "campaign of ideas" was conceived out of conviction rather than information. Among campaign decison-makers, the communication of strategies and tactics was so noisy that mistaken decisions were made about the Iowa and New Hampshire invitations (among others), possibly because Anderson himself gave contradictory signals.*

Communications were particularly weak between headquarters and field operations, both because resources of numbers and thus time were lacking, and also because resources of experience and expertise were short. Field workers were often volunteers or inexperienced in campaign politics, and the central staff had little direct knowledge beyond congressional campaigning. Jim Nowland, who had managed the exploratory committee, was the top professional because he had managed Senator Charles Percy's 1978 reelection campaign. This lack of resources affected output decisively, and it was soon apparent that Anderson's messages were communicated most effectively by television directly to the voters — a technology the campaign could not afford.

At first glance the prenomination Anderson campaign was a mixture of cybernetic contradictions. The candidate resisted corrective information and feedback lagged. He moved slowly and reluctantly to an independent candidacy. On the way, his adoption of a cross-over strategy was highly incremental and remedial in nature, moving him gradually and unconsciously toward the point when becoming an independent candidate seemed the only viable alternative left.† He had a determined confidence in his own judgments and skills, which sometimes led to dramatic success (such as at the end of the Iowa debate when he discarded a staff-prepared closing statement and made an extemporaneous one of his own — to spontaneous applause from the audience and national admiration), but more often resulted in continuing noise.

On the other hand, the campaign was unusually open to input in the form of new participants and thus new information. Its direct-mail, media, and strategic directors came into the campaign on their own, and it was an easy matter for local volunteers to advance from field workers to area managers. Thus in significant respects the campaign was an open system that experienced higher-order feedback as it adopted a new strategy and a new organization.

---

*It was, after all, not unreasonable to turn down the Iowa invitation, since Anderson was not competing in Iowa — even after the debate.

†The reluctance of Anderson to assume an independent candidacy is attributable more to his long Republican heritage and his loyalty to the party system than an inherent policy conservatism, which others have claimed.

Were the right things learned? The answer obviously depends on the goals of the system. The Republican primaries did not *prove* that Anderson could not mount a potent independent challenge in the general election, but they pointed to the need for very sophisticated analyses of public attitudes and electoral institutions that the Anderson campaign itself did not do.

NOTES

1. Not all of these individuals were with the campaign full time at the start. A slightly different staff is given in *Congressional Quarterly Weekly Report*, December 15, 1979, p. 2817.

2. For example, early in December Lyn Nofziger (press), Martin Anderson (issues), and Mike Deaver (fund raising) were fired following disputes with Sears. Ibid., p. 2830.

3. David Broder, et al., *The Pursuit of the Presidency 1980* (New York: Berkley Books, 1980), p. 127.

4. Richard Wirthlin, Vincent Breglio, and Richard Beal, "Campaign Chronicle," *Public Opinion*, February/March 1981, p. 4.

5. Broder, *Pursuit*, p. 140.

6. William H. Flanigan and Nancy H. Zingale, *Political Behavior of the American Electorate*, 4th ed. (Boston: Allyn and Bacon, 1979), pp. 122-23. Also see Norman H. Nie, Sidney Verba, and John R. Petrocik, *The Changing American Voter* (Cambridge, Mass.: Harvard University Press, 1976), Chapter 12.

7. During 1978 Bush spent most of his time campaigning for Republican congressional candidates, thus establishing political credit. See *Congressional Quarterly Weekly Report*, November 17, 1979, p. 2587.

8. Ibid., pp. 2587-92.

9. Elizabeth Drew, "Bush," *The New Yorker*, March 3, 1980, pp. 94-95; and *Congressional Quarterly Weekly Report*, January 5, 1980, p. 86.

10. *The New Republic*, March 8, 1980, pp. 8-12.

11. Drew, "Bush," p. 82.

12. Ibid., p. 92.

13. Ibid., p.. 86-87.

14. Broder, *Pursuit*, pp. 134-35.

15. *Congressional Quarterly Weekly Report*, December 1, 1979, pp. 2715-20.

16. *Congressional Quarterly Weekly Report*, December 15, 1979, p. 2830.

17. New York *Times*, January 21, 1980, p. A13.

18. Gerald Pomper, et al., *The Election of 1980* (Chatham, N.J.: Chatham House, 1981), p. 11.

19. *Congressional Quarterly Weekly Report*, March 15, 1980, p. 722.

20. This is an interesting illustration of the "senatorial life cycle" formulated by Donald Matthews in *U.S. Senators and Their World* (New York:

Norton, 1973), and noted again in the 1980 campaign by Charles E. Jacob, in Pomper et al., *The Election of 1980*, pp. 123-24.

21. *Congressional Quarterly Weekly Report*, November 10, 1979, pp. 2523-28; and December 15, 1979, p. 2830.

22. *Congressional Quarterly Weekly Report*, November 24, 1979, p. 2658.

23. *Congressional Quarterly Weekly Report*, December 8, 1979, pp. 2769-74.

24. *Congressional Quarterly Weekly Report*, December 15, 1979, p. 2830.

25. Broder, *Pursuit*, pp. 207-11.

26. Anderson did have a formal campaign staff during the summer and fall of 1979. William G. Bradford was the campaign manager and Dan Swillinger the campaign director. See *Congressional Quarterly Weekly Report*, November 3, 1979, pp. 2467-72.

27. E. J. Dionne, Jr., "Anderson and Independents," New York *Times*, March 6, 1980.

28. Following the Illinois primary, the media, which had been highly favorable to Anderson, turned against him. See Michael J. Robinson, "The Media in 1980: Was the Message the Message?" in *The American Elections of 1980*, ed. Austin Ranney (Washington, D.C.: American Enterprise Institute, 1981), pp. 208-9.

29. Broder, *Pursuit*, pp. 228-29.

5

The National Conventions

THE REPUBLICANS IN DETROIT

It is not unusual in presidential campaigns that the selection of the vice-presidential nominee provides some needed excitement. Certainly that was the case for Reagan's choice of George Bush as his running mate in July 1980. With the withdrawal of Bush on May 26, Reagan's last remaining opponent for the Republican nomination was removed. As the campaign had progressed, Bush had become increasingly aggressive in attacking Reagan's policy positions, and by May he had also developed an effective television format. He defeated Reagan in Pennsylvania (April 22), ran a close second in Texas (May 3), and won again in Michigan (May 20). Bush and his staff had expected the decisive Michigan victory to spur financial contributions, but this did not occur – possibly (as the Bush people believed) because the late-night television news reports stressed not Bush's victory but the fact that their projections showed Reagan now with enough delegates to win the nomination.[1]

Bush's withdrawal was a relief for the Reagan campaign, since its expenditures were now very tightly constrained by FEC limits. Furthermore, the campaign could use the time to shift gears for the general election and prepare for the national convention in the middle of July. Anticipating the difficulties of running against a sitting president, Reagan's aides began setting up committees of experts to advise the candidate across the whole range of policy issues. The function of these committees was not only to give actual advice, but also to impress commentators with the *breadth* of Reagan's policy review (the advisers numbered in the hundreds and reflected various policy perspectives) and the seriousness of his approach. Most of these experts were conservatives, but the campaign staff made sure to include enough of other persuasions so that the candidate would not be caught promoting ideas that most authorities viewed as plain silly.

A very large-scale population survey was also carried out, which, when combined with earlier poll data, was used to construct a comprehensive electoral strategy designed to get the campaign to October.[2] Finally, additional staff were hired, including some to deal with the mechanisms of the national convention. For example, William Timmons, a veteran of the Goldwater and Nixon campaigns, and who managed Ford's convention in 1976, was hired to do the same for Reagan. (He also became the political director of the subsequent campaign.) Mike Curb was brought in to handle the convention's program, including the entertainment. This part of the campaign system was working smoothly.

However, in significant respects the campaign drifted during June and early July. Detailed plans for such things as field operations, which could have been pressed forward, were not; efforts of platform control were relatively feeble; and major decisions were not treated with a sense of urgency — the selection of the candidate's running mate being the most obvious case in point.

It is difficult to know exactly why this occurred. Some insiders blamed Reagan himself, saying he was too inclined to leave it to others to initiate decisions.[3] Why, then, did the "others" lapse during this interim period? Part of the answer lies in the campaign and the political forces that were brought to bear upon the candidate and his staff at this time. While it can be said — following the New Hampshire reorganizations — that the campaign was generally of one mind during the primaries, once it was evident that Reagan would definitely be the Republican nominee, various elements of the Republican "coalition" intensified their efforts to gain access because this was the point at which several basic decisions would be made — those concerning the National Committee, the party platform, and, of course, the vice-presidential candidate.[4]

By far the most aggressive and organized effort was made by groups of the far right, now bolstered by a strong religious element manifested in the Moral Majority and Jesse Helms' Congressional Club. Degrees of conservatism were involved, and a generational quality also was present.* Elizabeth Drew described it this way:

> . . . [T]he Reagan people appear to be frittering. The campaign staff is ridden with tensions among the different generations of aides. Though some of the Reagan advisers are more conservative than others, the friction has less to do with ideology than with the nature and durations of the various people's ties to Reagan. Lines of authority are fuzzy at best.[5]

This division between the various "Reagan people" and ideologies led to conflicts that distracted the campaign from the business at hand. The mechanics of the convention were not a problem, but the political issues were. The first issue was whether Bill Brock would remain chairman of the Republican National Committee (RNC). Traditionally, the party's presidential candidate brings his own man or woman in to head the National Committee. Brock, however, had been almost universally praised for a superb job of building up the party organization, especially at the state and local levels. But the far right feared that Brock was not ideologically reliable, and that if Reagan lost the November election, the Reagan people being added to the RNC staff would be fired. With divided advisers, the candidate was pushed and pulled by seemingly irresolvable cross-pressures of party effectiveness, personal friendship, and electoral support – all heightened by the attention being given to the issue by the press. In a demonstration of incrementalism, Brock was kept on and a Reagan man – Drew Lewis – was appointed deputy chairman of the RNC, but only after much shilly-shallying that absorbed campaign time and reduced Brock's capacity to lead the RNC.

The second issue involved how far right the party platform should go. The central goal of the campaign staff was the election of their candidate, which generally called for moderation in the

---

*Drew saw Reagan's campaign (and the convention) composed of "old Reagan people and new Reagan people," both suspicious of the other. The old people were from past Republican campaigns, and tended to be more "political" and willing to compromise. The new people came into politics more recently, were from less affluent backgrounds, and were more intense in their ideology.

platform planks, but they were not prepared for the highly organized effort by Jesse Helms and his allies to fashion the platform in their image, again achieving ideological permanence from the Reagan campaign. Compared to 1976, Helms had started early:

> This time, much of the work had been done before the Convention. "We were able to work from inside," says James Lucier, Helms' chief legislative assistant. Helms was a member of the Platform Committee and Lucier served on its staff; Helms' aides tried to make sure that the correct people were assigned to draft certain sections. As the result of that, and of working . . . with allied groups, like the Moral Majority, Helms was able to insert "with God's help" in the preamble; eliminate the party's long-standing support for the Equal Rights Amendment; and add a call for a constitutional amendment prohibiting abortion, for a return to the gold standard, for strengthening relations with Taiwan, etc.[6]

While Reagan favored most of these positions, campaign strategists felt that stating them so baldly would needlessly offend important groups, such as women, whose votes would help Reagan's election, not to mention the plight of hundreds of other Republican candidates in moderate to liberal constituencies. The campaign staff managed to get some moderating language into the platform, but they clearly had been outmaneuvered by Helms' forces.[7] Here, as in other areas, the differences were less a matter of policy beliefs than of the importance of the policy statements compared to electing the candidate. While the fundamentalist religious element of the "new right" in the party was concentrating on how to lock Reagan into their preferred policy positions, the campaign was concentrating on the New Hampshire primary.

Nothing was more certain for the campaign, at least after the Florida and Illinois primaries, than that the issue of who would be the vice-presidential candidate would have to be faced and resolved. Moreover, there was an abundance of historical evidence from which lessons could be drawn. The campaign appeared to ignore all of this. Of course, the same forces that were involved in the previous two issues were also active here; but now there were more interests and alternatives available, so the chances for disorder were also greater. To ease decision-making, Reagan's staff constructed the usual lists of potential candidates — first a "long list," then a "short list."* The degree of their difficulties becomes clearer if we think of the five major values that were to be optimized. The vice-presidential candidate should: add — that is, bring additional votes — to the ticket; be personally compatible with the president; have a political philosophy consistent with the president's; not alienate any important segment of the Reagan "team"; and have the experience and skill needed to act as president.

As various interests were heard from, it became evident that the list confronted a type of "Arrow Problem"† in which no candidate achieved firm majority support, much less consensus. Of course, this was not a democratic election but the choice of one man: the presidential nominee. Yet Reagan sought at least a common acceptance among his close advisers. This by itself was not unusual, but other distinctive difficulties arose. Traditionally in convention politics the first value — that of adding to the ticket — has been by far the most important, with the idea of "balancing the ticket" reflecting this. John Kennedy, for example, chose Lyndon Johnson of Texas as his running mate despite their lack of personal closeness. To this end, Wirthlin had done polls, finding that only Gerald Ford helped appreciably with votes, and Ford seemed completely unavailable.

Yet electoral help was a matter of degree, and George Bush, the only candidate with the strength to defeat Reagan in any primaries, seemed the obvious choice. A poll of the convention delegates found him acceptable; the campaign staff rated him good politically;

---

*An indication of the names on the fluid long list are the following: Anne Armstrong, Howard Baker, George Bush, Gerald Ford, Guy Vander Jagt, Jack Kemp, Paul Laxalt, Richard Lugar, Donald Rumsfeld, and William Simon.

†Forumlated by Kenneth J. Arrow, in *Social Choice and Individual Values* (New Haven, Conn.: Yale University Press, 1963), the problem takes the following form in this case:

| | | Interests | | |
		1	2	3
Rankings of Candidates	First	A	B	C
A, B, C . . . n by	Second	B	C	A
Interests 1, 2, 3 . . . n	Third	C	A	B

In which the majority for every candidate is superceded by a majority for another candidate.

he did not offend the southern conservatives as did Baker; and he *was* available. Bush, however, was viewed by Reagan, largely on the basis of the Nashua, New Hampshire, episode, as not "gutsy" enough. He and Mrs. Reagan did not feel positive about the Bushes. Again, there is nothing novel about such feelings of personal incompatibility between campaign adversaries. The more significant factors involved Reagan's conservative associations. Hence the third and fourth values also hurt Bush, and virtually eliminated other "moderates," especially Baker. Not surprisingly, the conservatives on the list, such as Kemp, Laxalt, and Lugar, were hurt by not adding any electoral support to the ticket.

As the convention began, therefore, even though the campaign had had ample time to sort through the alternatives, Reagan was undecided, and his staff realized that "he'll be watched for the way he does this." To be sure, the campaign also wanted to use the *mystery* of who would receive the mantle as a source of suspense for a convention that otherwise was cut and dried; as Lyndon Johnson had no difficulty in doing in 1964. Sensing that Reagan's indecision was real, the opposing interests intensified the pressure on the candidate and his aides. All the potential running mates were scheduled to address the convention, and they all understood that the quality of their performance could be the decisive factor.* Since who would be the vice-presidential nominee was the only newsworthy uncertainty left, the media honed in on the question, thus generating even more "possibilities."

Now Gerald Ford entered the lists. Through a complex web of signals, such as statements by Ford supporters and hints by Ford himself (such as in his Monday night speech to the convention), it appeared that Ford was persuadable. Although a month before Ford had explicitly removed himself from contention (or availability), as the convention approached, friends of Ford suggested to the Reagan people that he should be asked again. At the convention some of Reagan's close advisers and friends, such as William Casey and William French Smith, were strong Ford advocates. Indeed, Casey had an analysis done on the implications of the

---

*Perhaps the most extreme case was the keynote speaker, Guy Vander Jagt, who was scheduled to address the convention on Tuesday evening. When the program began to run late, Vander Jagt called Reagan's suite to find out if the decision was still open before he agreed to delay his address until Wednesday.

Twelfth Amendment (both Ford and Reagan were residents of the same state). So Reagan decided to put the question to Ford, mostly as a formality to satisfy the proponents of the "dream ticket."

With the convention awash with rumors and speculations, Reagan met with Ford on Tuesday afternoon and asked him to be a candidate. There followed a day and a half of intense — almost wild — action, punctuated by a Ford interview with CBS anchorman Walter Cronkite, in which he spoke directly about "going to Washington," and did not deny Cronkite's suggestion of a "copresidency." Just after 10:00 P.M. (remember, this was the night of Reagan's nomination) CBS announced that it would be Ford. Shortly before midnight Reagan and Ford ended their negotiations, and Reagan phoned George Bush asking him to be his running mate. Reagan then drove to the convention to make the announcement. It was about 12:30 A.M. Elizabeth Drew, writing at the time, captured the significance of what was happening and reflected what many commentators were saying:

> It is hard to remember a night like this in politics . . . [Reagan], Ford, and Bush have been tarnished in the process. The whole thing suggests a picture of Reagan passively, without much thought, dealing out his Presidency; of Ford being tempted by a combination of duty and pride . . . ; of Bush having been embarrassed. It is a picture of some chaos. If they wanted Ford, why didn't they think of these things ahead of time?[8]

The Reagan campaign's handling of the national convention was a curious mixture of smooth efficient management and extremely fragmented political decision-making. Detailed arrangements for what the band should play and when, and how the singers should perform, were carried off almost without a hitch. The customary demonstrations for the candidates, and of party unity, seemed effortless. But the platform was not well controlled and the selection of the vice-presidential candidate was a breakdown of major proportions. There is the visual image of the candidate's top aides, for example, frantically casting about with representatives of Ford to devise ways for how he might serve as vice-president, while the convention is celebrating Reagan's nomination. Outlines of possible arrangements are typed, then modified and retyped, by the aides themselves so that security can be maintained. Should the vice-president be superdirector of the Executive Office, head of the National Security Council, or secretary of defense? Should he have veto power over certain appointments, receive all staff reports before the president, or direct all foreign affairs? Might there be "a head of state and a head of government"? Would Ford bring with him the secretary of state (Henry Kissinger) and the secretary of the treasury (Alan Greenspan)? How could the campaign system possibly make these decisions in the given circumstances?

Afterward there were as many versions of what happened as there were participants.[9] The Reagan campaign played the episode down, calling it "just batting ideas back and forth" and "brain-storming." Yet it seems clear that the negotiations were proceeding in earnest; that Reagan was planning to go to the convention with Ford; and that they were considering governmental arrangements that would have fundamental constitutional implications — and this on the part of two men who had not worked together before or had much admiration for each other.

We see in this episode a near cybernetic collapse because of overload. Messages about what the convention was doing, how political leaders on the floor and elsewhere were reacting, and what the media commentators were saying were coming in along with alternative vice-presidential proposals, the implications of which were very murky. Time was a matter of hours, and then of minutes.* Essentially, major systemic changes were being contemplated without an aggregate base of experiential or analytic information.

In the end, Reagan made the decision that was most incremental and most supported by his information and his ability to control. (He was confident that Bush would accept, but not at all sure that even an agreement could be reached with Ford by the next morning, the absolute deadline.) As Drew indicated above, however, the messages that went out to the national public (and other political leaders) were of bumbling indecision and fundamental ignorance of governmental institutions — despite the candidate's generally effective "unity" appearance at the end. The situation came about because the campaign received conflicting messages in the form of demands and requests that required painful decisions, which were deferred

---

*At one point, after Reagan's nomination, the demonstrators celebrating his victory were asked to continue in order to give the decision-makers back in the hotel more time to work out a solution.

in the hope that "something would work out." Instead the demands became more intense and the implications (and information needs) more complex. As an example of how "minor" factors become major considerations in such circumstances, when some Reagan aides heard that Henry Kissinger might come back on Ford's coattails, they were outraged, not only because they disapproved of Kissinger's policy views, but also because they aspired to the government positions at stake.[10]

Such motives of ideology and position had always been present in the campaign but were submerged in the contest for the nomination. Once Reagan's victory was assured, and the issues of vice-presidential selection emerged, they became virulent. Individual and group ambitions associated with the winning candidate certainly are not new in presidential politics, and they were long apparent in the Reagan campaign. A strong cybernetic campaign could easily have anticipated, and avoided, the near debacle of last-minute decision-making of 1980.

Equally important, the campaign did not foresee the impact of television on convention decisions. Struggling to carry out exceedingly complex negotiations in private, Reagan and his staff could not control the pressures generated within the media system to actually create events. For example, at 9:10 P.M., Dan Rather of CBS told Cronkite from the convention floor: "Walter, the number of sources on the floor who say a deal has been cut is increasing." Not mentioned was the fact that most of these "sources," like the leaders in their hotel suites, were getting much of their information from television reporters. It was almost a closed system of positive feedback. Reagan himself did not realize — and possibly neither did Ford — that the former President was asking as much as a "co-presidency" before seeing it on television.[11] When George Bush was interviewed by television reporters outside his hotel room after midnight, he expressed surprise at his selection because "you people were circulating a lot of rumors out there, and maybe they were based on a lot of fact."

There were several other aspects of the vice-presidential selection that are pertinent to our analysis. The first is Reagan's personal flexibility in the situation. He was willing to consider possible reorganizations of the presidency that, to say the least, were innovative. They involved major delegations of his own authority that, so far as we can tell, engendered no feelings of insecurity on his part.

Similarly, he was open to the often-diverse ideas of his advisers, while in the end achieving a reasonable resolution. As I have emphasized, there were negative implications in this behavior, yet the candidate's ability to hear and cope with such unusual messages was important.

Second, by contacting Bush, and then going personally to the convention, Reagan showed considerable skill in responding to, and controlling, a very difficult situation. In this respect, he demonstrated strong feedback and control under conditions of information overload and noise.

Third, this episode at least appeared to deliver a heavy blow to the campaign. Yet just as in the case of the Iowa loss, the campaign was able to bounce back, and perhaps learn, from the experience. Reagan's staff did not fall apart, and the candidate definitely did not: He delivered a very strong acceptance speech and "campaign kick-off" two evenings later. As a cybernetic system the campaign was able to survive the first two days of the convention and move forward.

Taken together, the campaign's handling of the national convention was mediocre. It relaxed too much following the end of the prenomination effort and suffered from its association with extremist elements. These caused internal friction and external embarrassments that impeded its control of events. Yet it demonstrated sufficient coherence and adaptability to limit its losses. Much of this was accomplished by the candidate, whose ability to communicate — to project the system's output — was extraordinary. Reagan's acceptance speech, which concluded the convention, was generally considered very effective by commentators, politicians, and pollsters alike. Hence, whatever the internal failures of the system before and during the convention, the effectiveness of key outputs from the candidate was high.

THE DEMOCRATS IN NEW YORK

There was a great difference between the challenges that the Democratic and Republican conventions posed to their respective candidates. The Republican convention was Reagan's convention. There were no opposition candidates and no major issues of policy threatened the party's standard bearer. The Democratic convention was literally the reverse. Faced with a strong opposing candidate, and sharply divided delegates, the management of the convention by Jimmy Carter's campaign may have set new records for thoroughness and control — a performance finally marred by the personal problems of its candidate.

Edward Kennedy not only continued his campaign through all the caucuses and primaries, but also renewed his efforts in the series of state conventions that followed in June and early July. Kennedy tried to persuade these meetings, which often were the last steps in an earlier series of caucuses, to select delegates supporting him. The campaign had some success in this, but nonetheless Kennedy arrived at the national convention in New York with 1,224 delegates to Carter's 1,982, with 1,666 needed for nomination. Persisting, Kennedy then began to work on the selected delegates, attempting to persuade them to shift from Carter to him. This effort ran headlong into party rule 11(h) requiring that "all delegates . . . shall be bound to vote for the Presidential candidate whom they were selected to support for at least the first convention ballot, unless released in writing. . . ." This rule, however, had not yet been adopted by the national convention, the supreme authority of the party. So the issue was whether the convention would adopt the rule as its own [Rule F (3)(c)], and this question — part of the traditional adoption of the rules — came before the convention on Monday evening (of its first day), August 11.

The Carter campaign had not paused or loosened up in May and June, after it became clear that the President had won enough delegates for renomination. Partly this was because the Kennedy challenge continued, but a more important reason was that the campaign leaders, especially Jordan and Caddell, saw the entire prenomination period as an integral and vital part of the general election campaign. Their conceptualization of campaign action and government action was equally integrated. We have already seen this in the President's use of government officials and grants during the primaries — a use that was accelerated during the final prenomination competition. The phrase "nothing was left to chance" aptly describes the Carter campaign during this period.

The campaign confronted two substantive issues simultaneously in Kennedy's convention challenge. One was the above-mentioned question whether delegates would be bound to their original pledges. The other was whether the party platform would contain planks supporting much more aggressive unemployment, wage and price, and similar programs favored by Kennedy. In a true sense, Kennedy brought the purposes of his entire primary campaign to the convention.

Both sides defined the rule issue in terms of high principle. The anti-Carter forces called for an "open convention" — a slogan that caught on and was generally used by the media — while Carter's supporters stood for "faithful delegates." Briefly, the open convention embodied the idea that since many delegates were elected earlier, when conditions were different, they should be allowed to reflect the changing conditions by changing their candidate. The idea of faithful delegates was that primaries and caucuses were conducted according to rules that specified that a delegate selected for a candidate would vote for that candidate, and "to change the rules after the game was played" was to break faith with the electors. Naturally, both of these ideas expressed values that almost all Americans agreed with — but not the Democratic convention.

As usual in convention politics, lofty statements of principle had little to do with the actual conflict, which was over who would be the party's candidate. This led to a fragmentation of the open convention forces that was strongly to Carter's advantage. In fact, despite his large delegate majority, Carter was in considerable difficulty as the convention approached.[12] Revelations about his brother Billy's abuse of presidential connections, and other misbehavior, had come out during the Republican convention in July; Democratic congressmen had been back in their districts during the July recess, finding what governors and other politicians had known: The President's support was at a very low ebb.* National polls showed Carter's popularity lower than even the year before. Fortunately for Carter, the population polled was not his delegates. These tended to have direct ties with the President, many stretching back to the 1976 campaign. Others were local mayors or party chairmen who had direct obligations to the President. Many Carter delegates were "amateurs" in politics, not long-time party regulars.[13]

In any case, the delegates found themselves overwhelmed by attention before the convention. Knowing that Kennedy was attempting

---

*On virtually every measure Carter's ratings were very low. On standard measures of approval, he had reached the lowest rating since the poll began in 1935. The Democratic Study Group on August 8 released polls showing Carter running behind Reagan in four-fifths of the districts surveyed.

to identify and break loose any delegates who were shaky, the Carter campaign set up an exhaustive monitoring, soothing, and reinforcing operation through which delegates were systematically contacted. Waverers were phoned by Mondale, Mrs. Carter, cabinet officers, and the President himself. Delegates were invited to the White House — 400 on August 1 alone — some two or three times, as were groups of party leaders (for example, county chairmen from New York State), and all were recorded on computers so that analysis and retrieval could be accomplished in moments. Seventy-five congressmen were brought to the White House to express their support for Carter. And on the Monday before the convention, the President held an effective press conference dealing with the problems of his brother.

We see in this very careful process of collecting information and using messages of control a cybernetic system at work. The campaign knew as accurately as possible where Carter stood in delegates and reacted to this information with precision and speed — an impressive example of feedback. In contrast, the open convention forces were accumulating problems from their constituent parts. To gain support for the principle, the Kennedy campaign encouraged the possibility that if the rule (that is, Carter) was rejected, the convention would be open to alternative candidates. Thus minicampaigns developed for Senator Jackson, Secretary of State Muskie, New York Governor Carey, and others — even Mondale. Yet what the Kennedy campaign was not able to accept was that their candidate had what we referred to earlier as a "high negative" — now reflected by the fact that the supporters of alternative candidates were frequently not supporters of Kennedy. Again, here is the description of Elizabeth Drew:

> It isn't surprising that Kennedy may not realize the extent to which support for Carter is not transferable to him, may not realize how much antipathy there is to him. In politics, as elsewhere, one can become so obsessed with reaching one's goal — so certain that if only X will happen the goal will be reached — that any number of things that happen will be assumed to be X.[14]

Thus as Kennedy's people publicly associated the open convention with Kennedy's own success, supporters of the other candidates turned away. The result was that the substantial disaffection from

Carter within the Democratic party, even among the delegates, could not coalesce around a *single* alternative. In the pressure cooker of Madison Square Garden as the convention began, the diverse factions, each needing large amounts of information about what the delegates were thinking and the other "candidates" were planning to do (so it would not be caught out in isolated opposition to the President) simply could not communicate sufficiently to take coordinated action.[15] To make matters worse, Carter was now in an ideal position to persuade with direct payoffs. In a massive operation, including on the convention floor, delegation leaders and individual delegates were offered jobs, grants, campaign positions, and so on, throughout Monday. The bargaining with and pressures on the delegates continued relentlessly, but Kennedy was in no position to compete.[16] On Monday night the motion to open the convention was lost by a vote of 1,390 to 1,936, only marginally different from the original delegate counts of Carter and Kennedy.[17] At 10:00 P.M. Kennedy announced the end of his campaign.

It is worth noting that the convention also reflected a problem that transcended the immediate controversy over delegate loyalty, a problem that was pointed up by the separation of Carter delegates from the concerns of many Democratic officials and party leaders. If delegates are merely agents of candidates,* what are the functions of the convention? If the convention is merely a place for candidates to give speeches, what are the functions of political parties, including the state parties in whose name caucuses and primaries are held? To be sure, these questions are leading, but their uncertain answers provide little encouragement to advocates of stronger political parties in American politics.

Just as the Carter campaign was prepared for Kennedy's delegate challenge, it was also prepared for his effort to "liberalize" the platform that had been drafted under Carter control. Even before the convention, the Carter forces had attempted to reach compromises with Kennedy on their platform differences, but to no avail. Caddell's polls showed that such Kennedy proposals as a $12 billion jobs program and wage and price controls were politically suicidal,

---

*Under the adopted rule, a delegate who did not vote as his candidate wished could be immediately replaced with a new delegate who would. Another way of putting it is that candidates have a certain number of convention votes, collected in primaries, and so on, but the individuals casting these votes are incidental.

not just in themselves, but also for what they would do to the federal budget that, in 1976, Carter had promised to balance by 1980. It was plain that public anger over inflation, and disillusionment with governmental interventions, were of overriding political import.[18] So the campaign was determined to head off Kennedy's more demanding economic and welfare proposals; but a number of these had considerable appeal to powerful segments of the Democratic coalition, such as organized labor, blacks, and residents of large Eastern and Midwestern cities. Thus Carter could easily offend important Democratic constituencies while trying to hold together an economic program that would affect the electorate as a whole. It was a dangerous situation in which Kennedy had more leverage than in his fight for nomination.

To cope with this threat (and also the open convention issue), the Carter campaign went to even greater lengths. Over 300 administration officials were circulated on the floor and meeting rooms of the convention. Furthermore, many of these people were coordinated to achieve systematic "use" of the television networks. Carter analysts calculated that the networks spent less than 10 minutes of every hour focused on the formal proceedings of the convention. The other 50 minutes were devoted to special interviews and commentaries, including many from the floor. Therefore, floor reporters were "tracked," and when they began to interview an opposition delegate or official, they were immediately offered a distinguished administrative official prepared with what Rafshoon called "talking points" to counteract negative views of the platform or Carter's performance. In the words of one Carter aide, "We are going to try to massively use the media."[19] We see here a cybernetic strategy to control the very media processes that were so damaging to the Reagan convention. Of course, in addition to this was the continuing employment of the resources of delegate persuasion that I have mentioned before.

Yet Kennedy's various "minority reports" on the platform were very difficult for the Carter campaign to control — not only because particular Democratic groups felt deeply about the policies, but also because the campaign needed the *appearance* of unity at the convention. To make matters worse, on Sunday Kennedy had extracted from Carter the requirement that two hours before the start of presidential nominations the candidates must state their positions on the party's platform in writing, thus limiting a candidate's ability to gloss over an issue. As the voting approached, Carter's forces held where they could, bargained where necessary, and were generally careful not to pressure their delegates unreasonably. Considering all the circumstances, including the fact that the vote was taken directly *after* Kennedy's withdrawal speech, the result was probably as much as could be achieved and was a mixture of diverse parts. Kennedy's jobs program was joined by federal funding of abortions, a denial of party financial support to candidates refusing to back the Equal Rights Amendment, and the rejection of the senator's comprehensive health insurance program. Carter's written statement before his nomination was able to finesse some of his disagreements with the final platform, and analysis indicated that the Democratic platform came closer to party and public preferences than did the Republican.[20]

On Tuesday night, in prime time, Kennedy spoke formally to the convention, withdrawing as a candidate and providing a dramatic high point for the proceedings. Realizing they would have to live with unwanted platform planks and give Kennedy his moment, Carter strategists had anticipated that Tuesday would "not be a good day," but they did not anticipate that Kennedy would rise to such an evocative and inspiring performance of an American political art form — leading numerous commentators to reach back to William Jennings Bryan's "cross of gold" speech in 1896 for a parallel. Moreover, the Carter campaign could not control the television cameras, which covered the entire address, cutting away only occasionally to scenes of transfixed or weeping delegates. The more than half-hour demonstration that followed was also given ample coverage, while not showing "that many delegates, perhaps the majority, were not involved in the noisy demonstration."[21] The message projected from the convention was of massive Kennedy skill and appeal.

The Carter managers ran out the remainder of the convention. On Wednesday evening the President was renominated, and on Thursday the Vice-President, after which both Carter and Mondale made their acceptance speeches and there was the traditional display of party unity. The last evening of a convention especially is considered the party's kickoff of its general election campaign, and the Carter forces clearly used it for this purpose. The speeches of the two candidates were strong and coordinated and included the basic theme of a "good future-bad future" that was carried through the subsequent campaign. Yet whether at the convention or watching it on television, the comparison between Carter and Kennedy could not be missed, and it was often mentioned by the media. Indeed, in the final unity demonstration, network commentators focused on how late Kennedy arrived, how undemonstrative he was toward Carter, and how the cheers for him seemed louder than those for Carter — all of which detracted from the President's kickoff image.

The Carter campaign's management of the national convention can hardly be faulted. Experience from past conventions was used to prepare ample networks of monitoring and control. Information about what was happening on the floor and podium, in surrounding hotels, on the television networks, and within the system itself was transmitted to the "nerve center" located in a group of trailers outside Madison Square Garden, and feedback was swift. Naturally, there were breakdowns and noise, but considering the nature of conventions, these were remarkably few and were quickly corrected. Yet the convention's cybernetic output obviously could have been better for Carter;* it was something that defied campaign control. The difficulties were inherent in the background and ability of Kennedy, the performance of the Carter administration, and the President's personal style. They also arose from the nature of the mass media.

What can we make of the Kennedy campaign, being carried all the way to the convention, almost to the last moment? It was a cybernetic system closed to certain types of external information and vulnerable to positive feedback that shifted its goals. Almost a prototype of a system of self-reinforcement, the campaign drew from the large array of available information the expectation that Carter's success could not hold; that the "bubble would burst." This phenomenon of mutual reinforcement is not uncommon among campaign decision-makers, and Hershey refers to it explicitly in her social learning analysis mentioned in Chapter 2.[22] Given the political experiences of the 1978-80 period, this expectation was not unreasonable initially, but as the preconvention primaries and

---

*Nevertheless, the impact on voter opinion was not all that bad. While Carter's poll ratings did not rise as much as Reagan's a month before, they did go up sharply during the Democratic convention, leaving the President within striking distance of Reagan.

caucuses unfolded, it became a mind-set. It also became more immediate. Thus as the convention began, Kennedy aides expressed their conviction that "something" would break, for how could the party nominate someone like Carter?[23] A plausible analysis became a conviction.

All of this was necessarily associated with the campaign's goals. Perhaps more than most candidates, Kennedy began the campaign with a complex set of goals, shaped by his family background and personal experiences. Thus in addition to winning the nomination, Kennedy wanted to demonstrate "character," to match his brothers, and to contribute to policies aiding the disadvantaged. These goals were mutually compatible and fit smoothly into a campaign system, the major purpose of which was to elect its candidate. The buffeting of the primaries, however, lowered the chances of winning and raised those of character refurbishment — by enabling Kennedy to show tenacity, resilience, and good humor in the face of adversity. Similarly, despite polls showing declining public support, and a turning away by other Democratic leaders, Kennedy made a point throughout his campaign of speaking for expanded government programs to help the poor, control inflation, and promote the nation's health — thus aiming at both his policy and character goals* while providing his campaign workers with reasons for continuing their efforts in the face of defeat.[24] Meanwhile, his election goal, generally unserved by his policy positions, was kept alive

---

*These themes can be seen in the closing words of Kennedy's address to the Convention:

> May it be said of us, both in dark passages and in bright days, in the words of Tennyson that my brothers quoted and loved and that have special meaning to me now:
>
> > I am a part of all that I have met . . .
> > Tho much is taken, much abides . . .
> > That which we are, we are —
> > One equal temper of heroic heart . . .
> >   strong in will
> > To strive, to seek, to find and not to yield.
>
> For me, a few hours ago, this campaign came to an end. For all those whose cares have been our concern, the work goes on, the cause endures, the hope still lives and the dream shall never die.

for the campaign by a few major victories and finally the remote prospect that Carter delegates could be shaken loose.

By this time the campaign was not able to perceive that to succeed on the open convention issue it would have to give up its nomination goal. The campaign had become for many of its participants — even aides such as Paul Kirk, who earlier had urged Kennedy to withdraw — a cause embodying the ideological position of the national party.[25] The goal of nomination remained but had become so infused by other goals that the informational link to the real political world had been short-circuited. Moreover, still another goal, familiar to campaigners, had become an integral part of the whole — defeating the opponent. Whether viewed as the bringer of personal pain through unfair exploitation of the hostages or of Kennedy's character, or as the underminer of the Democratic party, Jimmy Carter became a driving reason for carrying on.

It is hard to evaluate the Kennedy campaign in terms of all its goals or system functions. Of course, multiple goals are present in most campaigns; what distinguished Kennedy's was the importance of those other than election to the campaign system as a whole. Two or three of the others were future-oriented. Bolstered public images of Kennedy's ability and character, and ringing statements of party principles, for example, could affect events long after the 1980 election. The cybernetic operations in pursuit of these other goals were often impressive. Kennedy's dramatic speech to the convention was anticipated months in advance. Its contents were carefully selected and modified to fit the specific conditions of the convention at the time. Its delivery was practiced and learned from earlier successes and failures.

Overall, with one exception, the Kennedy campaign used its resources of communication to secure a large measure of its goals. The exception was, of course, the presidential nomination. There, its rigidities of dreams, biases, and commitments prevented it from taking those actions needed to win the open convention vote. Yet if these actions had been taken, would the vote have been won? If the vote had been won, would the open convention have refused to nominate Carter? To both questions, given the strength of the Carter campaign, and the weakness of other candidates, the answers are probably "no." So we are left with a campaign that was flawed and interesting and had no easy fixes.

NOTES

1. Elizabeth Drew, "1980: The Final Round," *The New Yorker*, June 23, 1980, pp. 68-69.

2. Richard Wirthlin, et al., "Campaign Chronicle," *Public Opinion*, February/March 1981, pp. 43-49.

3. One of these was John Sears, who, of course, had been fired after the New Hampshire primary but nevertheless had worked closely with Reagan since 1975. He discussed the condition of the campaign in the Washington *Post*, July 16, 1980, which appeared during the Republican convention. Also see Elizabeth Drew, *The New Yorker*, July 11, 1980, p. 56.

4. For a coalition analysis, see John Kessel, *Presidential Campaign Politics* (Homewood, Ill.: Dorsey Press, 1980), esp. Chapter 3.

5. Elizabeth Drew, "1980: The Republican Convention," *The New Yorker*, August 11, 1980, p. 38.

6. Elizabeth Drew, "Jesse Helms," *The New Yorker*, July 20, 1981, p. 84.

7. Some reports emphasized the "harmony" of the platform. See the *Congressional Quarterly Weekly Report*, June 28, 1980, pp. 1799-1800. But Michael J. Malbin, "The Conventions, Platforms and Issue Activists," in *The American Elections of 1980*, ed. Austin Ranney (Washington, D.C.: American Enterprise Institute, 1981), pp. 100-16, shows a variety of internal conflicts.

8. Drew, August 11, 1980, p. 60.

9. For example, *Congressional Quarterly Weekly Report*, July 19, 1980, pp. 1982-83; and Charles O. Jones, "Nominating 'Carter's Favorite Opponent': The Republicans in 1980," in *The American Elections of 1980*, pp. 92-96.

10. Ibid., p. 62.

11. The television commentators themselves were sensitive to what was happening. On NBC David Brinkley observed that television had become "something of an intercom" over which rumors "fly back and forth."

12. Three dozen Democratic congressmen signed a petition for the "open convention." *Congressional Quarterly Weekly Report*, August 2, 1980, pp. 2169-70.

13. Actually, half the Democratic delegates held some party office. Warren J. Mitofsky and Martin Plissner, "The Making of the Delegates, 1968-1980," *Public Opinion*, October/November 1980, p. 42. The delegates were probably even less "regular" in the preceding two conventions. Of the numerous studies, see, for example, John S. Jackson III et al., "Recruitment, Representation, and Political Values," *American Politics Quarterly* 6 (April 1978):194-96; Jeanne Kirkpatrick et al., *The New Presidential Elite: Men and Women in National Politics* (New York: Russell Sage Foundation, 1976); and Stephen J. Wayne, *The Road to the White House* (New York: St. Martin's Press, 1980), pp. 91-96.

14. Elizabeth Drew, "1980: The Democratic Convention," September 8, 1980, p. 46.

15. In the words of a Jackson supporter, "It's like trying to nail gelatine to the wall; everyone is ready to do something if someone else does." Drew, September 8, 1980, p. 56. This is a classic example of a convention problem often tackled with game theory. See Steven J. Brams and John G. Heilman,

"When to Join a Coalition, and With How Many Others Depends on What You Expect the Outcome to Be," *Public Choice* 17 (1974):11-25; Eugene B. McGregor, "Rationality and Uncertainty at National Nominating Conventions," *Journal of Politics* 34 (1974): 459-78; and Donald S. Collat, Stanley Kelley, Jr., and Ronald Rogowski, "The End Game in Presidential Nominations," *American Political Science Review* 75 (June 1981):426-35.

16. Yet by any other standard, the Kennedy effort was impressive. There were 120 Kennedy "whips" on the floor, communicating with the command post through 20 telephones. Carter had over 200 whips, but these did not include the 300 administration officials who were also being used. New York *Times*, August 12, 1980, p. B10.

17. For details, see the *Congressional Quarterly Weekly Report*, August 9, 1980, pp. 2268-76.

18. See, for example, Henry A. Plotkin, "Issues in the Presidential Campaign," in Gerald Pomper, et al., *The Election of 1980* (Chatham, N.J.: Chatham House, 1981), pp. 46-49; and Warren E. Miller, "Policy Directions and Presidential Leaders: Alternative Interpretations of the 1980 Presidential Election," paper delivered at the Annual Meeting of the American Political Science Association, New York, September 3-6, 1981, Table 12.

19. Drew, September 8, 1980, p. 50.

20. Adam Clymer, "A Platform as Vehicle for Unity," New York *Times*, August 13, 1980, p. B1.

21. Bernard Weinraub, "Carter Faces Problem," New York *Times*, August 14, 1980, p. B3.

22. Marjorie Randon Hershey and Darrell M. West, "Single-Issue Groups and Political Campaigns," paper delivered at the 1981 Annual Meeting of the Midwest Political Science Association, Cincinnati, April 15-18, 1981, p. 9.

23. In different ways various journalists commented on this aspect of the Kennedy campaign. For example, see Drew, September 8, 1980, p. 46.

24. This is not to say that Kennedy refused to modify policy positions for electoral purposes. For example, he dropped his early advocacy of gasoline rationing because it smacked too much of government overregulation.

25. *Time Magazine*, June 16, 1981, p. 12, makes it evident that there was considerable controversy within Kennedy's staff about whether he should withdraw following the primaries. Also see Drew, September 8, 1980, p. 46.

6

The General Election

CARTER

The Democratic national convention was treated by the Carter strategists as an integral part of the general election campaign. As far back as April, field workers had been sent out under the auspices of the Democratic National Committee (DNC) for campaign purposes, thus taking advantage of resources in addition to those provided by federal funding that became available only after the convention. Since early in the year, the campaign's leaders had been meeting daily at 8:00 A.M. in the White House office of Jack Watson (who replaced Hamilton Jordan as the President's chief of staff so that Jordan could direct the campaign full time). During the entire period Caddell's polling had continued, picking up public reactions to the primaries, to other relevant events, and to the Republican and Democratic conventions. The campaign knew with precision how Carter and Reagan stood — information that was used for continuous redevelopment of media strategy, including the themes of the Carter and Mondale acceptance speeches. The same information was used to guide the policy decisions of the federal government.

The use of governmental resources to influence campaign politics, which we have repeatedly noted in the prenomination campaign, manifested the thoroughly integrated concept the campaign strategists had of electoral influence. While some care was exercised to separate campaign operations formally from the White House (and other governmental agencies), the overlap of governmental and campaign decisions was very great. The usefulness of this conceptual and operation integration was initially learned by Carter and his aides in the 1976 campaign against Gerald Ford, and then confirmed by their experience as an incumbent administration. Ford's use of presidential prerogatives at first irritated Carter's staff and then impressed them with how effective it could be. As Caddell's polls showed how completely the President was held responsible by the public for the actions of his administration, advisers such as Jordan and Powell became convinced that wherever practicable the resource of incumbency must be used to the full.

The idea of government-in-the-campaign worked both ways and was consistent with the way federal resources were distributed by the Carter administration. Rather than developing an overall theory or design, the administration responded to demands and claims by states, localities, and groups. When the 1980 campaign got under way, Carter's staff was thus accustomed to this pattern, which was easily adapted to states or localities holding caucuses or primaries, and to special-interest and ethnic groups. An ethnic campaign committee was organized, and group representatives were given positions in the administration and invited to the White House – blacks, women, Poles, educators, environmentalists – the list was long. Certainly the Carter campaign did not originate this practice of stroking and rewarding groups, but it was started early in the administration, conducted systematically, and given administrative support. In the words of a White House official: "One of the real secrets of this Administration is that we've worked at constituency development: if you look down the list of organizations and constituency groups, you'll find policies to match. We've gone out to constituency groups and said, 'What are your needs?' "[1]

Carter's concern for these "constituency groups" provided the administration (and the campaign) with some direct local contacts, and presumably with considerable support from their memberships. It also produced policy fragmentation in the government, as it moved first this way then that in response to the diverse claims. No compelling overall thrust or theme was easy for the public to discern.

There were, of course, forces within the Carter administration – including the President – that sought and claimed comprehensive programs and planning; indeed, on the surface the Carter administration appeared to start off by overreaching itself in this respect, particularly with Congress. Yet even after such a program as energy had been laboriously formulated, it was partially dissipated by adjustments and exceptions in response to group pressures. Nor was this pattern confined to domestic policies alone. To be sure, this approach to public policy can be viewed as just another example of the well-known incremental and pluralistic character of the American system. The degree, however, and the resulting public perceptions of the presidency, were a distinct problem for the campaign. As we have already observed, by 1979 Carter was seen as a weak and indecisive President, and over a year later, with American hostages still held in Iran and the domestic economy in an inflationary shambles, the public image of Carter remained unrelieved.

Well informed by Caddell's polls, group contacts, and campaign workers in the field, Jordan and other Carter aides put together three components of the existing campaign to form a general election strategy following the national convention. It differed little from the strategy of a year earlier, except the targets were different. The first component was essentially managerial – a continuation of the painstaking attention to operational detail that we have seen from the start. The second component was the development of a positive theme for the second Carter administration. The third component comprised the attacks against the opponents, Anderson and Reagan – the "negative campaign."

Among the major lessons that campaign director Jordan had learned from previous campaigns was that "nuts and bolts count," and that incumbents have a big advantage in making them count more. Even at the previous low point in Carter's fortunes, when Kennedy was about to launch his campaign in August 1979, Jordan had argued that Kennedy would not be able to match the President's resources of time, expertise, and perquisites of influence. Despite the special hostage circumstances, the validity of this argument was seen as being demonstrated in the prenomination campaign. Knowledge of FEC financial regulations, and the staggering details of state delegate selection procedures; getting off to an early start by using White House staff, and keeping in mind that, like it or not, administration actions had campaign consequences; influencing caucuses and primaries, and the national convention, through the use of federal policies, programs, and jobs – all things we have already observed — were a prologue to the management of the fall campaign.

Let us consider a September campaign appearance by the President in Michigan.[2] The places were selected in order to celebrate the new cars coming off the assembly lines in and around Detroit, and to show the President's sensitivity to the unemployment problems of the auto industry. He arrived on Air Force One, which was closely followed by a plane carrying members of the national news media. He was met by local dignitaries and immediately inspected a group of cars from the five American producers. He toured an assembly line, drove one of the new cars, was praised by leaders of both management and labor for his aid to the industry, and announced agreements newly reached with Japan to limit auto imports. Local high school bands played. Local officials were present and expressed appreciation. Later the President held a "town meeting," at which the audience was swelled by advance men and local groups indebted to the President for past favors. Campaign staff helped choose those in the meeting who would ask questions. On and off during these events, Gerald Rafshoon's movie crews took pictures, some of which were subsequently used in Carter television commercials. The President also found time to grant special interviews to the local news media — all this in less than one day.

Many campaign purposes were accomplished in such appearances, the logistics of which were enormous and preceded by detailed planning. The appearances illustrate the inextricable relationship between the campaign's ability to carry out operations, to manage events, and to influence political effects. The appearances not only were publicized in depth over a large local area, but also were communicated nationally. Much of the message was symbolic. Even if the national media chose not to report Carter's remarks, the events spoke for themselves: in this case that the President was helping the auto industry; that he was supported by both industry and labor; and that he was concerned about the common man.

The Reagan campaign could and did carry out similar appearances, but Reagan did not come and go on Air Force One; did not announce national policies from lecterns bearing the presidential seal; did not hear "Hail to the Chief" from the bands; and was not so impressively surrounded by Secret Service agents. In short, Reagan was not the president. Field appearances enabled the campaign's managerial competence to exploit the symbols of the presidency, public- and private-sector accomplishments, group alliances, and the media for electoral benefits.

Cybernetically, the monitoring and control of this managerial component were very efficient. Considering the complexity of some of the operations, there was remarkably little noise or confusion. Once a strategic or tactical goal had been set, such as to keep track of public opinion, satisfy the wishes of particular groups, use government resources to persuade local politicians, or visit Detroit, implementation proceeded with careful provisions for feedback, including close communication with the campaign's central decision-makers. This does not mean that all decisions were made by a few people in Washington, since they would have been overloaded. Instead, leading "operating" staff were experienced and familiar enough with campaign strategy and organization that they had an effective understanding of what could be decided directly and what needed to be checked horizontally or vertically within the system. Of course mistakes were made, and there were surprises,* but mutual understanding and internal feedback enabled the system to correct itself and carry on without interruption.

We have already seen during the prenomination period that the campaign faced serious problems in finding one or more positive *themes* — persuasive reasons why the Carter administration should be continued. Caddell recognized this very early, and he and other strategists not only sought answers in analyses of public attitudes but also tried out various possibilities during the spring and summer. Caddell had suggested a general strategy in his memorandum to the President in the summer of 1979. Since Carter's accomplishments were not viewed favorably, why not focus the electorate's attention on the future, diverting it from the unpleasant present? Thus Carter might depict the 1980 election as "a choice between two futures." Caddell's idea was adopted by the campaign, but it remained to be converted into thematic phrases. The development of these was slowed by the initial Rose Garden strategy, which precluded the

---

*An extreme instance of a campaign surprise occurred on September 14 when Tim Kraft, national campaign manager, left the campaign following disclosures that he was under investigation for the use of cocaine. Kraft, along with Jordan and Robert Strauss, were at the core of the campaign system. What is more, he was responsible for field operations, which involved large amounts of detailed information about people and places. Kraft was replaced by Leslie C. Francis, who proceeded — hardly missing a beat.

trial-and-error testing that was possible in an extended series of stump speeches in the field. Surrogates, it turned out, could not capture enough media attention to "launch" a theme, even if they were as high ranking as Mondale.

Thus as spring advanced, Carter's strategists were anxious that he somehow get out of the White House to make his own case. (Some were also concerned that he would get rusty as a speaker and needed some practice before facing Reagan in the field.) Since the Rose Garden strategy had worked well against Kennedy, Carter's aides were of mixed minds about where and how it should end, especially because the original plan was for a limited version of the "working President" strategy to be followed in the general election. This was derived in large measure from what was judged the success of the 1976 Ford campaign. In any case, the need for the President to get into the field became more and more convincing, but it was hard to find a reason, since the hostages, for whose benefit the President was staying at his desk, were still in Iranian hands.

With the aborted hostage rescue attempt on April 24, followed by the resignation of Secretary of State Cyrus Vance, and the recruitment of Senator Edmund Muskie as Vance's replacement, Carter's advisers felt that these events had been sufficiently disruptive and damaging anyway, so that they might as well take the occasion to get the President out of the Rose Garden.* After an intensive analysis of the various alternatives that were available in the concluding June 3 primaries, the decision was reached to have Carter make his first "political" trip of the campaign to Columbus, Ohio. Prefaced by the rather embarrassing explanation after the April events that the problems facing the President had become "manageable enough now for me to leave the White House," Carter spoke on May 29, trying out the "we are turning the tide" theme.[3] This did not catch, and the effort to develop a theme moved to the national convention, where, in his acceptance speech, the President finally introduced his "good future-bad future" theme.

The positive-theme component of the campaign illustrates the cybernetic complexities and limits faced by the system. In contrast to its internal operations, here the campaign needed to communicate not with itself but with the electorate and through the media,

*The rescue mission, although unsuccessful, turned out to raise the President's standing in the polls.

but this was a process of great subtlety that, in simplified form, began with the actual performance of the government, continued with the expressive style of the President and the interpretations of the media, and ended with the receptiveness of the American voter. Although it tried, the campaign system could not control any of these elements, much less the last two, and they all were linked together with both information and noise. To develop an effective theme required a message that was sufficiently in phase with messages of administration performance so as not to be cancelled out or take on a negative meaning. Next, it needed to be expressed by the President in a manner to sustain, if not enhance, its information — keeping in mind that the message was essentially *about* the President: what *he* had achieved, what *he* knew or understood, and what could be expected of *him*. Then the message needed to be transmitted by the media, which meant decoding and coding (interpretation) before transmittal. Finally, the message needed to be in a form that would contain the intended information for the electorate, which meant being decoded by systems of attitudes, memories, and perceptions that comprise the voters.

While obviously complex, this process of communication is not impossible because it embodies numerous feedback loops that produce a great deal of mutual adjustment. Kennedy's speech to the national convention was an example of how a set of messages could be enhanced by a speaker's performance and then transmitted in a form (simultaneous pictures of Kennedy speaking and delegates reacting) that did not invite subsequent interpretations that would introduce contradictory meanings for the national television audience.

In the case of the Carter campaign, however, this communication process encountered two distinct breakdowns. The first was the President himself, an individual already described as a "loner," who lacked the personal style to project his message clearly to large audiences.* The second involved the personal feelings of coolness and skepticism toward Carter on the part of media commentators — attitudes growing out of the knowledge these persons had of White House manipulations combined, again, with Carter's lack of personal interaction with them. This produced a tendency on the part of

---

*Carter was at his best with small groups, where he could be very persuasive. It was for this reason that the campaign often chose the "town meeting" format for local appearances.

commentators to question the President's motives and purposes during the fall campaign. One of the more objective of the commentators put it this way:

> He does not know how to carry people along. He has little taste for the sweatiness and earthiness of politics; he seems to undervalue the emotional and psychological links between people that make things happen, and he seems to believe that arguments speak for themselves — that if you've made your argument, that's all you need to do. He doesn't seem to understand that people in political life act — or don't act — because of loyalty and affection and a whole range of psychological factors. . . . Perhaps he can't. Some people . . . think that the cold side of his nature and the engineer in him have taken over increasingly.[4]

The result was that even when the President would make a strong presentation of a positive message, it was often accompanied by media analyses of a questioning nature — analyses that the campaign considered were reducing the public impact of the message.

The problems of finding and projecting a positive theme were related directly to the third component, the negative side of the campaign. As early as the New Hampshire primary, Carter strategists made no secret of their satisfaction with the prospect of running against Reagan in the fall, seeing him vulnerable because of his extremely conservative positions, personal gaffes, and so on. Their success in focusing attention on Kennedy's character during the primaries (in turn consistent with earlier experiences in Georgia) encouraged them further, bringing them to a negative strategy that fit easily with the alternative futures theme.[5] Thus in his speeches, the President would draw extreme examples from the large collection of Reagan's past remarks to show the Republican candidate as a threatening menace — leaving the voters to decide if they wanted a future of *that*.

In the meantime, the press, quite aware of the use of the character issue in Carter's preconvention commercials, had become alert to this negative campaign. Exhibiting a sensitivity that had been heightened by Carter's tendency to make disparaging remarks about persons out of favor,* the commentators began talking and writing

---

*The most striking case was that of Cyrus Vance after his resignation as Secretary of State in April. Carter's comments about finding someone better able to manage foreign affairs smacked of "bad-mouthing."

about Carter's "mean streak," an issue that by September began crowding out the substance of the President's attacks on Reagan's extremist policy proposals.[6] Matters were made worse by a series of newspaper and television ads and remarks by the President, clearly implying that Reagan was a racist and a threat to world peace.[7] Naturally, this was an opening that the Reagan campaign quickly exploited. For Carter it tarnished a major positive aspect of his public image: that he was an honest, conscientious man.*

In a sense, their candidate, and how he was perceived by the media and the electorate, cast the participants in Carter's campaign as actors in a Greek tragedy. The organization was well established and efficient, and its patterns of decision were very well designed. With open channels and substantial resources of information, campaign leaders were remarkably well informed about relevant conditions and events, and their resources of action were formidable. Yet in the final two months they could do little with these resources to control the march of events.

The "presidential debates" were a case in point. From the beginning the Carter campaign made decisions about these based on intensive calculations of their probable electoral effects. The general, and widely recognized, rule was: If you're ahead don't debate. Thus Carter agreed to debate Kennedy in October 1979 but changed his mind in December. Kennedy, of course, continued to challenge Carter throughout the preconvention period, including during the time between the President's announcement that he could leave the White House and the end of the primaries. While Kennedy's challenges were not always reported to the public, they did not escape the news media.†

Following the conventions, John Anderson insistently called for a three-man debate, and a strategic minuet ensued. Reagan agreed, but Carter, though now behind in the polls, refused in

---

*It is interesting to observe how much attention the issues of "unfair attacks" received in this campaign, and how familiar Carter's tactics actually were in presidential campaigns: since World War II, for example, Truman against Dewey in 1948, Nixon against Humphrey in 1968, and, of course, Johnson against Goldwater in 1964 (when the latter was truly savaged). Commentators occasionally called attention to this in 1980, but with no apparent attention.

†Kennedy poured it on in the weeks before June 3. His last challenge was that if Carter would debate him, and then won a majority of the votes in all the June 3 primaries, he would concede Carter the nomination.

order not to strengthen Anderson's standing. Instead, he demanded a "head-to-head" debate with Reagan alone. There followed the Anderson-Reagan debate on September 21, which appeared to help Reagan and hurt Anderson and especially Carter.[8] Now Carter became increasingly boxed in. Alerted by his evident manipulations of the hostage issue during the primaries, journalists began calling attention to the transparent political motives of his debate proposals. So the public impression grew that Carter was "afraid" to debate.

Following the Anderson-Reagan debate, Carter (through campaign spokesman Strauss) stepped up his calls for a head-to-head debate, while Reagan, now leading in the polls, continued to demand that Anderson be included. By the middle of October, however, Anderson's decline in the polls left him ineligible to be included under the League of Women Voters' criterion, and Carter was caught.* The President's strategists had concluded from their analysis of past elections that challengers tended to be helped by debates and that incumbents usually regain support as the election nears. They had also become increasingly wary of Reagan's effectiveness as a performer. The challenge of a one-on-one had seemed useful in countering the avoidance or fear image, since Reagan seemed committed not to accept without Anderson, but it had all unraveled with Anderson's ineligibility, and Carter was left with no escape. The only question was when the debate would be held. (For their part, Reagan's advisers were uncertain about the size of his lead, a surprise move by the President, and so on, as we shall see later.) The debate was held on October 28, a week before the election, and contributed to Carter's defeat.

The issue of television debates was considered carefully by the Carter campaign throughout the campaign period. At every point of decision — and these points were numerous, sometimes continuous — impressive amounts of information were brought to bear. This ranged from historical analyses to Carter's own performance in past debates to current public opinions and attitudes. There were different points of view within the campaign leadership, and these were

---

*All the general election debates were sponsored by the League of Women Voters. Under a multitude of pressures, including minor parties seeking participation, the League dealt with the Anderson issue by declaring that he would be allowed to participate if a combination of opinion polls gave him 15 percent or more support. Anderson was approximately at that point early in September.

usually resolved through mutual adjustments and continuing references to the strategic situation. Decision-making was open and well-
informed. Nonetheless, as the campaign proceeded, the constraints
on the decision-makers grew, largely because of their previous
decisions, which were always subject to instant recall by the media.
The range of feedback was thus limited.

Carter's aides understood very well that the "meanness" image
hanging over the candidate would restrain his remarks, but they also
knew that they had succeeded, despite the price, in depicting Reagan
as uninformed and dangerous.[9] Their debate strategy, therefore,
was to have Carter emphasize these points about Reagan and act
presidential. Although they anticipated Reagan's ability to brush off
such attacks in part, Carter was not prepared for Reagan's skill at
turning the attacks against the President. With a characteristic grin
and shrug, and remarks such as "there you go again" [misrepresent-
ing Reagan's position], Reagan was able to suggest that Carter was
a petty distorter − hardly the image of a President. Reagan, meanwhile, came across as reasonable, understanding, and stable.

Could Carter's campaign have used better information and
control to "win" the debate? Possibly, but only if they had begun
long before, and been able to exercise greater control over their
candidate. Both Carter and Reagan reached the stage in Cleveland
(site of the debate) trailing records, styles, and public expectations.
It is easy to imagine different things both might have done to improve
their performances. Yet their styles of action were essentially set.
This was reflected in their preparations. Reagan approached the
event as a *performance*. He rehearsed for three days with live opponents (one of whom was David Stockman, later to become Reagan's
director of the Office of Management and Budget), videotape
replays, and advisers. Carter prepared too, mostly on substance, and
mostly by himself, and he continued to campaign. Reagan was well
rested, Carter was not.* In short, Carter's personality and style
imposed constraints on what and how much his campaign could do
to help him. Both sides understood the mutability of the electorate,
the volatility of public opinions and attitudes, and the critical nature

---

*One is reminded of the parallels with the classic first debate between
Kennedy and Nixon in 1960. Kennedy entered rehearsed and rested, while
Nixon scarcely interrupted his intense campaigning, and entered appearing
exhausted, even a bit haggard.

of the event. Yet in the end they had to use their candidates as they were.

Furthermore, how they "were" was partly a function of the attitudes and expectations of both the public and the media. Television viewers "looking for" something in the candidates were more likely to see it; and not only was the same thing true for media commentators, but also what they saw would be repeated for days after the debate, thus having a powerful effect on both viewers and nonviewers. On this score it was important that commentators were sensitive to the possibility of Reagan gaffes and Carter meanness.

As a cybernetic system the Carter campaign worked as effectively during the general election as it had during the preconvention and convention periods. Time and experience had enabled the campaign to recruit participants who were knowledgeable, competent, and sufficiently compatible so that communications were seldom interrupted by interpersonal conflicts. It is hard to overestimate the extent to which, directly and indirectly, the campaign's resources were derived from the presidency. Most of the top leaders had been together in the 1976 campaign to win the presidency. Almost without exception they had worked together in the White House.* This, plus being *in* the White House, facilitated communication and decision-making. They knew each other and were in close proximity. Meetings could be held easily and quickly, and the candidate was right there.

As the campaign advanced, the formal headquarters a few blocks from the White House grew in size and importance, but its separation did not impede the flow of messages because most of the leaders remained in the White House. Equally important, the President could be used for purposes of control. The party's national committee, although somewhat restrained before the nomination, was staffed by the President and could be used as an arm of the campaign. Of course, the programs of the federal government could also be controlled for campaign purposes — at least to a degree — a practice that continued through the general election.[10]

In other critical respects, communication and control, especially involving campaign output, faltered badly. The federal government was an enormously complex system of decisions and messages.

---

*Robert Strauss had not been a formal member of the White House staff, but had worked closely with the President in top-level positions.

Part of it the campaign could manage; the rest defied control — if only because the government itself lacked the capacity to solve the problems it faced. Yet the same persons who had led the government were leading the campaign, showing the striking discontinuity between the ability to do well in one but not the other.* As the government in general and Jimmy Carter in particular were perceived as failing, the campaign was to that extent immobilized in its efforts to build public support. Campaign decision-makers were well aware of these perceptions and, while having little success in improving the performance of government, were impressive in adapting the campaign to governmental events. Thus we have seen that after the American hostages were taken in November 1979 the campaign adjusted quickly and surely by holding the President in the White House and suggesting that policy criticisms, say by Kennedy, were improper if not unpatriotic.† But this ability to limit Carter's losses — even to derive benefits — from the hostage events did not extend to dealing with Iran, or to the actions of the media. By the fall both Iran and the media had become sources of negative information for Carter.

The campaign's relationship with the Democratic party, and specifically the DNC, was equally instructive. We have seen how precise efforts were made to *use* local party officials and the DNC to win and hold Carter delegates, to prepare for the national convention, to keep Anderson off state ballots, and so forth. Yet the flow of information (and resources) between Carter and his party tended to be primarily for purposes of Carter. As early as 1978, party officials at all levels were asking for more presidential attention and support, and by 1980 the DNC might have been an arm of the President's campaign, but it was not able to give much help to other Democratic candidates.[11] This lack of organizational muscle also

---

*The competence of the Carter campaign was highly respected, especially by opponents, but the irony of the situation was also seen. As a Kennedy aide put it after the New Hampshire primary, "If those guys could run the government as well as they run campaigns, the country wouldn't have any problems."

†Bear in mind that there were other instances. For example, at 7:00 A.M. on April 1, the morning of the Wisconsin and Kansas primaries, the President announced that Iran had taken a "positive step" — indicating that an agreement on the hostages was imminent. Obviously made early enough to capture the morning news broadcasts, this effort to influence primary votes, which it did, was transparent. It became more so when the positive step failed to materialize.

meant that the party arm was feeble in the presidential campaign as well. Just as in the case of the federal government, Carter and his aides had difficulty leading the party, which consequently was a smaller resource in the fall elections. It represented a weakness in the campaign's cybernetic control, and it was evident in the shortage of Carter volunteers (in contrast to the many Reagan enthusiasts) in campaign offices in many parts of the country.

Finally, and fundamentally, the campaign was not able to control its own candidate so that the projected messages (images) of his presidency could be more positive. We have seen many examples of this, and many more could be given. All serve to illustrate three major points. First, although for analytic purposes we may think of a campaign as a system of information, as our model shows, this system revolves around the candidate. *His* election is the manifest function of the system, and *he* personifies his campaign in the minds of the electorate.[12] A telling example of this point was the President's personal involvement in the negative campaign. It had been planned to have surrogates carry out the attacks on Reagan, leaving the positive high road to Carter.* However, when the media refused to report what the surrogates were saying, the campaign was forced to turn to its candidate to deliver the message, thus diminishing the "nonpolitician" image of the President.[13]

Second, the extent to which a presidential candidate can be adjusted or "molded" by his campaign staff — and thus his degree of feedback — depends on a number of personality, organizational, and status factors (as we shall also see in the case of Reagan). Not the least among these is whether the candidate is President of the United States. Moreover, given the historical model of a strong, independent personality, and the close attention of the media, the malleability associated with Harding or various fictional characters is both rare and risky.† In any case, it could not be attributable to Jimmy Carter.

---

*A classic example of this strategy was Vice-President Mondale's acceptance speech at the national convention. Following the equally classic model delivered by his mentor, Hubert Humphrey, against Goldwater in 1964, Mondale went through a litany of what "most Americans believe," adding after each, "But not Ronald Reagan." It was at once humorous and biting, showing Reagan as inaccurate, ludicrous, and extreme.

†An indication of Carter's nonmalleability is given in a report by Steven R. Weisman about Jody Powell, the President's press secretary, and the aide closest to him personally: "He is most attentive to the [phone] marked 'PRESUS' . . .

Third, how the candidate is perceived by the electorate can be affected by a highly cybernetic campaign, but it cannot be completely controlled. Even if large amounts of data and intensive analyses of public attitudes are used to shape messages about the candidate (such as Carter being depicted as knowledgeable, determined, and mature in the period following the embassy takeover and the Soviet invasion of Afghanistan), the media cannot be counted on to transmit them without a certain amount of noise. Just how much noise or malinterpretation depends too on other elements of the campaign itself, such as *past* messages that would have required great foresight to control (in order to convert them into effective *lead*). Finally, messages about the candidate also depend for some of their meaning on the actions of other systems, including other countries and opposition campaigns, which are virtually impossible to control.

The Carter campaign was thus a cybernetic system that functioned well but was degraded by elements within itself, events that preceded it, and outside forces that it could not manage. Together these created a flow of electoral circumstances that could not be overcome.

ANDERSON

John Anderson's general election campaign began late in April, well before those of Carter and Reagan, which depended formally on their parties' national conventions. In ways that are significant despite being obvious, the campaign shows how difficult it is for an independent candidate to be competitive in a presidential election, especially given the current rules of the game. It also illustrates less obvious organizational and strategic errors that an independent candidate is likely to make because of his other difficulties.

Let us consider first the rules of the game that stood in the way of Anderson. More important than any other is what might be called the general "two-party" rule. Despite the declining functions of parties in the electoral system, the fact is that in many respects

---

and which he answers 'Yessir,' with military correctness. To Powell and others, Mr. Carter is referred to as 'the Boss' or 'The President.' . . . It is never 'Jimmy' even in his most informal moments." New York *Times Magazine*, October 26, 1980, p. 76.

the Democratic and Republican parties are established *by rule* in presidential politics — rules that had powerful effects on the Anderson campaign.

Having announced his independent candidacy on April 24, John Anderson might have been expected to get a running start on Carter and Reagan, who still faced numerous state primaries and conventions, and of course their respective national conventions. However, not only did all of these events serve to keep the two candidates before the eyes of the public, but also upon their nominations they were automatically placed on the ballots of all the states. Anderson, in contrast, was faced with having to qualify in every state according to a particular set of procedures, if procedures existed at all. Michigan, for example, had procedures for parties only, not for an independent candidate; so a special party had to be formed.[14]

The first and unavoidable step, therefore, was to get on the ballots, and the step was difficult. It could not be eased by formulating a single strategy, since each state had different rules. What is more, by the time Anderson announced, the filing deadlines had already passed in five states, including the important state of Ohio. Then there were other state restrictions that seemed to apply to Anderson — for instance the "sore loser" statutes, which prohibited candidates who had previously run in a party primary from running again.

It was evident that these legal impediments could not be overcome by enthusiastic volunteers alone. Expertise was required, and this was expensive. As we have already seen, the campaign hired the Washington law firm of Arnold and Porter to do the ballot access research and Washington attorney Mitchell Rogovin to direct the detailed legal effort — an effort that was made greater by the DNC's determined challenges in state after state (under the direction of the Carter campaign). In the end, Anderson won every challenge and succeeded, but not until the end of September and the drain of most of his money and time — resources that could not be used for other campaign purposes, such as public exposure.

The second set of rules concerned campaign financing. As an independent, Anderson would not receive the $29.4 million (plus the $4.6 million for the national party) subsidy given both Carter and Reagan. At the same time, his contributions were subject to the same limits as they were earlier (such as no more than $1,000 from any one person and so on), thus preventing him from becoming financially competitive through large contributions from wealthy individuals and forcing him to allocate resources to collect resources. (A few wealthy individuals, such as Norman Lear and Stewart Mott, did make substantial independent contributions in Anderson's behalf.) Of course, the FEC record-keeping and reporting requirements also applied fully. In addition, since the campaign had already started to raise most of its money through direct-mail solicitations, still another federal regulation worked against Anderson. While the major party candidates could mail campaign literature for 3.1 cents per ounce, others who had not received more than 5 percent of the vote in 1976 had to pay 8.4 cents, a substantial difference, especially for a campaign that was very short of money and personnel.

The third rule could not have been more obvious. A presidential ticket required a vice-presidential candidate. Indeed, a few states had this requirement as a formal law, making it necessary for Anderson to find a running mate before his ballot access effort could be completed. Once again, while for the Carter and Reagan campaigns the process of recruiting vice-presidential candidates might be painful and disruptive, it was institutionalized and brief. Not so for Anderson, who confronted far more than the usual problems. Added to the normal requirements of personal compatibility, bringing votes to the ticket, and so on, whoever was Anderson's choice faced a career problem. Whereas numerous Republican and Democratic politicians would have been quite willing to run even on a losing ticket with Reagan or Carter, because of future rewards within their parties, for such a partisan to run with Anderson could just as well be political suicide. Thus Anderson needed to find someone who was publicly attractive but not aspiring to higher elective office as a Democrat or Republican.

A fourth set of rules reflected a different part of the two-party system already mentioned. In all the states and thousands of local communities the Democratic and Republican parties had some semblance of organization. As hollow and feeble as these organizations might be, they did provide some points of contact for the national campaigns. And occasionally a local organization would be quite robust — able to provide substantial numbers of workers and effective services. Thus as soon as they were nominated, Carter and Reagan, with no personal effort, had national organizations that Anderson lacked. Of course all the candidates had the state and local units of their own campaign organizations, built up during the contest for nomination. Yet here again Anderson was far behind because his campaign had not been very extensive and at least some of his local activists were loyal Republicans who refused to turn against their party.

Related to Anderson's organizational disadvantages were the party identifications and expectations of the electorate. Despite the softening of party identification in the United States — something that was extremely important to Anderson throughout his campaign — more or less two-thirds of the electorate identified themselves as Democrats or Republicans.[15] This psychological attachment has tended to be the most important single factor in presidential elections.[16] Furthermore, the *expectation* that only a major party candidate had a chance of winning a presidential election was even more deeply ingrained. For those who had this expectation, it was irrational for all but the most alienated to choose Anderson, since a rational voter would support the least bad of those candidates who had a reasonable chance of winning.[17]

There were early (April to June) indications, however, that this last rule was shaky, as public opinion polls showed considerable dissatisfaction with the probable major party nominees, Carter and Reagan, and Anderson received about 20 percent support among the three. Then, in May, an ABC/Harris poll was released that had asked who voters would support "if Anderson actually had a chance of winning?" The result nationally was Reagan 35 percent, Carter 31 percent, and Anderson 29 percent. In the eight largest states, it was Anderson 36 percent, Carter 31 percent, and Reagan 29 percent. Ignoring the very slippery logic of such a question (since under what conditions would Anderson "actually have a chance of winning"?), the Harris news release of May 15 concluded that "Anderson now possesses the potential for being the first independent to win the White House in American history."

Probably this Harris poll was the most widely discussed of those taken in the 1980 campaign. It provided at least a temporary indication that Americans might change their voting behavior with a change in the rules* and a very large morale boost for those

---

*This cannot be pushed very far, however, since the "rule" was in fact a pattern of expectations, and the "break" comprised only answers to a "suppose that" question. It was interesting primarily because of the circular pattern of inferences that followed.

activists either already working, or considering working, in the Anderson campaign.

It was in this opinion context that the Anderson campaign was begun. As we have already seen, its leadership group was very modest in size, having been reduced after Anderson withdrew from the Republican contest and several members of his staff resigned rather than go on with an independent effort. Moreover, the top leadership was to a large extent self-recruited, and it was now joined by Washington lawyers and David Garth, a New York political consultant of high repute, but also of high demands for authority. Thus the new campaign was led by people who, for the most part, had not worked together before and had little experience in presidential elections.

Getting on state ballots was necessarily the first order of business, and raising money either the first or second. Because some type of petitioning was required in almost all the states to get on the ballot as an independent, this function was coupled with building state and local organizations. Anderson was receiving favorable, and relatively extensive, coverage in the media.[18] Volunteers were relatively abundant, especially in key industrial states. As it developed, the unprecedented ballot access effort was impressive. Yet it did not go quickly; it drained away over half of the campaign's resources; and it did not create an effective grass-roots organization.

The trouble was threefold. First, the new campaign was faced with "doing everything at once." To be sure, some of this was true for all campaigns, but for Anderson's in the spring and summer of 1980 it was worse. Anderson had to get on the ballot, raise very large amounts of money, write a platform, keep track of domestic and international events, build an organization, and find a running mate — all as soon as possible. The Carter and Reagan campaigns had done these things over a period of years.

Second, the campaign was experiencing internal conflicts. Garth was accustomed to selling his services as a full package, with his firm doing everything from polling to media commercials.[19] In style and reputation he was a powerhouse. His forte was in constructing a candidate's image through the mass media, after careful analysis of both the candidate and the constituency. He demanded control over his campaigns in order to prevent conflicting messages from being projected to the electorate. Under the circumstances it was inevitable that conflicts would occur between Garth and some of Anderson's older staff.[20] Such conflicts should not be seen only as differences of personality and style. These are always present in campaigns but with time and experience can be "shaken out," as they were in the Reagan campaign. The difficulty for Anderson was that the infusion of new and demanding staff occurred suddenly and very late, when the pressures were high and the leadership group was quite small.[21] Most of these people were not only notably independent-minded but also had political backgrounds considerably to the left of the candidate's.

Third, the resources of the campaign were far too few to support the functions that needed to be performed. Thus field volunteers were used quite effectively when the ballot access effort was underway in a state, but the staff resources were too few and inexperienced to maintain the organization after the access drive had moved on. Volunteer workers would find themselves relatively cut off, unable to get quick, authoritative responses from the Washington headquarters. For their part, the central decision-makers were continually worried about money and overloaded by the pressures of time. Following the May-June high point, the growth of direct-mail contributions slowed, and the polls began to show a wavering in Anderson support. A ten-day television commercial to raise funds was used between July and August, but it cost more than it brought in, forcing the campaign to cancel or defer major events designed to gain publicity. During much of July and August it found itself forgotten by the media, which were concentrating on the Republican and Democratic national conventions. This naturally affected both public attention and contributions, which fell in August, rose in September, and fell again in October.

Nevertheless, the Anderson campaign continued to develop during July and August. As the Democratic convention was ending, Anderson announced the appointment of Mary Crisp — until a few weeks before the cochairman of the Republican party — as his national chairman. This was quite a coup, since Mrs. Crisp left her Republican position over the issues of abortions and equal rights for women — issues that could be expected to draw support to Anderson.[22] By the end of August, Anderson had recruited Patrick Lucy, former governor of Wisconsin and deputy manager of the Kennedy campaign, as his running mate. But this was followed by a major shake-up of the campaign staff. The deputy campaign director (Ed Coyle), treasurer (Francis Sheean), and schedule organizer (Michael Fernandez) left, and the press secretary was replaced. Tom

Mathews assumed the press position and David Garth moved in to take full control of the Washington headquarters and campaign operations.

At this point, with Anderson's ratings in the polls gradually sinking to the 14-15 percent range, the campaign was heavily dependent upon the decisions of others — on the television networks for coverage of his campaign appearances, and on the League of Women Voters (and Carter and Reagan) for his participation in the hoped-for presidential debates. Ironically, the very success of the campaign in such states as New York, where Anderson was nominated by the Liberal party, convinced Carter to persist in refusing to participate in a debate that included Anderson. Even without Caddell's more precise findings, this decision by the Carter campaign can hardly be considered unreasonable. For example, a poll taken for Senator Jacob Javits of New York in late July showed Carter running *fourth* in a field of Reagan, Anderson, and Undecided (in that order). Unless Anderson could achieve a major breakthrough in public support that would enable him to overtake and pass one of the other major candidates, any indication of strength on his part could be counted on to generate countermeasures by either Carter or Reagan, or both.

As we have seen, however, Anderson's participation suited Reagan's strategic needs, and a League-sponsored debate between the two was held in Baltimore on September 21. Anderson's performance appeared strong to commentators on the scene (and to Anderson TV parties around the country), but Reagan again showed his ability to impress a mass television audience, and the debate did not produce the sharp rise in public support that the campaign was depending on.

Anderson did not get another chance to confront either one or both of the major party candidates on national television, and the last month of his campaign was anticlimactic. Excluded from the second presidential debate because of low poll ratings, Anderson found these measures of public support continuing to fall until they stood at between 5 and 9 percent (depending on which public poll is referred to). The campaign's fund-raising efforts through direct mail never flagged, going on to the end with a mixture of frustration and success. By mid-September his "list" had stabilized and thus the same people received plea after plea (including requests for loans to be repaid with federal funds after the election), while their response progressively declined. The Federal Election Commission agreed that Anderson would be treated as a third-party candidate, and he was thus eligible for federal reimbursement funds based on his percentage of the vote in November (5 percent or more). Eventually, the campaign raised a total of $7.3 million, $2.7 million of which were federal funds, and spent $6.5 million — a very modest amount covering the campaign from beginning to end. Lacking finances, the campaign was unable to run the Garth television commercials designed to build up Anderson's public image (and support) before the fall. Several of these ads were eventually shown in the waning days of the election, affecting at best 1 or 2 percent of the popular vote, and thus the amount of federal reimbursement funds.

Underlying every other problem for the campaign was the question of credibility: How could Anderson expect to win? Except for a brief period in May and June, the question was ever-present, restraining contributors, potential workers and voters, and the internal morale of the campaign itself.[23] It became more nagging during September and October. As he campaigned in the field, Anderson's greatest irritation was to be asked why he was running, prompted by the obvious possibility that he might cost Carter the election while having no chance himself. From the start Anderson insisted that he was running to win; that he would not be a "spoiler"; and that he was conducting "a campaign of ideas." Yet by October it was evident that Anderson would not win. Then the repetition of the question aggravated the irritation because it indicated that the ideas part of the campaign was no longer of much interest to the media — thus suggesting to both the candidate and those around him that there was little purpose to the enterprise.

Nevertheless, the campaign continued. Numerous commentators pointed out that this was necessary to capture enough votes to qualify for the federal funding that would cover the campaign's debts — comments that further demeaned the effort. Surely that explanation was plausible, especially since no secret was made of the campaign's interest in the reimbursement funds.* It did

---

*This was made explicit in a concluding series of direct-mail solicitations, in which previous contributors were asked to give again — but now much larger amounts in the form of loans, which would be repaid after the election with funds from the reimbursement subsidy.

not, however, get to the central characteristics of John Anderson as a candidate, or of his campaign.

Cybernetically, Anderson's "National Unity" campaign was a failure. It was a system that lacked resources of information and was relatively weak in communication and control. We saw earlier that the general election campaign originated on the initiative of Tom Mathews in consultation with a small group of people — Anderson, his wife Keke, a few aides from the primary campaign, and other "outsiders," such as David Garth and Norman Lear. The newcomers represented anything but Republican thinking; they were liberals, whose work had been for Democrats and reformist causes.[24] Anderson had "caught the attention of some homeless artisans and angels of the New Politics."[25] Thus the independent campaign was launched with strong elements of imagination, reform, and untested hypotheses about American politics.

Based on a series of "what ifs," a campaign scenario was constructed that was then refined into a strategy. We might think of each major factor usually needed for a successful presidential campaign — such as resources of money and people, an attractive candidate, favorable public attitudes, media, and so forth — as taking a range of values. That is, the candidate could be more or less attractive and still win (if the other factors were strong enough to compensate). The Anderson strategists were generally well-informed about the range of values but chose to place their campaign in decidedly optimistic positions on each range or scale. For example, given the possible proportions of the electorate that were disgusted with the major party candidates, and therefore supposedly susceptible to Anderson's appeal, the upper rather than the lower part of the range was selected as a basis for planning. These assessments of political reality tended to be justified by a commitment to reform, and by the view that Anderson embodied the qualities needed in American politics.

As the campaign was put into operation, it soon became evident that a number of its optimistic assumptions were probably invalid. Feedback, however, was impaired by a lack of money, experience, and available corrections. What, for example, was the campaign to do when desperately needed news coverage of Anderson was lost to the Democratic and Republican national conventions? Or when the ballot access effort proved more expensive (and difficult) than anticipated? In controlling operations, feedback often required the addition of new staff, the replacement of existing staff, or more lawyers, more publicity, more telephones, and so on. These resources of information and control were meager, a shortage compounded by the lack of systematic polling that might have provided the campaign a more accurate picture of its electoral environment.

As for higher-order feedback, or learning, the difficulties were even greater because the appropriate adjustments might challenge "true beliefs" of the campaigners. For example, as evidence accumulated that what Mathews had supposed was a large "middle" group of "available dissidents" actually was not that large, was the campaign prepared to shift to the ideological extremes, or to just stop altogether? Neither alternative was acceptable to the chief decision-makers, and more refined feedback needed large amounts of the information mentioned above. Learning did take place in the campaign. There was, of course, the basic change in the system when the independent candidacy began; but during the general election campaign the most visible instances occurred with the formulation of the platform and the staff reorganization of August. In every case, however, the quality of the learning was highly uncertain because the amount of information upon which it was based was so limited.* This should not detract from the cybernetic nature of Mathews' late February analysis that began the change from a Republican to an independent campaign:

> Mathews began by comparing Anderson to a man speaking to a roomful of people who sat politely, their hands folded in their laps, listening to his message, but not responding. But, Mathews said, the man's voice is being piped into another room filled with more people and they were going crazy, yelling, cheering, jumping up and down. Those people, Mathews told Anderson, were not Republicans, and they were the audience he believed Anderson should begin to appeal to more directly in his campaign.[26]

Unfortunately, Anderson's attentive and responsive audience needed great expansion before it would constitute a competitive electoral base.

---

*It is interesting to note that the major source of empirical information about the electorate was responses to the early direct-mail solicitations. Mathews was quite systematic about his, testing 16 different mailing lists and comparing their returns with those from many others used in his business.

At the core of the campaign system was the candidate himself. A man of great knowledge and pride, Anderson could appear intelligent, principled, and courageous but also humorless, preachy, and self-righteous. Many viewers perceived him with a combination of these qualities when he debated Reagan on September 21. Well informed, he liked to speak extemporaneously, especially at field appearances. Sometimes, as we saw in the Iowa debate, statements of great eloquence would result, but often the speeches would meander and lose their audiences. When Anderson attempted to correct this by using staff-prepared copy based especially on the detailed campaign platform, the statements usually were ignored by the media. Of course part of the problem lay in the media, but another part was in the nature of the candidate. The following reflects the characterizations of various journalists who traveled with the campaign, and we see again that it was a bad year for "loners":

> Anderson's loner quality has made him difficult for his would-be managers to manage. . . . Candidates do need advice. It is difficult to tell when advice becomes manipulation, and apparently Anderson thinks it does very soon. "He's exasperating, maddeningly self-directed," says one of his would-be advisers. Another describes him as "unpenetrable."[27]

Plainly, one of the very qualities that made Anderson appealing to many Americans, the image of being one's "own man," did not lend itself to the adaptability needed to suit diverse audiences and a very sensitive press. This was critical, since Anderson *was the message*. No party symbol or phalanx of spokesmen were there to supplement his personal appearances as sources of information for the electorate. This was especially true given the lack of media advertisements.

The messages Anderson sent out were decoded and interpreted in various ways by the media and different segments of the electorate. Loyal Democrats, for example, and some loyal Republicans, "heard" Anderson as a "spoiler." He no longer had a traditional party identification through which, for partisans, only favorable messages would be filtered. It turned out that, apart from an understanding and appreciative audience of well-educated, relatively affluent, and independent-minded citizens, Anderson's messages lacked compelling meaning for the American electorate.[28] In some respects he replaced Jerry Brown as the "new class" candidate of 1980, even though this did not fit Anderson's basically conservative style. Anderson's inability to adjust his message thus limited his campaign's success in reaching out to other population groups and a larger electorate.

For the most part the media were kind to Anderson, partly because he was a "new" quality in the political landscape. Indeed, one study shows that he received a more favorable press than any other candidate during the preconvention period,[29] but the amount of media coverage was always less than that of the leading contenders of the time, and this disparity increased after the national conventions. It is fair to say that through most of 1980 Anderson was covered more fully and favorably than would be expected for a candidate of his electoral support.

Interestingly enough, in the final days of the campaign Anderson suddenly seemed to relax. He became more open, humorous, and self-depreciating in manner, and he delivered some of the best speeches of his campaign. This feedback evidently occurred because the candidate realized not only that the election was lost but also that at least for the accompanying journalists his pattern of action was not communicating what he wanted it to. By then, however, the campaign was losing cohesion as its members began attending to their personal futures, which clearly would not be in an Anderson White House. The campaign ended as it had begun, with limited input, restricted feedback, and output resources that were far too small to communicate effectively with the American electorate. John Anderson received 6.6 percent of the popular vote.

REAGAN

No campaign demonstrated the centrality of the candidate in a more interesting way than Ronald Reagan's. One element of this, which had been seen on and off during the primaries, reappeared vividly during the period following the Republican convention, when the campaign was attempting to set the stage for a wider effort in September and October by solidifying its conservative and Republican base. This was Reagan's tendency to make "gaffes." The problem had nagged the campaign from the start, when John Sears attempted to deal with it by keeping the candidate's field appearances to a minimum before the Iowa caucuses. As we saw, that tactic failed and was replaced by barnstorming in New Hampshire.

Now in August, George Bush visiting mainland China in an effort to give the Republican ticket an apperance of greater foreign policy expertise, Reagan, in a series of field appearances, became bogged down in issues of U.S. relations with the Nationalist government on Taiwan.* Reagan's remarks, in addition to undercutting Bush, made the candidate seem uninformed about the actual formal status of U.S.-Chinese relations.

Next, caught in an unexpected joint appearance with a television evangelist, the candidate appeared to associate himself with the radical right — at the same time when campaign strategy called for the construction of a "programmatic and unifying" image (in response to the thrust of the Carter and Mondale convention speeches, which painted Reagan as an absurdly right-wing figure). Finally, there were Reagan's statements that the Vietnam War was a "noble cause," and that air pollution was caused mainly by volcanos and trees.† Consequently, by the end of August media attention was focused not on policy and performance problems of the Carter administration but on Reagan misstatements.

The campaign's reaction to this unfavorable situation (Carter had almost drawn even to Reagan in the polls at this point) reflected

---

*Conservative Republicans had long advocated U.S. recognition of the Nationalist government rather than the Communist government on the mainland. Nixon's reopening of relations between Washington and Peking seemed to quiet the Nationalist faction in the party, but the faction remained.

†Air pollution provided one of the few cases of humor in the campaign. At an appearance in Steubenville, Ohio, Reagan got off on a rambling discussion of pollution, in which he observed that Mount St. Helens had produced more sulphur dioxide than automobiles in the United States over a ten-year period. He also repeated a previous statement that trees were generating 93 percent of the nitrogen oxides in the air. Then the next day he said that air pollution in California had been "substantially controlled" during his administration (at the very moment when Los Angeles was under a smog alert). A few days afterward, at a campaign stop in California, the candidate confronted a sign attached to a tree reading: "Chop me down before I kill again."

Both the Carter campaign and environmental scientists from around the country reacted loudly and swiftly to these statements, and Reagan tried to squirm out where he could, usually making matters worse. For example, the day after his comment about California air pollution, he denied having said it was substantially under control.

its own analysis both of its candidate and of the fact that there had been another organizational slump within the campaign following the national convention. The candidate's speeches, which were written in the Arlington, Virginia, headquarters, appeared to be less at fault than the lack of field checks before they were delivered — since Reagan himself had inserted the "noble cause" line, for example. It was also believed that the candidate's scheduling and advance work (resulting in his sharing a platform with the evangelist) had been too loose.* At the same time, Reagan's aides realized (with some bitterness) that the media representatives traveling with the campaign were now working at a higher level of intensity than during the primaries.

"Packaging" corrections were made. The speech-writing schedule was pushed back so that more of the candidate's advisers could review the drafts before they were delivered. Ron Walker, who had been Nixon's chief advance man, was brought in to handle the same position for Reagan. Stewart Spencer, a veteran public relations man from California, who had managed Reagan's 1966 and 1970 gubernatorial campaigns, and who had worked in Ford's campaign in 1976, was assigned to travel with the candidate. Spencer had actually been with the campaign since the summer but had not been in the traveling unit. He combined experience, seniority, and personal closeness to Reagan, so that he could exert more influence on the candidate to avoid mistakes. (During the preceding weeks, junior staff traveling with Reagan had been unable to keep him away from questioning reporters and thus occasions for gaffes.)

The task of making Reagan less accessible to the media was by no means left to Spencer alone. All other senior staff in the traveling party, including Press Secretary Lyn Nofziger, were involved. The candidate's aides were particularly determined to keep national "pool" reporters (whose responsibility was to stay near the candidate and report closeup events to the other journalists) at bay, since they were more sophisticated than members of the local media. Patently this was an effort to restrict the flow of information about the candidate, allowing him to appear only in easily controlled "set" pieces.

As the campaign progressed through September, Reagan's general election standard "stump speeches" were perfected. They differed

---

*Interesting enough, this also was a very bad period in John Anderson's scheduling, with the candidate often finding himself in places of little political significance. This was followed by the late-summer organizational shakeup.

from those of the primaries in being more moderate, more directed to independents and weak Democrats.[30] To keep the media interested, inserts, usually framed in Arlington, were strategically added. The charge that Carter was guilty of a "cynical misuse of power" in revealing that the United States had developed the "stealth bomber" was an example.* It was a time of thrust and parry between the two campaigns, with each attempting to keep the other off balance, and to be prepared to counter any statement by the other *before* the traveling press asked. It was a time when media attention seemed absorbed in Carter's "meanness" and Reagan's gaffes. It is also important to note that through his standard speeches Reagan developed the major phrases and stories that would appear later in the presidential debates and in his half-hour television commercials. They were an excellent illustration of feedback.

After the moderate organizational shakeup at the end of August, worked out in a meeting between Reagan and his top aides at his northern Virginia home, the campaign assumed a pattern of operation that continued to the election. Major strategic decisions were made at the Arlington headquarters. There, poll data were also received and analyzed; public policy research was conducted and integrated with input from the numerous policy advisory teams; media ideas were originated; speeches were written; and the field organizations were directed.

But coordination was erratic. William Casey, formally in charge of the headquarters, lacked the personal vigor and political skill to pull the diverse operations together, and communications often flowed around rather than through him. Such decisions as whether the stump speeches should be more or less conservative usually involved a good deal of give and take, and sometimes were modified by the candidate in the field. As a whole, decision-making was slowed by a cumbersome, often divided organization, yet there was considerable flexibility. For example, after the flap over Reagan's charge that Carter had begun his campaign on Labor Day in Tuscumbia, Alabama, "the city that gave birth to ... the Ku Klux Klan," the decision was made at headquarters to issue an apology, which

---

*"Stealth" was a technology involving various electronic devices that had the effect of making a plane invisible to enemy radar. It was "leaked" by the Carter campaign in an obvious effort to blunt Republican assertions that U.S. defenses had been allowed to deteriorate.

was done, but against the wishes of the traveling team, who nevertheless took it in stride. The campaign was now focused on the goal of victory, with ideological and procedural issues softened as much as possible.

Following the prenomination campaign, Richard Wirthlin had become the campaign's leading (but not sole) strategist. At every point his polls were brought to bear upon the definition of the situation and the decisions to be made — not just to respond to issues but also to create issues. Although Wirthlin's survey questions did not achieve the subtlety of Caddell's "semantic differential" variations, his polling was definitely competitive in terms of frequency, accuracy, and speed and complexity of analysis. Furthermore, in terms of analysis, Wirthlin accomplished what may fairly be termed a technical breakthrough of his own by refining the simulation of electorates. Originally developed as the "Simulmatics" project by a team of academic researchers for the 1960 Kennedy campaign,[31] the analytic approach had generally lain fallow, partly because of its size and expense. Essentially it involved the use of an extended series of surveys to build a very large computerized memory of how various segments of the electorate responded to different issues and events. Wirthlin's 1980 version, complete with an oversized electronic display enabling campaign strategists to view results directly, was used to simulate electoral responses to themes or issues — thus giving decision-makers the ability to "test" possible actions before they were taken. Because Wirthlin had considerable state-level data, he could also predict how the electoral vote would be affected. This was a dramatic use of computerized survey information that magnified the potential of current polls as an aid to decision-making. It was a cybernetic triumph.

The campaign was particularly strong in field organization. As we noted in our earlier review of the preconvention campaigns, Reagan's own state and local organizations had been built up gradually through the 1970s, nurtured by his occasional speaking appearances, and exercised in both the 1976 and 1980 primaries. Based on long-term ideological loyalty, the enthusiasm of these workers was now heightened by the prospect of final victory. During the summer these Reagan activists were integrated with the state and local organizations that had been built up by the Republican National Committee for more than a decade. One of the important reasons for keeping Bill Brock as RNC chairman was his proven effectiveness in continuing to strengthen the party's organization.[32] By September an elaborate and well-financed get-out-the-vote plan was underway, aided by the 1979 amendments to the Federal Election Campaign Act that allowed virtually unlimited local party contributions of certain types (which the Republicans were in a much better position to take advantage of than the Democrats). To all of this was added the media contributions of "independent PACs" that were almost entirely in support of Reagan.[33] The integration of the Reagan and Republican party organizations was by no means perfect, but it was very good and vastly superior to its Democratic counterpart. Moreover, it was aided by a systematic effort in the campaign to schedule Reagan appearances in areas, such as Philadelphia, where the get-out-the-vote project needed a boost.

Not surprisingly, the campaign's aggressive effort to "protect" the candidate from the press was quickly noted and soon began to draw negative commentary by journalists in all the media. Often at Reagan's appearances the protection was patently obvious, with Nofziger pushing and shouting "No interviews" when reporters happened to get within earshot of the candidate — giving commentators ample reason to speculate about whether Reagan was being patronized by his aides; whether this separation from the press was designed to hide serious weaknesses of the candidate; and whether this presaged a similar pattern in the White House. Naturally, the media's concern with these issues — and the "human interest" aspects of the protected candidate — distracted them from the points the campaign was attempting to make, and the campaign complained to the media that too little attention was being given to the substance of Reagan's attacks on Carter (just as later the Carter campaign would complain that the media should pay less attention to their candidate's meanness and more to Reagan's record). In short, minimizing Reagan's gaffes projected a negative image of its own.[34]

There were continuing disagreements among and between the traveling and headquarters staffs about how vigorous this candidate protection effort should be. Essentially, the issue was not settled but resolved when the campaign responded to a Carter assertion that Reagan was being "muzzled" by holding a press conference and then going on to debate Anderson. Reagan, too, would sometimes just break out of his protective ring and disarm his critics. For example, after visiting a Lithuanian community in Chicago:

When Reagan begins to answer a question from a local radio reporter ("What did you think of your welcome here?"), Nofziger and another aide almost have apoplexy. "*No interviews!*" Nofziger shouts, waving his arms and diving for the reporter. "Just let me reply to this one," Reagan says to Nofziger calmly, and then he says, "Most heartwarming. . . ."[35]

With an inextricable combination of "personal" and policy issues then competing for attention (for example, Carter's meanness; Reagan's militarism; Carter's incompetence; Reagan's simple-mindedness; Carter's inflation; Reagan's Kemp-Roth economic ideas mired in the past; and so on), the media seemed to follow a pattern of focusing on the President's foibles for four or five days, then switching to Reagan's, then back to Carter's. It was evident that neither campaign was able to control either the "herd" tendency of the media or their inclination to favor "personalized" stories rather than stated policy positions.

The major question that confronted the campaign approximately from mid-September to mid-October was whether Reagan should debate the President. This, in turn, was closely linked to fears of an "October surprise." The early position that the candidate was eager to debate, but only if Anderson was included, compromised the opposing arguments of Reagan's top advisers. One side, including Casey, Meese, and, at the start, Wirthlin, argued that Reagan needed to meet Carter in order to overcome his "presidential" advantage. It was a "higher risk" position. The other side, including Timmons, Spencer, and Nofziger, maintained that the risks were too high, since the President had the advantage of inside information and Reagan was ahead anyway. All agreed on the desirability of including Anderson, since Wirthlin's polls were showing the same thing as Caddell's — that Anderson would draw more votes away from the President. Debate proponents, however, were afraid that by insisting on Anderson's participation, the campaign might allow Carter to slip away.

Decision-making on this issue was highly incremental. The candidate's position was shaped and reshaped in response to changing poll results, Carter's position, suggestions by the League of Women Voters, changing assessments of advisers, and of course media commentary. Reagan's own stance was generally cautious. He felt that the inclusion of Anderson not only would serve as a buffer against Carter's known ability to command details, but also would assist Anderson in stripping liberal voters from the President. There was respect for Anderson's debating skills within the Reagan camp, but little fear, since the two had debated before in New Hampshire and Illinois, with no ill-effects on Reagan.* Thus the decision to debate Anderson alone on September 21 was easy — giving Anderson public exposure and reminding the viewers that once again the President was avoiding an open confrontation, just as he did against Kennedy. When it became evident, following the Reagan-Anderson debate, that the candidate had gained against *both* opponents (and that Anderson was unlikely to maintain sufficient poll rating to qualify under the League's rules), the differences between the high- and low-risk advisers continued but were eased somewhat by the stronger showing of Reagan in Wirthlin's polls compared to those of the public polling agencies.

Overhanging campaign strategists throughout this September-October period was the specter of an event generated by the president that would alter the basic dispositions of the electorate — specifically one involving the release of the American hostages in Iran: an "October Surprise." Because the strategists were convinced that the Carter campaign would try *something* of this sort — a move over which Reagan had no control — it had been decided in June to begin talking to the press about the "surprise" in order gradually to move the idea into public, and at least media, consciousness. The aim was to create a public sensitivity so that if there was a presidential announcement that the hostage crisis had been resolved, it would be seen as a campaign gimmick. In addition, most of the strategists expected a Carter surge in the last week of the campaign. This was based, first, on long-term evidence that marginal voters turn to the incumbent near the end, and, second, on the tendency of wavering Democrats to "return home." (The Carter campaign was anticipating the same movement of the electorate for the same reasons at this point.) These expectations, difficult to refute, were the basic grounds for the high-risk argument that even a moderate lead in the polls could not be counted on and that Carter had to be confronted directly.

The "battle of the commercials" also proceeded through September and October, with the ads for both sides containing accurate

---

*In Illinois the other candidates concentrated on John Anderson, considered the front-runner, attacking him for his "non-Republican" positions, and so forth.

indications of their current strategies. Reagan's ads were produced by Peter Dailey, who was virtually as efficient as Rafshoon in moving from strategic decisions to commercial productions and airings. In this arena, too, the expectation of a final Carter surge led the campaign to budget considerably more money for advertising in the final two weeks than did the Carter campaign.[36]

At the beginning of October, campaign decision-makers formally reviewed the strategy for the final weeks.[37] In addition to the question of debating Carter, both the media and travel schedules were reviewed so that state targeting could be revised to match developing electoral dispositions in the field. This major review, long scheduled as part of Wirthlin's overall design for the campaign, did not mean the end of adjustments. As the intense polling of the final two weeks showed additional states falling into the competitive category, some media were diverted into these also.

In any event, during the first two weeks of October, despite a series of new commercials (by both sides), there were some indications in public polls that Carter was once again closing the gap. In fact, Wirthlin did not agree with this assessment. His polls showed Reagan maintaining a six-point lead (Reagan 43 percent, Carter 37 percent, Anderson 10 percent, and Undecided 11 percent), and doing even better in electoral votes.[38] Nevertheless, in view of the electorate's "volatility," which had been so widely observed over the preceding year, Wirthlin was not able to assure the other decision-makers that this lead could be held. Feeling that the time could be better spent on other things, however, Wirthlin now opposed the debate, as did his counterpart, Caddell, in the Carter campaign. Yet just as Carter was trapped by earlier events, Reagan's campaign could not throw off the conviction that Carter would attempt a break in the hostage situation before the election. The timing of the debate was therefore important, with Reagan's people trying to position it as close to the election as possible. Carter wanted it earlier so that there would be more time to overcome any ill-effects and to benefit from the expected last-minute Democratic swing.

On October 21 the two campaigns compromised. The debate was scheduled for October 28, a week before the election. In the words of John Osborn writing in The New Republic, "it no longer was a matter of one wanting a debate, the other ducking a debate. Both Carter and Reagan, frightening close in the polls, were afraid not to debate."[39] While Reagan's aides remained divided, and his chief strategist had switched to opposing the debate, the basic logic of the situation overcame the opposition. The campaign had not proceeded smoothly according to plan. Gaffes had distracted public attention in August, and then there was the "muzzling of the candidate" issue in September. Despite a heavy concentration on Carter's record in the early October commercials, and the effort to make the candidate look more moderate, Carter had at least partially succeeded in making Reagan look "dangerous" to many voters. Wirthlin's own polls showed that 54 percent of the electorate agreed with that description.[40] Thus the campaign's strategists saw the debate as a means to "absorb the uncertainty" that they had as practicing politicians, despite the formidable resources of information in Wirthlin's polls and simulations. Their strategy for the debate was to have the candidate hammer away at the economy and show, both in manner and content, that he was peaceable and presidential.

The last week before the election was more satisfying to Reagan than to Carter for some very definite cybernetic reasons. Convinced as they were that Carter would attempt to pull a favorable event out of his presidential hat, Reagan's strategists did considerably more than plant the expectation of a "surprise" in both media and public consciousness. Information input and output of the campaign reached exceptionally high levels in the last ten days. Major inputs were of two types. The first was field operations, which are estimated (from Wirthlin's polls) to have made at least twice as many voter contacts as those of the Democrats.

The second type comprised Wirthlin's public opinion polls, which were less extensive than Caddell's before the general election as a whole, and more extensive after the middle of October. During this period both campaigns were essentially polling continuously, but Wirthlin was "tracking" 10 of the large states and 11 of the smaller ones, while Caddell concentrated on the largest states alone. (Of course, in both cases the national public as a whole was also being covered.) These inputs provided the campaign with a relatively exact picture of opinion and electoral vote situations, enabling it to adapt quite specifically, even in particular states.

Feedback was completed by the provision for large amounts of output. Of the campaign's total $15 million media budget, $6 million was spent in the last ten days, with media content and targeting based on both polls and field reports. The content was indicative of the campaign's most basic resource. Wirthlin had found as early as February that Reagan was "well known but not known well." This condition would make him vulnerable to Carter's negative message that he was erratic and dangerous, especially when it came to war and peace. Hence the campaign's television concentrated on Reagan himself in rather sophisticated productions. As Wirthlin explained, "our ads were about as exciting as milk and bread. We used head-on shots. Reagan was placed in a study. We were positioning Ronald Reagan as the President."[41]

These commercials were produced in the normal 30- and 60-second lengths, but also in major half-hour presentations, particularly in the three or four days preceding the election. All were designed to give the electorate information about the candidate directly, without fancy elaborations, thus reducing the credibility of the Carter messages (in speeches and commercials) that Reagan was a dangerous man.

The campaign's strategy was to use the debate for the same purpose. While Carter might have more details of government operations and world conditions, Reagan was to come across as a person who was reasonable, who could be understood and trusted, and who was *presidential*. Joined to this media output was that of another type — the intensive get-out-the-vote effort mentioned earlier. Together, these provisions of carefully tailored information to the electorate were rather complex feedback designed to protect the campaign against last-minute events that Carter might be able to manipulate. It was an impressive cybernetic plan, carried out to sharply limit the opposing campaign's ability to adapt.*

Even so, it is misleading to see the campaign as controlling events for which it could do little more than prepare. Specifically, these include the media's growing sensitivity to Carter's use of the hostage situation for political purposes. In the final campaign period, while Caddell's polls showed little diminution in the public's perception of the President's trustworthiness, there was little doubt about the

---

*As late as the middle of October the campaign made detailed provisions for the "surprise" last-minute return of the hostages. A special group constructed a complete strategy, including media productions and messages to the press, that would go into effect upon the announcement of the event. It was never used and its specific contents remain confidential.

media's *readiness* to interpret a last-minute hostage release in political terms.*

Second, because of various earlier positions taken on debating Kennedy, Anderson, and Reagan, the Carter campaign felt itself locked into the debate, even though it realized that the debate could not be won.[42] Third, although Wirthlin's polls showed Reagan with a steady and relatively comfortable lead, Caddell's polls did not; and more significantly for the Reagan campaign, neither did most of the public surveys at the time. Given the inherent uncertainties in sample surveys that we discussed in Chapter 1, most Reagan decision-makers decided it was safer to risk a debate than the *possibility* that vote dispositions were closer than Wirthlin calculated. Fourth, Reagan personally wanted to debate Carter at this point.

Finally, there was the Anderson factor. While both Caddell and Wirthlin found that electoral support for Anderson was fading by the first week of October, both also found, as earlier, that this support was not consistent across the states. Thus, small as it was, Anderson's support could have been a major factor in terms of electoral votes *if* the separation between the two major candidates was actually narrower than Wirthlin's polls showed.

The Reagan campaign closed with the accelerating and hectic activity so traditional in American politics, though now made more dramatic through the technology of high-speed jet aircraft. On the last day of the campaign the candidate made personal appearances in three states and spanned over half the country,† and in the evening he was seen for half an hour on nationwide television — in a program taped several days before and purchased with the resources the campaign had reserved for the end.

---

*Indeed, media commentators were commonly doing this in virtually all their speculation about reports and rumors about U.S.-Iranian negotiations. For example, a frequent point was that the Iranian government realized that it would be more difficult to deal with a Reagan administration than with Carter's, which presumably was much more willing to "deal" in order to salvage its desperate electoral situation. Thus the internal logic of this political situation constrained the Carter campaign whatever it did.

†Illinois, Oregon, and California. Carter's last day was even more ambitious. He touched down in six states from Ohio to Oregon to Washington, D.C. All three candidates kept up a fast pace throughout September and October; Carter especially. When he moved into the field, it was not uncommon for him to visit two or three states each day.

The electoral effects of this output "blitz" are quite uncertain, particularly since the movements of public opinion during the final week were seen differently by different pollsters.[43] There is general agreement, however, that Reagan's lead widened markedly between Sunday and Tuesday (election day), but the evidence indicates that this was a result not of Reagan or Republican popularity but rather of pent up frustrations with Carter's inability to control either the domestic economy or Iran.[44]

Looking back over Reagan's general election campaign, we see a cybernetic system that was strong but hardly an unrelieved triumph. We have already noted that its inputs of information were large and well-financed and that this information was used continually to make output adjustments — in short, feedback. Yet top-level decisions — the conversion of input into output — were often tortuous, affected by unwieldy organization and the difficulties key aides Casey and Meese had in coping with the demands of campaign politics. The internal management of the system lacked the cohesiveness and precision of the Carter campaign. On the other hand, mistakes were rarely repeated and feedback continued. A principal reason for this internal resilience was the ability to avoid ideological rigidities. Despite the conservative beliefs and associations of the candidate, which we saw could be sources of trouble in the primary and convention periods, campaign decision-makers were open to adjustments in the moderate direction. Underlying this was, first, the experience and expertise of middle-level campaign leaders (and the enthusiasm of field volunteers), who kept operations in high gear, even as top leaders vacilated; and, second, the willingness of the leadership to bring talented operatives into the campaign, including persons whose past loyalties had been to other candidates — perhaps the most notable instance being James Baker, who had been George Bush's chief of staff and who advanced quickly to a senior position in the campaign by October. These experienced and pragmatic leaders facilitated the flow of messages and the use of feedback with the goal of winning the election.[45]

A key element of the campaign that enhanced its cybernetic qualities was Richard Wirthlin's strategic planning. In this respect, Wirthlin did for Reagan what Jordan and Caddell did for Carter. Wirthlin's strategies were consistently based on the best available information, and his plans made explicit provisions for feedback and learning. Comparable to Jordan's in the Carter campaign, Wirthlin's strategic thinking provided some "lead" for the system, enabling it to anticipate difficulties before they occurred — the use of television commercials to increase the electorate's information about Reagan and of the news media to prepare for an "October surprise" being outstanding examples.* Of course his computer simulations were another. In a sense, Wirthlin, even though he was personally overextended, brought informational *stability* and focus to the system that otherwise lacked unified direction.

By far, however, the cybernetic goat and star of the campaign was its candidate, Ronald Reagan. Within his widely touted reputation as the "great communicator" was also the fact that Reagan was the message that the campaign had the most trouble controlling. Before any help from Carter, Reagan brought to the campaign a firmly established image of an extreme conservative (and an actor) that was decidedly unfavorable for many Americans. The campaign's cybernetic triumph was in limiting its losses from this image, an image that was worsened by the candidate's gaffes.[46] The central fact about these gaffes was that they almost always reflected the candidate's true beliefs or actual misinformation. Thus the campaign was faced with the dilemma of continuously balancing the negative message of a "muzzled" candidate with the negative messages of the candidate's own views. To the extent that it moved toward the first, a "packaged" candidate, information was obviously reduced or distorted, probably both.

The other side of Reagan was his unusual ability to "slide off" attacks and to project a positive message *in conjunction with* opposing candidates.[47] In no debate or joint appearance during the entire campaign was Reagan bested in the eyes of the public, and usually, as in the case of Carter, the attacking opponent came off looking worse than Reagan. As a campaigner, he took advice from his aides and adapted to different situations. Thus Reagan had better cybernetic qualities than Carter, which had the effect of limiting the negative evaluations he would otherwise have suffered.[48] In the whirlwind of the concluding weeks of the campaign and the decisive Republican victory on November 4, Reagan's ability to attract voters

---

*It is to be noted that these actions were begun long before the fall campaign. Media designed to provide background information about Reagan (his gubernatorial performance, and so on) were used in the primaries, and the October surprise was started in June.

appeared larger than life. More careful analyses now suggest that the major accomplishment of the Reagan campaign was to so communicate that Jimmy Carter was not prevented from losing the election. Considering that Ronald Reagan brought so many vulnerabilities into the campaign that the early prospects of his nomination had delighted Carter strategists, this was no mean feat.[49]

Yet if Reagan as a candidate was not an unalloyed success, the dimensions of his electoral victory were unquestionably formidable. He won 51 percent of the popular vote compared to Carter's 41 percent and carried every state except Georgia, Hawaii, Maryland, Minnesota, Rhode Island, West Virginia, and the District of Columbia (see Appendix D). Most striking was the consistency of the Republican gains in every region of the country. The popular early-summer speculations that the candidacy of John Anderson would deprive any candidate of an electoral vote majority, and throw the election into the House of Representatives, turned out to be quite idle. Reagan won 489 electoral votes to Carter's 49 and none for Anderson. Moreover, the efforts of the Reagan campaign to support and use the Republican party appeared to pay rich partisan dividends as the election returns showed a rising tide that lifted Republican boats across the nation.[50] The new President was thus presented with a Republican Senate and a compliable House of Representatives, which, though Democratic, had ample respect for Reagan's appeal.

In the final analysis, however, it was not Reagan but Carter's failure to pull out of his policy quagmire that convinced almost half the electorate it was "time for a change."[51] For a critical number of these voters, wary or fearful of Reagan, the campaign succeeded in imparting the image of a candidate that was *acceptable*. This was the major extent of its cybernetic impact. The administration of Jimmy Carter demonstrated that major discontinuities can exist between campaign expertise and governmental effectiveness. In the case of Ronald Reagan, it remains to be seen how much learning there is by his administration from his campaign, or whether the cybernetic pattern will just be repeated.

NOTES

1. Elizabeth Drew, "1980: The President," *The New Yorker*, October 20, 1980, p. 187.

2. Much of this episode is drawn from ibid., pp. 180 ff.

3. Elizabeth Drew, *The New Yorker*, June 23, 1980, pp. 73-74.

4. Drew, October 20, 1980, pp. 195-96.

5. Significantly, this pattern was established in Carter's gubernatorial campaign against Carl E. Sanders in Georgia. This led reporter Steven R. Weisman, writing in October 1980, to conclude: "By now, the three Georgians [Carter, Jordan, and Powell] are so confident in their instincts to go for the jugular that they stand by their tactics and pay little heed to the pieties of newspaper columnists and editorial writers who deplore their negative campaigns." "The Power of the Press Secretary," New York *Times Magazine*, October 26, 1980, p. 74.

6. James Reston of the New York *Times* observed: "Back on the press plane, enroute to Washington, the reporters analyze all this. It is astonishing how hostile most of them are about Carter personally. They agree that Reagan is unduly absorbed in the past, and offers many dubious remedies . . . , but somehow they still don't believe in Carter." New York *Times*, October 15, 1980, p. A31.

7. Probably the most dramatic instance was an advertisement placed in 100 newspapers about the middle of September aimed at black readers. It claimed that the Republicans were attempting to defeat Carter because of his record of appointing blacks and advancing civil rights and social welfare programs. When the Republicans objected, the ad was quickly withdrawn.

8. The New York *Times*/CBS News poll showed that Reagan went from four points behind Carter to five points ahead (40 percent for Reagan, 35 percent for Carter), while Anderson stayed at 9 percent. Campaign polls showed the same pattern, except that Anderson's ratings showed some decline. Positive assessments of Anderson as a debater did not seem to convert into support. See *Congressional Quarterly Weekly Report*, September 27, 1980, p. 2831.

9. Various public and private polls showed that in October Reagan was weakest on the war-peace issue. "Face Off: A Conversation with the President's Pollsters Patrick Caddell and Richard Wirthlin," *Public Opinion*, December/January 1981, p. 10.

10. Gerald Pomper, et al., *The Election of 1980* (Chatham, N.J.: Chatham House, 1981), p. 79.

11. See "Republican Groups Dominate in Party Campaign Spending," *Congressional Quarterly Weekly Report*, November 1, 1980, pp. 3234-39.

12. This point might seem more obvious than it is. In strong party systems, for example, many citizens vote for the party's candidate more than the *person* of the particular candidate. Nineteenth-century American parties were much more important in election campaigns than they are today. See Stephen J. Wayne, *The Road to the White House* (New York: St. Martin's Press, 1980), pp. 155-57.

13. "A Conversation with the President's Pollsters," p. 10.

14. Collecting over 1 million petitions alone was a formidable task. *Congressional Quarterly Weekly Report*, May 17, 1980, pp. 1315-18.

15. Warren E. Miller, "Policy Directions and Presidential Leadership: Alternative Interpretations of the 1980 Presidential Elections," paper delivered

at the 1981 Annual Meeting of the American Political Science Association, New York, September 3-6, 1981, Table 2. Actually, these identification figures have been quite stable for a decade.

16. William H. Flanigan and Nancy H. Zingale, *Political Behavior of the American Electorate* (Boston: Allyn and Bacon, 1979), Chapter 6.

17. Anthony Downs, *An Economic Theory of Democracy* (New York: Harper & Brothers, 1957), Chapter 3.

18. Michael Robinson, et al., "The Media at Mid-Year: A Bad Year for McLuhanites?" *Public Opinion*, June/July 1980, pp. 41-45.

19. Sidney Blumenthal, *The Permanent Campaign* (Boston: Beacon Press, 1980), Chapter 4.

20. Tensions within the Anderson campaign also involved the role of Keke Anderson as well as Garth. See *Newsweek*, June 9, 1980, pp. 28 and 32.

21. Virtually all of Anderson's top staff joined the campaign in May or after, some in July and August. *Congressional Quarterly Weekly Report*, September 27, 1980, pp. 2833-38.

22. Leslie Bennetts, "Mrs Crisp, Ex-GOP Aide, to Direct Anderson Race," New York *Times*, August 15, 1980, p. B3.

23. "John Anderson Still Trying to Dump His 'Spoiler' Image," *Congressional Quarterly Weekly Report*, September 27, 1980, p. 2833.

24. David Broder et al., *The Pursuit of the Presidency 1980* (New York: Berkley Books, 1980), pp. 222-23.

25. *Newsweek*, June 9, 1980, p. 28.

26. Broder, *Pursuit*, p. 227.

27. Elizabeth Drew, *The New Yorker*, October 13, 1980, p. 156.

28. Everett Ladd and G. Donald Ferree, Jr., "John Anderson: Candidate of the New Class?" *Public Opinion*, June/July 1980, pp. 11-15.

29. Robinson, et al., "The Media at Mid-Year," pp. 41-45; and Michael J. Robinson, "The Media in 1980: Was the Message the Message?" in *The American Elections of 1980*, ed. Austin Ranney (Washington, D.C.: American Enterprise Institute, 1981), pp. 208-10.

30. Elizabeth Drew, "1980: Reagan," *The New Yorker*, September 29, 1980, p. 112.

31. Ithiel de Sola Pool, Robert P. Abelson, and Samuel Popkin, *Candidates, Issues and Strategies* (Cambridge, Mass.: MIT Press, 1964 and 1965).

32. "National Committee Given Major Role in Fall Campaign," *Congressional Quarterly Weekly Report*, July 19, 1980, p. 2011.

33. Independent committees spent over $10 million in support of Reagan compared to less than $100,000 for Carter. Terence Smith, "Financing Campaign '80: Would You Believe Half a Billion?" New York *Times*, November 23, 1980.

34. Drew, September 29, 1980, pp. 115-16.

35. Ibid., p. 119.

36. There is some disagreement about just how large the difference was in terms of electoral impact. Compared to Reagan's expenditures of $6 million on media, Carter spent about $4.5 million. In a postelection assessment, Wirthlin thought this difference was significant, while Caddell thought it was not. "A

Conversation with the President's Pollsters," p. 63. Robinson, "The Media in 1980," Chapter 6, argues that the media had little electoral impact in 1980 as a whole.

37. In the initial June plan, the campaign was divided into three periods: from the end of the primaries to September 7; from September 8 to October 16; and from October 17 to November 4. Each period had a major purpose. That of the last period was to attack Carter aggressively and turn out the Reagan vote. See Richard Wirthlin, et al., "Campaign Chronicle," *Public Opinion*, February/March 1981, pp. 44-45.

38. Ibid., p. 47. Also, Elizabeth Drew, "1980: The Election," *The New Yorker*, December 1, 1980, p. 158.

39. *The New Republic*, November 1, 1980, p. 9. Albert R. Hunt also emphasizes the pressures of uncertainty upon the Reagan strategists in "The Campaign and the Issues," in *The American Elections of 1980*, pp. 166-68.

40. Drew, December 1, 1980, p. 160.

41. *Public Opinion*, December/January 1981, p. 10; and also February/March 1981, p. 47.

42. Ibid., December/January 1981, p. 11.

43. See Everett C. Ladd and G. Donald Ferree, "Were the Pollsters Really Wrong?" *Public Opinion*, December/January 1981, pp. 12-23 (which includes results of the major public polls).

44. Ibid.

45. "Ron Reagan's Inner Circle Combines 'California Mafia' with Nixon and Ford Alumni," *Congressional Quarterly Weekly Report*, pp. 2913-22.

46. Warren E. Miller, "Policy Directions and Presidential Leadership: Alternative Interpretations of the 1980 Presidential Elections," paper delivered at the 1981 Annual Meeting of the American Political Science Association, New York, September 3-6, 1981, Tables 27, III-3, III-4, and III-5.

47. Drew, December 1, 1980, p. 155.

48. An interesting finding by researchers at the Survey Research center of the University of Michigan was that changes in the comparative evaluation of the candidates through 1980 were generally caused by negative changes in the assessment of Carter rather than positive changes in Reagan's direction. See Miller, "Policy Directions," pp. 25-26 and 37.

49. James Reston, "Carter's Secret Weapon," New York *Times*, March 21, 1980, p. A27. A similar point is made by Charles O. Jones, "Nominating 'Carter's Favorite Opponent,' " in *The American Elections of 1980*, Chapter 3.

50. The Republicans gained 33 seats in the House of Representatives, more than in any election since 1966. In the Senate their numbers were increased by 12, giving them control for the first time since 1954. On the state level, there were 13 gubernatorial contests, of which Republicans won 7, for a net gain of 4. Perhaps equally significant, the GOP gained an additional 189 state legislative seats, increasing the number of states from 12 to 14 where Republicans controlled both houses of the legislature, and from 5 states to 7 where party control was divided. The significance of these gains for the Republican party arises from the fact that state governments are responsible for the legislative (including congressional) redistricting required as the result of the 1980 census.

51. William Schneider, "The November 4 Vote For President: What Did It Mean?" in *The American Elections of 1980*, p. 247.

7
Conclusions

In a number of respects the presidential campaigns of 1980 demonstrated interesting similarities. These reveal a significant amount of common understanding about when and in what manner campaigns should be organized and how they should be run – significant but not complete. The "rules of the game" in the form of state caucuses and primaries, sources and requirements of financing, functions of the media, and so on, were generally recognized. Yet how candidates "played" by these rules was quite variable. As in other games, skill, experience, and ingenuity made a difference.

Often the lack of resources made it impossible for a candidate to follow the rules, to exploit opportunities. A major reason for this was that decisions to launch campaigns frequently seemed to be governed by other considerations. More often than not these were matters of personal circumstances and psychology rather than objective appraisals of the political situation. This calls attention to the presidential candidates not covered in this study – Republicans Benjamin Fernandez and Harold Stassen and Democrat Lyndon La Rouche, for example – persons who ignored the rules of the game and ran in a world partly of their own.[1] They illustrate the diverse motivations in presidential campaigns.

Little variation was seen in the approaches to campaign management and organization, and the contrasting styles of decision-making found in earlier years were almost entirely missing in 1980.

Campaign organizations followed loosely centralized designs in which the desirability of central control was never challenged but seldom carried out with much determination. Decisions were overwhelmingly incremental and were arrived at through mutual adjustment. Sharp differences in ideology were present in 1980, yet these had little effect upon patterns of organization and were not associated with varying commitments to synoptic or incremental decision-making. Comprehensive planning was the norm in 1980. Indeed, the campaigns characteristically, if not always successfully, began by formulating comprehensive strategies or plans to guide their actions. In practice, these were usually changed or departed from, perhaps with disappointment but not with bitter resistance. Where differences in management or organization or decision-making did occur, they arose primarily from scarce resources and not intentional design. There seemed to be only one blueprint for campaign organization in 1980.

When the campaigns are considered in terms of cybernetics, however, many more differences emerge. A major reason for this lies in the nature of the model. For example, a cybernetic campaign requires not only that it collect enough resources (inputs of money, staff, and information) to maintain a viable system of internal action (decisions and output) but also that its output messages affect the political environment to achieve its goals. While this is hardly an original idea, the cybernetic model makes the system's impact an integral part of the campaign and calls attention to the readiness of citizens to receive and respond to campaign messages. It is thus evident that past experiences and information predispose voters to hear some messages better than others, or to distort their meanings, thereby contributing to sharp differences in the cybernetic quality of campaigns. Among other things, a perfect cybernetic campaign requires continuous monitoring of the electorate (and other targets) in order that outputs are coded and transmitted with optimal effects — a tall order to be sure, but one that helps us understand why John Connally, with abundant resources of output, had so little success in winning delegates.

With this reminder of the characteristics of the cybernetic model, the following are the major conclusions drawn from the 1980 campaigns stated in cybernetic terms.

Sufficient resources for decisions and communications are essential. Defining resources quite narrowly to include money (which can buy other resources), staff (excluding the candidate), and data about the political environment, it is clear that the successful campaign must have the ability to know a good deal about public attitudes and opinions, other campaigns, world events, and so forth; to make decisions about these as they relate to the election; and to communicate directly to the electorate. Furthermore, lesser-known candidates need greater resources than their better-known competitors (assuming equal levels of approval). Attractive candidates — Anderson and Baker, for example — may get some help from the news media, but in the end they must be able to get their messages out with resources of their own in order to make themselves credible (worth helping) by the media and contributors. As a rule, the greater resources of information a campaign has, the more it is able to collect, and vice versa.[2]

The candidate is the message. Although other messages — about issues, endorsements, relevant events, and even the candidate — affect the electorate, these work only as supplements to the direct statements and actions of the candidate.[3] Both news media and voters perceive the presidency as an individual role, so that the person aspiring to fill that role is the central focus of media and voter attention. Other elements, such as the candidate's party, ideology, or associations, may be separated analytically from the candidate, but voters tend to see the candidate as a composite message that includes all these elements. Thus the campaign may make many other statements, but unless these are also expressed by the candidate, they have much less effect. This was dramatically illustrated by the Carter campaign during the spring.

Similarly, the internal operations of the campaign system are affected more by the candidate than any other factor. There can be significant variations in this, especially as the campaign grows in size, but these are dependent on the candidate's ability to delegate authority and are limited by the media's insistence on seeing the candidate directly. Candidates are more able to delegate authority to those they trust; in short, to those with whom communication is strong. Hamilton Jordan's role in the Carter campaign is a notable case in point.

Above all, internal communications that enable the campaign to influence its candidate are critically important. In fact, since the candidate is the dominant message, breakdowns in communication and control with and over the candidate constitute breakdowns in campaign feedback as a whole. Thus the "he wears no man's collar" image may impress the media, but unless the candidate accepts staff advice and other input, the campaign will suffer, and usually to a considerable extent. The campaigns of Anderson, Carter, and Connally are examples.

Internal campaign communication and decision-making are enhanced by common experiences and beliefs of its staff. If campaign staff have worked in campaigns before, they not only have knowledge that increases their ability to make appropriate decisions, but also have the basis for mutual understandings that ease communication and decision-making. This is particularly true if they have *worked together in past campaigns*, which also increases the likelihood that they have values in common. Anderson and Carter, especially, illustrate this in different ways. In any case, value or belief conflicts constitute impediments (noise) to the flow of messages and break up networks of communication. This can be temporarily overcome by an overriding purpose, such as the election of the candidate, but the potential distrust and incompatibility remain, often to be reasserted when the common purpose is either achieved or weakened, as was the case in the Reagan campaign. It is to be remembered that presidential campaigns face enormous performance demands: to build field organizations, deal with the news media, produce commercials and buy media time, arrange for massive public opinion polls, transport large numbers of people from place to place, raise millions of dollars, cope with FEC regulations, and so forth — and to do these things quickly and in the face of political competition. The knowledge (information) about how to handle these operations is best acquired through experience.

Older campaigns are likely to run better than younger campaigns. Like members of most organizations, it takes time for campaigners to learn their tasks and to work together. Because these tasks tend to be multiple and demanding, and campaigns tend to be open systems, overloads and mutual incompatibilities are common and usually lead to multiple breakdowns in communication and control. With the passage of time, staff adjustments (feedback) and individual learning occur. These can sharply increase the flow of information and the efficiency of decision-making. How quickly and well this takes place depends heavily on the experience and sensitivity of the campaign's chief of staff (or others who perform this organizational role).

Since the demands of a long series of separate state caucuses and primaries impose extremely heavy requirements of knowledge and expertise on campaign decision-makers, emphasizing the benefits of mutual experience is another way of saying that getting an early start, and thus "easing into" these various operations, pays cybernetic dividends.[4] This can be seen most clearly in the Bush, Carter, and Reagan campaigns.

The news media comprise a separate system that must be accommodated and cannot be controlled. Because the news media have high credibility and large audiences, they are of overwhelming importance in communicating with other systems that are necessary to the campaign's success (such as contributors, local volunteers, and voters). This is especially true during the prenomination campaigns. However, the media have purposes and standards of their own, which do not permanently coincide with those of the campaign. Newspeople are self-conscious about these and react negatively to being manipulated or "used," as both the Carter and Reagan campaigns found out. Thus feedback mechanisms must be constructed to monitor and adapt to media actions that are usually difficult to predict. Moreover, the media are complex and variegated in themselves, which also limits the possibilities of control by the campaign. All in all, although how the media treat the campaign depends on its cybernetic quality, the precise actions and effects of the media in particular situations remain part of the cybernetic mysteries of American politics.

Public opinion polling is essential for effective decision-making and control. The technology of opinion polling makes it possible to adapt campaign operations and output to changing conditions of the electorate. In fact, the need for competent polling is acute because citizens now have weaker political "anchors," such as party identification. This was seen in what was often called the "volatility" of political opinion during the 1980 campaign. Public surveys taken by major firms, such as Gallup, cannot be used as a substitute for the campaign's own polls, since their questions are not tailored to the campaign's particular needs, their sampling designs will not match the needs of the campaign, and their timing is usually too infrequent. Similarly, "amateur" or cut-rate polling costs too much in unreliable information to be worth the financial savings.[5]

Most of the prenomination campaigns undervalued regular systematic monitoring of public opinion — Anderson, Connally, and

Kennedy being conspicuous examples. Polling must be done with professional competence and major amounts of campaign resources should be allocated for this purpose. Moreover, the person(s) in charge of the operation should be immediately involved in the formulation of campaign strategies so that poll information is not distorted or lost before it can be used. Such arrangements were present in both the Carter and Reagan campaigns and were a major reason for their competitive success.

Comprehensive strategic planning is useful, but only if subject to feedback. To formulate an overall strategy in some detail, based on sophisticated analyses of the best available information, can be very helpful to the campaign. Such comprehensive planning serves to make strategic assumptions (about sources of electoral support and financing, and schedules of organization, for example) explicit, and to identify expected difficulties and required accomplishments at a time when commitments to action are less intense. Essentially, it provides the campaign with a type of "lead" so that future problems can be anticipated and prepared for. The danger in such a plan is that it will replace reality and become a self-fulfilling prophecy that moves further and further away from actual political conditions (akin to *positive* feedback). Therefore, feedback, especially higher-order feedback (learning), is critically important in order that the campaign not get caught up in repeating its mistakes. The strategic planning of Hamilton Jordan (for Carter) and Richard Wirthlin (for Reagan) was an outstanding example of this conclusion.

Campaigns are always threatened by commitments and expectations that cut off reality. Related to the preceding point is the well-known tendency of campaigners to become so emotionally attached to their enterprise that negative information is filtered out and feedback short-circuited. This could be seen clearly in the Anderson, Connally, and Kennedy campaigns. An associated phenomenon involving other systems (particularly the press and contributors) is so-called *momentum,* in which a series of feedback loops occurs, based more or less on reality. The reverse of momentum is the disintegration that occurs when campaign expectations are not met, the disappointment leading to lower performance (output), leading to lower effects, and so on. The overall problem is endemic because campaigns tend to attract participants motivated by personal commitments to a "cause" (either a candidate or ideology, or both) rather than by more neutral monetary rewards. Position goals, such as White House staff jobs, tend to cause less distortion of reality than ideology. Therefore, campaigns motivated by intense commitments to ideology or personality are especially vulnerable to the unreality problem. The correction is a more experienced and professional staff.

Local field organizations are an important element of campaigns. With the arrival of political television (that is, news reports and campaign commercials) and other mass media, it became fashionable to think of presidential campaigns as battles of television (and radio) commercials. In the long series of caucuses and primaries, however, the 1980 campaigns taught that a good media campaign would be defeated by a good media and good grass-roots campaign.[6] This is because the communication (both input and output) and control possible through workers going door-to-door, and phoning friends and neighbors, cannot be replaced by television ads (but see below). For caucuses, field organizations are indispensable.[7] Strong field organizations cannot be created overnight and require considerable resources of time, skill, and local participants to construct. Then, however, they have the potential to produce more resources than they consume (as in the Republican case in 1980). Consequently, campaigns such as Carter's and Reagan's have inherent advantages over those that are started late and without established ties to state and local activists.

From the start of formal competition, campaigns need direct communication with the voters to be competitive. This is a fairly complex point, since it means not only that mass media technology must be in hand as early as the first caucuses (Iowa in 1980), but also that extensive personal appearances by the candidate are needed. In no sense does this contradict the points above, for there is a cybernetic link between the two. Local activists now use their candidate's media appearances as a resource of support, providing evidence for all to see that their local cause is credible.* The push and pull of intense prenomination competitions and voter responses has left campaigns facing public expectations that media appearances are a necessary signal that the candidate is worthy of consideration. At the same time, with the exception of the President, candidates are "expected" to appear personally, presumably to demonstrate their

---

*The phenomenon of local activists gathering to watch their candidates perform in televised debates is now common in electoral politics.

true interest in the state or locality.[8] Numerous examples of this point occurred during the prenomination campaigns of 1980, with the Iowa caucuses being as clear as any.

The Democratic and Republican parties do not control nominations; they monopolize elections. According to the classic observation of E. E. Schattschneider that "he who can make nominations is the owner of the party," the 1980 campaigns seemed to leave the parties in limbo.[9] Candidates certainly did not await their party's call but took it upon themselves to create their own self-contained campaigns through which they struggled for nomination and defined their own versions of their party's platform.

Yet the major parties remained systems of information and control that had a profound influence on campaigns. Candidates ran for president by competing for the Democratic and Republican nominations through party institutions, with party activists, and the necessary approval of party voters. When one of the candidates, rejected in this process, sought the presidency as an independent, he confronted a network of rules, expectations, and loyalties that hamstrung his campaign. John Anderson showed that even in their weakened state the major parties placed a winning cybernetic campaign by an independent candidate virtually beyond reach.[10]

For their part, the major party nominees left no doubt about the differences between their parties and made determined efforts to use their parties in their campaigns. Ronald Reagan, as head of his party, appeared to encourage a return to Republican identification for the first time in almost half a century.[11] Thus by 1980 the parties had adapted and stabilized their operations in terms of the rules of the game of the late 1970s.

The more complex the campaign, the more probable its breakdowns (that is, the failure of complex systems). This restatement of the Second Law of Thermodynamics, basic to cybernetics, signifies that as modern campaigns incorporate more sophisticated technology and complicated operations, they should expect more lapses and errors. Evidence of this proposition is very impressionistic because the smaller campaigns of 1980 experienced so many cybernetic failures due to a lack of resources. Nonetheless, it is interesting to note the considerable number of lapses that did occur in the highly controlled yet complex Carter and Reagan campaigns that were larger. The "solution" to the "law" is, of course, the increased provision for feedback. In short, modern complex campaigns need more self-correcting mechanisms in order to cope with the increased probability of failures.

Looking at the presidential campaigns of 1980 from the perspective of cybernetics suggests still another conclusion. Any expectation that experts in political communication are on the verge of controlling elections is at best premature. The major campaigns had great difficulty controlling their own candidates, not to mention actions of the past that saddled such candidates as Carter, Connally, Kennedy, and Reagan with negative images that resisted change. There is no doubt that all the campaigns tried to present their candidates in the best possible light. Their success varied, but substantial misrepresentations succeeded only partially and for limited periods of time. Though far from perfect, self-correcting mechanisms exist within the electoral system as a whole.

The model cybernetic campaign was not achieved in 1980. As we have seen, there were many reasons for this. Some involved conditions and circumstances that impeded the flow of information and the operations of feedback. Most of these are subject to improvement. Others, however, were "built-in" motivations to reduce or distort information for the advantage of a campaign. No one, including James Madison, has yet discovered how these can or should be removed from a democratic system. One thing is clear: If the model cybernetic campaign ever does occur, its theory will make it benign.

NOTES

1. Republicans Fernandez and Stassen and Democrat La Rouche were not simply persons who ran in one or two states. All began early — Fernandez in 1978 — and persisted to the end of the primaries. These were not treated as "serious" candidates by the media and thus received almost no news coverage. Fernandez, in particular, defeated some of the "major" candidates in a number of primaries. For a comprehensive list of the early candidates, see *Congressional Quarterly Weekly Report*, November 1, 1979, p. 2228.

2. The continuing importance of money in campaigns has been documented repeatedly. It is even more important, and difficult to collect, under the new FECA regulations. A brief insightful view of how things look from the inside is Robert J. Keefe, "Presidential Campaign Strategy and the Law," in *Parties, Interest Groups, and Campaign Finance Law*, ed. Michael J. Malbin (Washington, D.C.: American Enterprise Institute, 1980), pp. 233-37.

3. The direct perception of the candidate as a "total" person may have a lot to do with the level of trust voters have. There is an interesting discussion

of trust (and other voter models) and the electorate in Jeffrey A. Smith, *American Presidential Elections* (New York: Praeger, 1980), esp. Chapters 5 and 6.

4. The other side of the coin is that the fresh ideas and enthusiasm of "unjaded" campaigners — amateurs — can bring new information and vigor into the system. This point is capsulized by the point that veteran campaigners, like generals, "are always running the last campaign."

5. Campaign polling was quite widely discussed in the political media during 1980, and campaign pollsters appeared to be forming a type of professional community of their own. See *Congressional Quarterly Weekly Report*, March 15, 1980, pp. 723-27; and "Face Off: A Conversation with the President's Pollsters Patrick Caddell and Richard Wirthlin," *Public Opinion*, December/January, 1981, pp. 2-12 and ff.

6. Michael J. Robinson argues that the media had little effect on electoral outcomes in 1980. See "The Media in 1980: Was the Message the Message?" in *The American Elections of 1980*, ed. Austin Ranney (Washington, D.C.: American Enterprise Institute, 1981), Chapter 6.

7. An unsung triumph in Carter's prenomination campaign was the work of his field operatives in the caucus states. Almost invisible compared to the primaries, state caucuses often went through several stages that continued through the preconvention period. Had Kennedy's primary campaigns not faltered, Carter's superiority in the caucuses could have been a key factor in securing his renomination. For an excellent picture of the complexities of the caucus states, see *Congressional Quarterly Weekly Report*, December 29, 1979, pp. 2957-65.

8. It is difficult to sort myth from reality around these phenomena. Do voters really make a negative assessment of candidates who, though appearing on television, do not make personal visits to the state? Or is it just that candidates who do make personal appearances also receive significantly more media coverage? And so on. In any case, on the Republican side, some of Bush's late victories were in states where he had done much more personal campaigning than Reagan.

9. E. E. Schattschneider, *Party Government* (New York: Holt, Rinehart and Winston, 1942), p. 64.

10. This was very specific in the case of the Democratic National Committee, which challenged Anderson's efforts to get on the ballot in many states.

11. Ellis Sandoz, "Revolution or Flash in the Pan?" in *A Tide of Discontent: The 1980 Elections and Their Meaning*, ed. Ellis Sandoz and Cecil V. Crabb (Washington, D.C.: Congressional Quarterly, 1981), pp. 15-16.

Appendixes

APPENDIX A
Primaries and Selected Caucuses of 1980

					Democratic				Anderson	Republican						
Date	State	Caucus[a]	Primary	Primary Turnout[b]	Brown	Carter	Kennedy	Un.[c]		Baker	Bush	Connally	Crane	Dole	Reagan	Un.[c]
1/21	Iowa	X		—		59.1	31.2	9.6	4.3	15.7	31.5	9.2	6.7	1.5	29.4	1.7
2/3	Arkansas[d]	X		—						4.0	1.0	1.0			6.0	
2/10	Maine	X		—	11.6	45.2	39.4	3.8								
2/17	Puerto Rico		X	—						37.0	60.1	1.1		.2		.9
2/26	New Hampshire		X	39.4	9.6	47.5	37.3		9.8	12.9	22.7	1.5	1.8	.4	49.6	
3/4	Massachusetts		X	30.4	3.5	28.7	65.1	2.2	30.7	4.8	31.0	1.2	1.2	.2	28.8	.6
3/4	Vermont		X	29.3	.9[f]	74.1	25.5	9.5	29.0	12.3	21.7	1.3	1.9	.1	30.1	
3/8	South Carolina		X	—						.5	14.9	29.9			54.4	
3/11	Florida		X	24.9	4.9	60.7	23.2		9.2	1.0	30.2	.8	2.0	.2	56.2	
3/11	Alabama		X	16.6	4.0	81.6	13.2			1.0	25.9	.5	2.4	.3	69.7	
3/11	Georgia		X	16.1	1.9	88.0	8.4		8.4	.8	12.6	1.3	3.2	.1	73.2	
3/16	Puerto Rico		X	—	.2	51.7	48.0									
3/18	Illinois		X	29.0	3.3	65.0	30.0		36.7	.6	11.0	.4	2.2	.2	48.4	
3/25	Connecticut		X	16.9	2.6	41.5	46.9		22.1	1.3	38.6	.3	1.0	.2	33.9	
3/25	New York		X	—	W[e]	41.1	58.9			W		W	W	W		
4/1	Kansas		X	27.3	4.9	56.6	31.6	5.8	18.2	1.3	12.6	.7	.5		63.0	2.4
4/1	Wisconsin		X	44.6	11.8	56.2	30.1	.4	27.4	.4	30.4	.3	.3		40.2	.3

(continued)

Appendix A, continued

Date	State	Caucus[a]	Primary	Primary Turnout[b]	Democratic				Republican							
					Brown	Carter	Kennedy	Un.[c]	Anderson	Baker	Bush	Connally	Crane	Dole	Reagan	Un.[c]
4/5	Louisiana		X	14.4	4.7	55.7	22.5	11.6			18.8		W		74.9	5.3
4/22	Pennsylvania		X	33.0	2.3	45.4	45.7	5.8	2.1[f]	2.5	50.5	.9			42.5	
5/3	Michigan		X	—		47.1	48.6									
5/3	Texas		X	19.7	2.6	55.9	22.8	18.7	W		47.4				51.0	1.5
5/6	District of Columbia		X	15.1		36.9	61.7		26.7		66.1		3.6			
5/6	Indiana		X	30.1		67.7	32.3		9.9		16.4				73.7	
5/6	North Carolina		X	22.3	2.9	70.1	17.7	9.3	5.1	1.5	21.8	.7	.3	.5	67.6	2.7
5/6	Tennessee		X	15.3	1.9	75.2	18.2	3.9	4.5		18.1				74.1	
5/13	Maryland		X	21.2	3.0	47.5	38.0	9.6	9.7		40.9		1.3		48.2	
5/13	Nebraska		X	31.5	3.6	46.9	37.6	10.4	5.8		15.3		.5		76.0	
5/20	Michigan		X	10.3	29.4			46.4	8.2		57.5 W				31.8	
5/20	Oregon		X	33.9	9.7	58.2	32.1		10.1		34.7		.7		34.7	
5/27	Arkansas		X	—	4.1	60.1	17.5	18.0								
5/27	Idaho		X	29.2		62.2	22.0	11.8	9.7		4.0		.8		82.9	2.6
5/27	Kentucky		X	13.2		66.9	23.0	8.0	5.1		7.2				82.4	5.1
5/27	Nevada		X	21.4		37.6	28.8	33.6			6.5				83.0	10.5
6/3	California		X	34.4	4.0	37.7	44.8	11.4	13.6		4.9				80.2	
6/3	Mississippi		X	—							8.3		.9		89.1	2.6
6/3	Montana		X	36.0		51.6	37.2	11.2			9.7				87.3	3.0
6/3	New Jersey		X	15.5		37.9	56.2	3.5			17.1				81.3	

6/3	New Mexico	X	24.9		41.9	46.1	6.1	12.1	9.9	7.5	63.7	2.2
6/3	Ohio	X	26.5		51.0	44.1			19.2		80.8	6.5
6/3	Rhode Island	X	6.3	.8	25.8	68.3	2.0		18.6		72.0	6.5
6/3	South Dakota	X	32.2		45.9	48.2	5.9	6.3	4.2	.5	82.1	5.8
6/3	West Virginia	X	33.1		61.9	38.1			14.4		85.6	
	TOTAL		25.3									

[a]Only those caucuses are included that received substantial public attention or are otherwise noteworthy (for example, Arkansas provided Connally's only delegate). Usually the date given is that of the first of a series of caucuses. The percentages given are based mostly on votes for delegates and are thus approximations in some cases. Primaries are also of several types, including some for delegates only, some for candidates only, and some for candidates in one party and delegates in the other party. There are many other differences as well, including states with primaries for one party and caucuses for the other.

[b]Covers both parties. Calculated by dividing the total number of votes cast in both parties' primaries by the estimated voting-age population in each state. Primary states that are blank had missing data.

[c]This category is a very mixed bag, including Uncommitted, No Preference, and None of the Candidates.

[d]These are numbers of delegates. Percentages could not be calculated.

[e]W indicates the time when the candidate formally withdrew from contention. In several cases they had stopped campaigning weeks before.

[f]Write-in vote. Most went unreported in the states.

Sources: Congressional Quarterly Weekly Reports, including final report of "official results" on July 5, 1980, pp. 1870-71; and Austin Ranney, ed., The American Elections of 1980 (Washington, D.C.: American Enterprise Institute, 1981), Appendix C., Table C-1.

APPENDIX B
Percent of Total Votes in Primaries

Democrats	Percent	Republicans	Percent
Carter	51.2	Reagan	59.7
Kennedy	37.6	Bush	24.0
Brown	2.9	Anderson	12.3
La Rouche	0.9	Baker	1.4
Kay	0.3	Crane	0.8
Finch	0.3	Connally	0.6
Others	0.2	Fernandez	0.2
No preference	6.6	Stassen	0.2
		Dole	0.0
		Others	0.3
		No preference	0.5

Source: Congressional Quarterly Weekly Report, July 5, 1980, p. 1868. Percentages are based on various data bases. Relationships are precise.

APPENDIX C
Systems for Choosing National Convention Delegates

State, District, Territory	1968	1972	1976	1980
Alabama	DP	DP	OP	OP
Alaska	PC	PC	PC	PC
Arizona	(D)P (R)PC	PC	PC	PC
Arkansas	P	PC	OP	(D)OP (R)PC
California	PP	PP	PP	PP
Colorado	PC	PC	PC	PC
Connecticut	PC	PC	PC	PP
Delaware	PC	PC	PC	PC
District of Columbia	PP	PP	PP	PP
Florida	PP	PP	PP	PP
Georgia	(D)P (R)PC	PC	OP	OP
Hawaii	PC	PC	PC	PC
Idaho	PC	PC	OP	(D)PC (R)OP

(continued)

APPENDIX C, continued

State, District, Territory	1968	1972	1976	1980
Illinois	DP,PC	PP	OP	OP
Indiana	OP	OP	OP	OP
Iowa	PC	PC	PC	PC
Kansas	PC	PC	PC	PIP
Kentucky	PC	PC	PP	PP
Louisiana	P	PC	PC	PP
Maine	PC	PC	PC	PC
Maryland	(D)P (R)PC	PP	PP	PP
Massachusetts	PIP	PIP	PIP	PIP
Michigan	PC	OP	OP	(D)PC (R)OP
Minnesota	PC	PC	PC	PC
Mississippi	PC	PC	PC	(D)PC (R)DP
Missouri	(D)PC,P (R)PC	PC	PC	PC
Montana	PC	PC	OP	OP
Nebraska	OP	OP	OP	OP
Nevada	PC	PC	PP	PP
New Hampshire	PIP	PIP	PIP	PIP
New Jersey	PIP	PIP	PIP	PIP
New Mexico	PC	PP	PC	PP
New York	DP,P	DP,P	DP	(D)PP (R)DP
North Carolina	PC	PP	PP	PP
North Dakota	PC	PC	PC	PC
Ohio	OP	OP	OP	OP
Oklahoma	PC	PC	PC	PC
Oregon	PP	PP	PP	PP
Pennslyvania	PP,P	PP	PP	PP
Rhode Island	(D)P (R)PC	PIP	PIP	PIP
South Carolina	PC	PC	PC	(D)PC (R)OP
South Dakota	PP	PP	PP	PP
Tennessee	PC	OP	OP	OP
Texas	PC	PC	OP	PP
Utah	PC	PC	PC	PC

(continued)

APPENDIX C, continued

State, District, Territory	1968	1972	1976	1980
Vermont	PC	PC	PC+	PC+
Virginia	PC	PC	PC	PC
Washington	(D)PC,P	PC	PC	PC
	(R)PC	PP	PP	PP
West Virginia	PP	PP	PP	PP
Wisconsin	OP	OP	OP	OP
Wyoming	PC	PC	PC	PC
Puerto Rico	(D)P	PC	PC	OP
	(R)PC			
Total of all primaries	17	24	30	37

Notes: Delegates are chosen by:

PC = Party caucuses and conventions.

P = State party committee.

PP = Party presidential preference primary, open to registered party members.

PIP = Presidential preference primary, open to registered party members and independents.

OP = Presidential preference primary, open to all registered voters.

DP = Direct primary; no presidential preference, open to party members.

PC+ = Vermont, 1976 and 1980: both parties elected delegates in local caucuses; Democrats held a nonbinding presidential preference primary; Republicans held a presidential preference primary binding on 10 of 19 delegates if one candidate received at least 40 percent of the votes.

(D) = Democratic

(R) = Republican

Source: Adapted from Austin Ranney, ed., *The American Elections of 1980* (Washington, D.C.: American Enterprise Institute, 1981), Appendix D.

APPENDIX D
1980 Presidential Election

State	Carter Percent Popular Vote	Carter Number Electoral Votes	Reagan Percent Popular Vote	Reagan Number Electoral Votes	Anderson Percent Popular Vote	Anderson Number Electoral Votes	Turnout
Alabama	47.4	—	48.8	9	1.2	—	49.9
Alaska	26.6	—	54.6	3	7.1	—	60.0
Arizona	28.2	—	60.6	6	8.8	—	49.8
Arkansas	47.5	—	48.1	6	2.7	—	53.5
California	35.9	—	52.7	45	8.6	—	50.9
Colorado	31.1	—	55.1	7	11.0	—	58.3
Connecticut	38.5	—	48.2	8	12.2	—	60.6
Delaware	44.9	—	47.2	3	6.9	—	55.9
District of Columbia	74.9	3	13.4	—	9.3	—	35.4
Florida	38.5	—	55.5	17	5.1	—	54.2
Georgia	55.8	12	41.0	—	2.3	—	44.1
Hawaii	44.8	4	42.9	—	10.6	—	46.5
Idaho	25.2	—	66.5	4	6.2	—	69.5
Illinois	41.7	—	49.6	26	7.3	—	58.9
Indiana	37.7	—	56.0	13	5.0	—	58.1
Iowa	38.6	—	51.3	8	8.8	—	62.6
Kansas	33.3	—	57.9	7	7.0	—	59.9

(continued)

229

APPENDIX D, continued

State	Carter Percent Popular Vote	Carter Number Electoral Votes	Reagan Percent Popular Vote	Reagan Number Electoral Votes	Anderson Percent Popular Vote	Anderson Number Electoral Votes	Turnout
Kentucky	47.7	—	49.0	9	2.4	—	51.4
Louisiana	45.7	—	51.2	10	1.7	—	55.8
Maine	42.3	—	45.6	4	10.2	—	66.1
Maryland	47.1	10	44.2	—	7.8	—	50.7
Massachusetts	41.7	—	41.8	14	15.2	—	58.8
Michigan	42.5	—	49.0	21	7.0	—	59.7
Minnesota	46.6	10	42.7	—	8.6	—	69.4
Mississippi	48.1	—	49.4	7	1.3	—	54.2
Missouri	44.3	—	51.2	12	3.7	—	58.8
Montana	32.4	—	56.8	4	8.0	—	64.7
Nebraska	26.0	—	65.6	5	7.0	—	56.2
Nevada	27.4	—	63.6	3	7.2	—	47.0
New Hampshire	28.4	·	57.7	4	12.9	—	58.8
New Jersey	38.6	—	52.0	17	7.9	—	55.3
New Mexico	36.8	—	55.0	4	6.5	—	53.1
New York	44.0	—	46.7	41	7.5	—	48.0
North Carolina	47.2	—	49.3	13	2.8	—	45.8
North Dakota	26.3	—	64.2	3	7.8	—	64.3
Ohio	40.9	—	51.5	25	5.9	—	55.5

230

Oklahoma	35.0	—	60.5	8	3.3	—	54.4
Oregon	38.7	—	48.3	6	9.5	—	62.7
Pennsylvania	42.5	—	49.6	27	6.4	—	52.6
Rhode Island	47.7	4	37.2	—	14.4	—	60.5
South Carolina	48.2	—	49.5	8	1.6	—	43.1
South Dakota	31.7	—	60.5	4	6.5	—	67.1
Tennessee	48.4	—	48.7	10	2.2	—	50.8
Texas	41.4	—	55.3	26	2.5	—	47.7
Utah	20.6	—	72.8	4	5.0	—	67.9
Vermont	38.4	—	44.4	3	14.9	—	59.8
Virginia	40.3	—	53.0	12	5.1	—	48.8
Washington	37.3	—	49.7	9	10.6	—	59.6
West Virginia	49.8	6	45.3	—	4.3	—	54.5
Wisconsin	43.2	—	47.9	11	7.1	—	66.2
Wyoming	28.0	—	62.6	3	6.8	—	54.2
Totals	41.0	49	50.8	489	6.6	—	54.0

Source: Compiled by author from official state returns (Washington, D.C.: U.S. Federal Election Commission, December 29, 1980).

Index

Abelson, Robert P., 43
Accountants for the Public Interest, 46
Agranoff, Robert, 43, 51-52
Aldrich, John, 56-57, 82
Alexander, Herbert E., 43, 45
Allison, Graham, 81
Ambramson, Paul R., 42
Anderson, Arthur, 45
Anderson, John: cybernetic system, 142-44, 189-90; general election campaign, 181-92, 194; New Hampshire primary, 122, 141; obstacles, 181-84, 188-89; personal style, 139, 140-43, 191-92; and the political parties, 25, 27, 142, 143, 223-25; prenomination campaign, 139-42; public approval, 18, 140-41, 184, 187; staff, 140 145, 185, 186-87
Anderson, Keke, 140, 189, 208
Anderson, Martin, 123, 144
Anderson, Thelma, 42
Armstrong, Anne, 150
Arrow, Kenneth, J.: Arrow problem, 150
Arterton, F. Christopher, 43, 45, 82
Asher, Herbert, 44
Axelrod, Robert, 82

Bailey, Douglas, 137
Baker, Howard H., 119; New Hampshire debate, 122; campaign, 135-36, 137; cybernetic system, 138
Baker, James, 127, 204
Barber, James David, 43
Barone, Micheal, 116

Barron, James, 46
Beal, Richard, 144
Bennetts, Leslie, 208
Berelson, Bernard, 42
Bibb, John F., 26, 45
Big Mo, 131
Black, Charles, 120, 122, 124
Bloom, Melvyn H., 44
Blumenthal, Sidney, 44
Boulding, Kenneth, 83
Bourne, Dr. Peter, 93
Bradford, William G., 145
Brams, Steven J., 47, 56, 165
Braybrooke, David, 81
Breen, Jon, 122
Breglio, Vincent, 144
Brinkley, David, 165
Brock, Bill, 148, 196
Broder, David, 115
Brown, Jerry, 113; Anderson and, 191-92; Carter and, 91, 113; cybernetic system, 114-15
Brzezinski, Zbigniew, 96
Buchanin, Bay, 120
Burke, Rich, 99
Buckley v. *Valio*, 28, 30-31, 33, 37
Burns, James MacGregor, 94, 116
Bush, George, 119, cybernetic system, 128-30, 131; New Hampshire debates, 122-23, 125; personal style, 129-30; prenomination campaign, 127-28, 131, 146; primary victories, 122; and Reagan, 146, 150-51, 152, 153-54, 193

Caddell, Patrick, 87, 88, 93, 156, 171; as Carter pollster, 99, 108,

112, 159, 167-69, 187, 202-3
campaign theory: tests to apply,
50; organization approach, 50-54;
decision making approach, 54-55;
rational choice theories, 55-57;
game theory, 56-57; electoral
coalitions, 57-58; campaign resources, 59, 60; the cybernetic
campaign, 67-80, 212-13
Campbell, Bruce A., 42
Camp David Domestic Summit, 93-94
Carey, Hugh, 43
Carp, Bert, 108
Carter, Billy, 157-58
Carter, Jimmy: and Baker, 135; and
Brown, 114; Camp David Summit,
93-94; cybernetic system, 89, 91,
93-96, 97, 106-7, 158, 160-61,
162, 171-73, 178-81; and Democratic party, 88, 92, 161, 179;
general election campaign, 167-81;
Georgians, 87-88, 92; and Iran,
96-97, 172, 179, 199, 204; and
Kennedy, 99, 104-5, 108, negative campaign, 169, 174-75, 177,
180; personal style, 88, 91-94,
108-9, 131, 173-74, 176-77, 181,
203; prenomination campaign, 89-
90, 97, 104-5, 107-9, 111-12, 156,
162; public approval, 87, 91-92,
94, 96, 99, 102, 105, 157-58,
162, 169, 174-78
Carter/Mondale Reelection Committee, 88
Carter, Rosalynn, 93-94, 95, 97, 158
Casey, William, 123, 151, 198, 204
Cavala, William, 44
CBS/New York Times poll, 98 (*see
also* technology)
Ceaser, James W., 44
Chappaquiddick, 98-99, 100
Chicago convention of 1968, 21
Clark, Dick, 99

Clem, Alan L., 63-64
Clymer, Adam, 46, 166
coalitions, electoral (see campaign
theory)
Collat, Donald S., 166
Committee for Reelection of the Presi-
dent, 88
Common Cause, 47
Compliance Review Commission, 22
(*see also* electoral rules)
computers: use of (see technology)
congressional campaigns, 8-9, 13, 31,
59, 63-64, 65 (*see also* electoral
rules, technology)
Congressional Club, 38, 148
Connally, John B., 85, 119; personal
style, 131, 133-35; prenomination
campaign, 131-35, 137, 138; staff,
132; cybernetic system, 134-35
Converse, Philip E., 42
Coppola, Francis Ford, 113
Cotter, Cornelius P., 26, 45
Cousins v. *Wigoda*, 25
Coyle, Ed, 186
Crabb, Cecil V., 220
Crane, Philip M., 119; New Hampshire
primary, 122, 129, 136; prenomination campaign, 135-37; cyber-
netic system, 138
Crisp, Mary, 186
Cronkite, Walter, 10, 152, 154
Crotty, William, 44-45, 46
Crouse, Timothy, 111
Curb, Mike, 147
cybernetic campaign: boundaries, 77;
description, 67-71, 78-80, 212-19;
and the news media, 76-77;
problems, 8; and staff relations,
77-78 (*see also* individual candi-
dates)
Cyert, Richard M. 81

Dailey, Peter, 200

Daley, Richard, 21, 25
Daugherty, Anthony, 114
Deardourff, John, 137
Deaver, Michael, 120, 123, 144
debates, 175-77, 187, 198-201
Dees, Morris, 99
Delegates and Organization Commission, 26
delegates to national conventions (see electorial rule, prenomination)
Democratic Party of the United States of America v. *Bronson C. La Follette*, 25-26, 44
Democratic platform (see political parties)
demographic factors, 2, 9; age, 3-4; education, 4-6; geographic factors, 7-9; family changes, 7; population mobility, 2-3, 6-9
Dennis, Jack, 46
d'Estaing, Valéry Giscard, 121
Deutsch, Karl W., 84
De Vries, Tom, 118
Dewey, Thomas, 175
Dionne, E. J., Jr., 44, 145
Dobelle, Evan, 88-89, 95
Dole, Robert, 119; prenomination campaign, 137; cybernetic system, 138
Donilon, Tom, 95
Downs, Anthony, 55-56, 82, 84
Drayne, Dick, 99
Drew, Elizabeth, 102-3, 105, 109, 117, 129-30, 144, 148, 152, 158, 165-66, 207, 208

Easton, David, 82
Edelman, Peter, 99
Edwards, James, B., 133
Eizenstat, Stuart, 92-93, 96, 108
electoral rule changes: delegate regulation, 23-25; and Democratic party, 21-33; and Humphrey, 21;

McGovern-Fraser Commission, 21-22, 25; other commissions, 22; for primaries, prenomination campaigns, 23-38; Republican party rules, 26
electoral votes: population shift, 8; and Anderson, 203; in 1980 election, 206
Ellen, Marlene, 42
entropy (see cybernetic campaign)

Fallows, James, 86-87, 92-93, 115
FEC (see Federal Election Commission)
FECA (see Federal Election Campaign Act)
Federal Election Campaign Act (FECA), 28; amendments, 28-31; Brown and, 114; Bush and, 129; Kennedy and, 100; Reagan and, 127
Federal Election Commission (FEC), 30-32, 37, 88, 113; Anderson and, 188; Reagan and, 146
feedback (see cybernetic campaign)
Fenno, Richard F., Jr., 62, 115
Fernandez, Benjamin, 211
Fernandez, Michael, 186
Ferree, G. Donald, 43, 209
Finance, campaign: and campaign theory, 58-60; federal administration, 31-33, 188; and media, 137; resources, 212; rules for, 28-31; state regulations, 33 (*see also* electoral rule, preprimary, political parties, technology)
Flanigan, William H., 42
Ford, Gerald (Jerry): and Carter, 168, 172; decision not to run, 120; handicaps, 91, 98; and Reagan, 168, 172
Francis, Leslie, C., 171
Franks, Martin, 108

Fraser, Donald, 21
Froman, Lewis A., Jr., 83

Gaby, Daniel M., 81
Gage, John, 99
Gallup, George, 15, 215
game theory, 1-2, 40-41, 79-80, 165, 181-84 (*see also* campaign theory)
Garth, David, 20, 142, 185-87, 188-89
Gaudet, Hazel, 42
general elections (see individual candidates)
Georgians (see Carter, Jimmy)
Goldwater, Barry, 48, 54, 55, 147, 175, 180
Goodman, Robert, 127, 129
Graber, Doris A., 43
Gramen, Rex, 108
grassroot caucus, 27-28
Green, Mr., (see Breen, Jon)
Greenspan, Alan, 153
Gregg, Hugh, 129
Gresham, Thomas: Gresham's Law, 17
Guetzkow, Harold, 84
Guzzetta, S. J., 81

Halperin, Morton H., 82
Harrison, Gail, 108
Hart, Peter, 112
Harwood, Richard, 115
Heard, Alexander, 45
Heilman, John G., 165
Helms, Jesse, 38; and Republican platform, 148-49
Hennessy, Bernard C., 43
Herrnson, Paul S., 45
Hershey, Marjorie Randon, 61-63, 82, 162
Hess, Stephen, 83
Huckshorn, Robert J., 52-53, 59-60, 81
Humphrey, Hubert: and Carter; defeat by Nixon

Humphrey, Muriel, 97
Hunt, Albert R., 209
Hunt Commission, 40
Hunt, James B., 40

incumbency, 85, 87, 91; Carter and, 157-60, 167-71, 178-79; Reagan and, 120 (*see also* Rose Garden, Iran)
input, and output (see campaign theory)
Iowa debate, 104, 113, 126
Iran (see Carter, Connally, Kennedy, Rose Garden)

Jackson, John S., III, 165
Jackson, Henry, 158
Jacob, Charles E., 145
Jacobson, Gary C., 31, 45
Jarvis, Howard, 114
Javits, Jacob, 187
Jewish vote (see demographic)
Johnson, Haynes, 117
Johnson, Lyndon, 48, 54, 55, 150-51, 175
Jones, Charles O., 82
Jordan, Hamilton, 87-95, 108, 156, 167-69, 171, 204, 207, 213

Kayden, Xandra, 45, 52
Keating, Charles, Jr., 132
Keech, William, R., 82
Keefe, Robert J., 219
Keene, David, 125, 127
Kelley, Stanley, Jr., 43, 44, 166
Kemp, Jack, 150-51
Kennedy, Edward (Ted): and Brown, 113; and Carter, 99, 104-5; Chappiquiddick, 98, 100; cybernetic system, 101-2, 103-7, 112, 162-64; and Democratic party, 97, 99; personal style, 98, 100-1, 102-3, 104-5, 108-9, 161-62;

prenomination campaign, 99-109, 111-12, 155-56, 158-61, 166; public approval, 98, 102, 103, 106, 158; staff, 99-100, 102, 107-12

Kennedy, John, 2, 98
Kennedy, Joseph, 98
Kennedy, Robert, 21, 98
Kessel, John, 57-58, 82
King, Anthony, 46
Kingdon, John W., 61-62, 82
Kirk, Paul, 99, 164
Kirkpatrick, Evron M., 46
Kirkpatrick, Jeanne, 165
Kissinger, Henry, 153-54
Kraft, Tim, 88-89, 92, 95, 171

Ladd, Everett C., 209
La Follett, Robert M., 25
Lake, James, 123
Lamb, Karl A., 44, 48, 54-55, 67, 79
Lance, Bert, 93
La Rouche, Lyndon, 211-219
Latus, Margaret Ann, 47
Laxalt, Paul, 120, 150-51
Lazarfeld, Paul F., 42
League of Women Voters, 176, 187, 198
Lear, Norman, 141, 142, 189
Lederman, Susan S., 42
Lengle, James I., 44, 81
Leuthold, David A., 59-60, 83
Lewis, Drew, 148
Lindblom, Charles E., 54, 81
Lipset, Seymour Martin, 44
Lipshutz, Robert, 92
Literary Digest poll, 15 (*see also* technology)
Longley, Charles H., 45
Loomis, Burdett A., 52, 81
Lucier, James, 149
Lucy, Patrick, 186
Lugar, Richard, 150-51

MacLeod, Michael, 140
Madison, James, 219
Mahe, Eddie, Jr., 132
mailing lists (see technology)
Maisel, Louis, 83
Malbin, Michael J., 219
March, James, 52, 82
Mathews, Tom, 141-42, 186-87, 189, 190
Matthews, Donald, 82, 144
Mayhew, David, 83
media, 108-12, 138; and debates, 175-78; news media, 76-77, 197, 215; public opinion polling, 15-19, 124-25, 194-96, 201, 215-16; television, 10-12, 154, 160 (*see also* campaign theory, individual candidates, prenomination campaigns, technology)
Meese, Edwin, 120, 123, 198, 204
Mencken, H. L., xi
Mikulsky, Barbara, 22
Mikulsky Commission, 22 (*see also* electoral rules)
Mileur, Jerome M., 83
Miller, Warren E., 166
Mitofsky, Warren J., 45, 165
Moe, Richard, 95, 107
Mondale, Walter: and Carter, 93, 95, 97, 105, 107-8, 158; and the Democratic convention, 161-62, 167, 180
Moore, Frank, 92-93
Moral Majority (see prenomination campaign, Reagan)
Morgenstern, Oskar, 42, 80
Mott, Stewart, 140
Mudd, Roger: and "60 Minutes," 100, 102, 106
Mueller, John E., 140
Muskie, Edward, 158, 172
McCarthy, Eugene, 21
McDonald, John, 128

McGinnes, Joe, 43
McGovern-Fraser Commission, 21-22,
    25 (*see also* electoral rules)
McGovern, George, 11, 14, 21-22, 99
McGregor, Eugene B., 166

Napolitan, Joe, 20
National Conservative Political Action
    Committee, 38 (*see also* polit-
    ical parties)
national conventions: and Carter, 167;
    Chicago convention of 1968, 21;
    comparison of, 155-56; function
    of, 159; and Reagan, 155 (*see
    also* electoral rules, individual
    candidates, media)
negative campaign (of Carter): 169,
    174-75, 177, 180
New Hampshire primary, 12, 122,
    125-26
New York *Times*/CBS poll, 18, (*see
    also* technology)
Nie, Norman H., 42
Nimmo, Dan, 36, 46
Nixon, Richard, 2; use of television,
    11, 177; and Reagan gaffe, 193
Nofziger, Lyn, 120, 123, 194, 197-98
Nowland, Jim, 141, 143

October surprise, 198-99, 202
O'Hara Commission on Rules, 22 (*see
    also* electoral rules)
O'Hara, James, 22
Orren, Gary, R., 46
Osburn, John, 200

PAC (see political action commit-
    tees)
Page, Benjamin I., 56-57
Paige, Glenn D., 82
Palmer, Charles, 99
Parker, Carey, 99
Parkinson, Hank, 81

Patterson, Thomas E., 43, 111
Pelham, Thomas, 109
Percy, Charles, 143
Petrocik, John R., 42
platform, of political party (see polit-
    ical parties)
Plissner, Walter, 45
Plotkin, Henry, 166
Podesta, Tony, 99
political action committees, PACs (see
    campaign finance, political parties
political parties: analysis of decline,
    34-41; Democratic party and its
    candidates, 88, 91-92, 97-99, 114,
    178-80, 181-82; effect on federal
    candidates, 39-40, 181-82, 197;
    party platforms, 147-49, 156,
    159-61; Republican party and
    Reagan, 119-20, 197 (*see also*
    electoral rules)
polling, public opinion (see media)
Polsby, Nelson W., 44, 63-64
Pomper, Gerald M., 42, 81
Pool, Ithiel de Sola, 43
Popkin, Samuel, 43
Powell, Jody, 88, 92-93, 95, 108,
    168, 180
prenomination campaigns (see individ-
    ual candidates)
Pressman, Jeffery, L., 82
primaries, presidential (see electoral
    rules, prenomination, and individ-
    ual candidates)

Quinn, Thomas, 114

Rafshoon, Gerald, 92, 95, 108, 160,
    170
Ranney, Austin, 46
Rapoport, Anatol, 81
Rather, Dan, 154
Reagan, Nancy, 151
Reagan, Ronald: and Bush, 121-23,

130, 146, 150-51, 152, 153-54, 193; and Connally, 133; cybernetic system, 121, 124-27, 153-55, 195-96, 201-5; and Ford, 119-20, 151-54; general election campaign, 192-206; October surprise, 198-99; and Republican party, 119-20, 125, 147-49, 155; personal style, 120-22, 124-26, 147, 152, 154-55, 192-93, 197-98; prenomination campaign, 121-27, 146-54; public approval, 120, 125, 200, 205-6; staff, 120, 123, 126, 147-49, 194-96; and the vice presidency, 147, 149-54

Reed, T. R., 100

Reimer, Rita, 46

Republican platform (see political parties)

Reston, James, 209

Richards, Richard, 46

Riker, William H., 55

Robbin, Jonathan, 43

Robbins, Steven, 99

Robinson, Michael J., 117

Rogovin, Mitchell, 182

Rogowski, Ronald, 166

Ronstadt, Linda, 114

Roosevelt, Franklin, 15

Rose Garden strategy (see Carter, Jimmy)

Rubenstein, David, 108

Rule 29 Commission, 26 (*see also* electoral rules)

Rumsfeld, Donald, 150

Salzner, George T., 83

Sanders, Carl E., 207

Sandoz, Ellis, 220

Sanford, Terry, 22

Sanford Charter Commission, 22 (*see also* electoral rules)

Savage, Robert L., 36, 46

Scalia, Antonin, 45

Schattschneider, E. E., 218, 220

Scheinbaum, Stanley, 142

Schellhardt, Timothy D., 116, 117

Schlesinger, Steven, 99

Schneider, William, 210

Schram, Martin, 117

Schweiker, Richard, 121

Sears, John, 121-24, 126, 192

Shaddeg, Stephen, 81

Shafer, Bryon E., 44, 81

Shah of Iran, 117

Sharpansky, Jay, 46

Sheehan, Francis, 186

Shrum, Robert , 99

Simon, Herbert A., 82

Simon, William, 150

Simulmatics (see campaign theory)

"60 Minutes" (see Mudd, Roger)

Smith, Mary Louise, 128

Smith, Paul A., 44, 48, 54-55, 67, 79

Smith, Steven, 99

Smith, Terence, 115, 208

Smith, Tim, 95

Smith, William French, 151

Snyder, Richard C., 82

Sorauf, Frank J., 45

Southwick, Tom, 99, 101

Spencer, Robert C., 52-53, 59-60

Spencer, Stewart, 194, 198

Stassen, Harold, 211, 219

Sterns, Richard, 99

Stevens, Liz, 99

Stockman, David, 177

Stone, Jane, 46

Strauss, Robert, 89, 95, 178

student vote, 6; and Anderson, 141 (*see also* demographic)

Sullivan, Denis G., 82

Supreme Court decisions (see electoral rules, political parties)

Swillinger, Dan, 145

Tayler, Donald W., 82
technology, politically relevant changes in: computers, 14-16; mass mailing, 13-15; professional consultants, 19-20, 136; public opinion polling, 15-19, 215-16; television, 10-12; transportation, 12-13 (*see also* general elections, media, prenomination)
Terra, Daniel, 120
Thurmond, Strom, 133
Timmons, William, 147, 198
Treusch, Mark H., 81
Truman, Harry, 12, 175

Udall, Morris, 140
Ujifusa, Grant, 116

Vance, Cyrus, 172, 174
Vander Jagt, Guy, 150, 151
Verba, Sidney, 42
Vidal, Gore, 141
Viguerie, Richard, 20, 136
Von Neumann, John, 42, 80

Waddington, Sarah, 95
Wagner, Carl, 99
Walker, Ron, 194
walkie-talkie, 10

Wallace, Irving, 141
Walsh, Jack, 116
Watergate, 28
Watson, Jack, 90, 167
Wayne, Stephen J., 43
Weaver, Warren, Jr., 42
Weber, Max, 52, 92
Weinraub, Bernard, 166
Weisman, Steven R., 116, 180, 207
Wertheimer, Fred, 46
West, Darrell M., 83
whistle stop, 12-13 (*see also* technology)
White, John C., 88
White, Theodore H., 42, 48
Wiener, Norbert, 72, 77, 79-80, 83
Wildavsky, Aaron, 44, 63-64
Wilson, James Q., 81
Windsor, Larry, 99
Winograd Commission, 22 (*see also* electoral rules)
Winograd, Morley, 22
Wirthlin, Richard, 120, 122-25, 126, 196, 198-202, 203, 204
Wise, Phil, 95

Yates, Drummond, Jr., 47

Zingale, Nancy H., 42

About the Author

PAUL A. SMITH is a Professor of Political Science at the State University of New York at Binghamton. He received his Ph.D. from Princeton University and has also held academic positions at Columbia College, Dickinson College, and Grinnell College.

Dr. Smith coauthored *Campaign Decision-Making* with Karl A. Lamb and his edited or contributed to several other volumes. His articles have appeared in such journals as *Midwest Journal of Political Science, Journal of General Education*, and *Western Political Quarterly*. He has also given numerous papers on political parties, community politics, and environmental policy.